VOCABULARY
& SPELLING
SUCCESS

VOCABULARY & SPELLING SUCCESS
IN 20 MINUTES A DAY

6th Edition

LEARNINGEXPRESS®

NEW YORK

Copyright © 2014 LearningExpress, LLC.

All rights reserved under International and Pan-American Copyright Conventions.
Published in the United States by LearningExpress, LLC, New York.

Library of Congress Cataloging-in-Publication Data:

ISBN 978-1-57685-967-4

For more information or to place an order, contact LearningExpress at:
  80 Broad Street
  4th Floor
  New York, NY 10004

Contents ▶

CONTENTS

Introduction ▶

The words we use to communicate every day are important in every aspect of our lives. From relaxing, to working, to studying, to taking tests, we use words to share with others how we feel, what we think, and why we think that way. Without words, it is difficult to express our ideas to the rest of the world. The more words we know—the larger our vocabulary—the more clearly we can communicate with others. Our vocabularies reveal our knowledge to the world; therefore, a person with a large vocabulary has the advantage of self-expression.

This book will help you learn the words you need to know to successfully express yourself in school, work, and your personal life. The words in this book have been carefully chosen to help you learn what you need to know to pass any test—from standardized tests, to civil service tests, to college entrance exams, and to professional job interviews—and continue to build your vocabulary, even after you have finished using this book.

In each of the following chapters, you will complete practice exercises that have been created specifically to help you understand words inside out. You will learn pronunciation, spelling, context, definitions, word parts, denotation and connotation, synonyms, and antonyms. The word lists are grouped into categories, so you will be able to associate them with like words and remember them more easily. There is also a crossword puzzle at the beginning of chapters 4–18 to introduce you to the new words before you begin to work on the practice exercises. Then, you can take the Posttest at the end of the book and gauge how much you've really learned about words and how you have improved your vocabulary.

How to Use This Book

Build Your Vocabulary

No matter what language a person speaks, he or she uses three different types of vocabularies:

- A **speaking** vocabulary—words and expressions we use every day to communicate
- A **listening** vocabulary—words and expressions we have heard but may have never used
- A **reading** vocabulary—words and expressions we have encountered in print but have neither heard nor used

One of the best ways to increase your vocabulary is to make a conscious effort to move words from your listening or reading vocabularies to your speaking vocabulary—the words you not only understand, but also use. This book is especially helpful because the exercises you complete help you *use* your new vocabulary words so you know them cold. Suddenly, you'll find yourself speaking and writing with these new words, and you will also find that reading will become much easier as you begin to recognize more and more words.

Test makers try to assess how well you have absorbed your language and how well you can use and identify the words you know to express yourself and understand others. Each lesson in this book will help you show test makers and prospective employers that you know how to communicate clearly and effectively, and that you understand what others are communicating to you. Once you have learned the vocabulary words and completed the exercises in this book, you'll have what you need to ace any exam or job interview.

Write It Down

If this book is yours, write in it as much as you like. Write your answers in the blanks indicated and write notes to yourself in the margins. It is meant for you to consume. Pull out important details from the surrounding text to make them more visible and accessible to you. Underline or highlight information that

seems important to you. Make notes in the margins that will help you follow what's important as you practice and learn your new words.

Make Flash Cards

If you are having trouble remembering words, even after the drills and practice exercises in the book, buy some index cards and make flash cards for yourself. Write a vocabulary word on one side of the card, and then write its definition, synonyms, antonyms, and other essential information on the other side of the card. You can carry the cards with you to review when you have a free moment.

Ask for Help

Enlist a friend or relative to help drill you on any word with which you are having trouble. You'll be surprised at how much more you will remember if you share what you know with someone else, and if they help you come up with clues to help jog your memory.

Keep a List

In addition to the words you learn in this book, make a list of flash cards of new, useful words that you encounter at work, at school, on TV, in your reading, or even at home. They will more than double the benefit you will get from using this book.

How the Book Is Set Up

Each chapter of this book that contains a word list starts with a crossword puzzle to help you get acquainted with your new words. Do your best to fill it in; if there are some words you don't recognize, you can flip to the next page, where you will find the full definition, pronunciation, and part of speech of each word in the word list. Take a good look at how each word is pronounced, especially the accented syllables. You should pronounce each word aloud several times. The sentence following each definition illustrates the word's meaning. You should fill in the blank inside each sentence with the correct word from the list. It is a good idea to say the entire sentence aloud.

Second, you will encounter several words from the vocabulary list in context. If you do not remember the meaning of the words, you should circle any clues in the text that might help you figure out the meaning of these unfamiliar words.

Then, you will read and fill in the blank to complete the sentence by selecting the best choice from the vocabulary list on which you are working. Read each sentence slowly and carefully. There are usually clues within each sentence that tell you which word from the list is the best choice.

Next, you will encounter exercises that revolve around synonyms and antonyms. You will read a group of words and decide which one is not a synonym. Then, you will read a group of words and select the word from the vocabulary list that is most nearly opposite in meaning from the entire group of words.

You will also complete matching, true/false, and choosing-the-right-word exercises that will help you reinforce the meanings of each new word you have learned. Then, at the end of the book, you will take a 75-question posttest so that you can see how much you've learned as you've worked through this book.

The pretest that follows this Introduction will help you see how good you are at identifying unfamiliar words. Then, Chapters 2 and 3 will teach you about the basics of vocabulary. In Chapter 2, you'll learn important vocabulary terms and about language origins. In Chapter 3, you'll learn important spelling rules to help you become a better speller, even on those tricky or foreign words. Then, you'll get to the word lists. The 15 vocabulary list chapters consist of helpful exercises to drill you on new words, so that by the end of each lesson, you'll know them inside out. Finally, completing the posttest will show you how far you've come, and how well you know your new words.

You can also refer to Appendices A and B to learn important studying strategies and find out about other valuable resources.

Self-Analysis

Find out how you feel about your own vocabulary with the following self-assessment. Put a check next to the sentences that best describe your own vocabulary habits.

_____ **1.** I feel confident that I express myself clearly in speaking.

_____ **2.** I sometimes feel uncomfortable when I know what I want to say but just can't think of the right word.

_____ **3.** I notice unfamiliar words in print and wonder about their meanings.

_____ **4.** Sometimes I come across unfamiliar words in print and feel that I should know them.

_____ **5.** I remember words that I had on vocabulary quizzes and tests at school.

_____ **6.** If I write down new words, I can learn them.

_____ **7.** If I come across an unfamiliar word in print, I will look it up in the dictionary.

_____ **8.** If I come across an unfamiliar word in print, I will ask someone to tell me the meaning.

_____ **9.** If I hear an unfamiliar word in conversation or on TV, I will ask someone to tell me its meaning.

_____ **10.** If I hear or see an unfamiliar word, I am usually too embarrassed to ask for or to look up its meaning.

Your answers to these questions should give you a good sense of how you feel about and use your vocabulary.

VOCABULARY
& SPELLING
SUCCESS

1 ▶ PRETEST

Before you start your study of vocabulary, you may want to get an idea of how much you already know and how much you need to learn. If that's the case, take the pretest in this chapter. The pretest consists of 50 questions introducing you to many of the words you will learn as you complete the exercises in this book. Even if you get all the questions on this pretest right, it's almost guaranteed that you will find a few words in this book that you didn't know before. On the other hand, if you hardly know any of the words on the pretest, don't despair. Out of the many words in this book, you're sure to find a few that you are already familiar with, and that will make the going easier.

Use this pretest just to get a general idea of how much of this book you already know. If you get a high score on this pretest, you may be able to spend less time with this book than you originally planned. If you get a lower score, you'll be amazed at how much your vocabulary will improve by completing the exercises in each chapter.

1. (a) (b) (c) (d)
2. (a) (b) (c) (d)
3. (a) (b) (c) (d)
4. (a) (b) (c) (d)
5. (a) (b) (c) (d)
6. (a) (b) (c) (d)
7. (a) (b) (c) (d)
8. (a) (b) (c) (d)
9. (a) (b) (c) (d)
10. (a) (b) (c) (d)
11. (a) (b) (c) (d)
12. (a) (b) (c) (d)
13. (a) (b) (c) (d)
14. (a) (b) (c) (d)

15. (a) (b) (c) (d)
16. (a) (b) (c) (d)
17. (a) (b) (c) (d)
18. (a) (b) (c) (d)
19. (a) (b) (c) (d)
20. (a) (b) (c) (d)
21. (a) (b) (c) (d)
22. (a) (b) (c) (d)
23. (a) (b) (c) (d)
24. (a) (b) (c) (d)
25. (a) (b) (c) (d)
26. (a) (b) (c) (d)
27. (a) (b) (c) (d)
28. (a) (b) (c) (d)

29. (a) (b) (c) (d)
30. (a) (b) (c) (d)
31. (a) (b) (c) (d)
32. (a) (b) (c) (d)
33. (a) (b) (c) (d)
34. (a) (b) (c) (d)
35. (a) (b) (c) (d)
36. (a) (b) (c) (d)
37. (a) (b) (c) (d)
38. (a) (b) (c) (d)
39. (a) (b) (c) (d)
40. (a) (b) (c) (d)

41. (a) (b) (c) (d) (e) (f) (g) (h) (i) (j)
42. (a) (b) (c) (d) (e) (f) (g) (h) (i) (j)
43. (a) (b) (c) (d) (e) (f) (g) (h) (i) (j)
44. (a) (b) (c) (d) (e) (f) (g) (h) (i) (j)
45. (a) (b) (c) (d) (e) (f) (g) (h) (i) (j)

46. (a) (b) (c) (d) (e) (f) (g) (h) (i) (j)
47. (a) (b) (c) (d) (e) (f) (g) (h) (i) (j)
48. (a) (b) (c) (d) (e) (f) (g) (h) (i) (j)
49. (a) (b) (c) (d) (e) (f) (g) (h) (i) (j)
50. (a) (b) (c) (d) (e) (f) (g) (h) (i) (j)

Pretest

Choose the best word to fill in the blank. Mark your answers on the answer sheet on page 3 by darkening the corresponding oval.

1. When I received my term paper back, my teacher's comments on it were so _____ that I had to ask him to explain each one.
   a. disinterested
   b. copious
   c. audible
   d. illegible

2. The _____ data supports the belief that there has been an increase in population.
   a. nominal
   b. demographic
   c. pragmatic
   d. puerile

3. The veterinarian came out and told the cat's owner that the animal's _____ for recovery is good.
   a. prognosis
   b. etymology
   c. pragmatism
   d. euphemism

4. Because I didn't want anyone else to be able to uncover the meaning of my note, I wrote a _____ message only he could understand.
   a. chronic
   b. agoraphobic
   c. cryptic
   d. incisive

5. Scientists research gene _____ in fruit flies to see how genes change from one generation to the next.
   a. remittance
   b. mutation
   c. mediocre
   d. cliché

6. The hotel tried to _____ their mistake by giving us a suite at a reduced price.
   a. debut
   b. rectify
   c. recapitulate
   d. exempt

7. The theater's acoustics were awful; the actors' voices were barely _____.
   a. equity
   b. audible
   c. bandwidth
   d. abrogate

8. In court, the witness committed _____ when she lied to the judge.
   a. perjury
   b. solace
   c. mimicry
   d. rancor

9. The _____ in her letter was so lovely that I read it over and over.
   a. nepotism
   b. prose
   c. hyperbole
   d. guffaw

10. The one year the company did not break even was just a/an _____.
    a. acme
    b. facetious
    c. syllogism
    d. anomaly

Choose the word that is closest in meaning to the bold word.

11. purge
   a. cite
   b. purify
   c. perspective
   d. decimate

12. parity
   a. equality
   b. mimicry
   c. antipathy
   d. sympathy

13. furtive
   a. open
   b. demote
   c. secret
   d. utopia

14. pathos
   a. loyalty
   b. fidelity
   c. pity
   d. epitome

15. audacious
   a. badinage
   b. guttural
   c. bold
   d. stolid

16. controversy
   a. antecedent
   b. debate
   c. excessive
   d. sympathy

17. staid
   a. pallor
   b. sham
   c. sober
   d. elite

18. addle
   a. stolid
   b. empiric
   c. ruminate
   d. muddle

19. erudite
   a. genteel
   b. scholarly
   c. garrulous
   d. bequest

20. tenet
   a. belief
   b. antecedent
   c. teleology
   d. demote

Choose the word that is most nearly the opposite of the bold word.

21. feisty
   a. staid
   b. relevant
   c. tangential
   d. hot

22. bigotry
   a. prognosis
   b. open-mindedness
   c. badinage
   d. parity

23. agonize
   a. blasé
   b. rectify
   c. enjoy
   d. trivial

24. élan
   a. fidelity
   b. ingenue
   c. error
   d. frumpy

25. bane
   a. solace
   b. crux
   c. pun
   d. downfall

26. banal
   a. puerile
   b. trite
   c. fresh
   d. obtuse

27. addle
   a. expose
   b. confuse
   c. muddle
   d. fluster

28. extricate
   a. remove
   b. entangle
   c. malaise
   d. gauche

29. paradox
   a. contradictory
   b. mysterious
   c. enigma
   d. evidence

30. purloin
   a. larceny
   b. wallow
   c. return
   d. plausible

Choose the word that is spelled correctly.

31. a. percieve
   b. achieve
   c. reciept
   d. hygeine

32. a. knarled
   b. blight
   c. alite
   d. fraut

33. a. indeight
   b. indite
   c. indight
   d. indict

34. a. narrled
   b. gnarled
   c. gnarlled
   d. narled

35. a. curiculums
   b. curriculmns
   c. curriculas
   d. curricula

36. Spike was the most _____ dog you could ever wish for.
   a. peacable
   b. paeceable
   c. paecable
   d. peaceable

37. Spending your summer in Spain will be a great
_____ for you to improve your Spanish.
a. opportunity
b. opportuneity
c. oportunity
d. oportuneity

38. Al and Jane hired attorneys, and together, the
_____ added up to over $10,000.
a. lawyer's bills
b. lawyers' bills'
c. lawyers' bills
d. lawyers bills

39. The county commissioners said _____ going to
discuss the taxation issue at the meeting next
week.
a. they're
b. there
c. their
d. thei'r

40. In order for Scott to receive his two master's
degrees, he had to write two different _____ .
a. theses
b. thesis
c. thesis'
d. thesis's

Match the word in the first column with the correct
definition in the second column.

41. consummate   a. elegant

42. copious   b. steal

43. euphemism   c. inactive

44. mediocre   d. inelegant

45. urbane   e. complete

46. gauche   f. embodiment

47. inert   g. abundant

48. epitome   h. average

49. mete   i. allocate

50. purloin   j. inoffensive expression

Answers

1. d	**26.** c
2. b	**27.** a
3. a	**28.** b
4. c	**29.** d
5. b	**30.** c
6. b	**31.** b
7. b	**32.** b
8. a	**33.** d
9. b	**34.** b
10. d	**35.** d
11. b	**36.** d
12. a	**37.** a
13. c	**38.** c
14. c	**39.** a
15. c	**40.** a
16. b	**41.** e
17. c	**42.** g
18. d	**43.** j
19. b	**44.** h
20. a	**45.** a
21. a	**46.** d
22. b	**47.** c
23. c	**48.** f
24. d	**49.** i
25. a	**50.** b

2 ▶ VOCABULARY TERMS AND LANGUAGE ORIGINS

Without words, without writing, and without books there would be no history, there could be no concept of humanity.

—HERMANN HESSE, author (1877–1962)

CHAPTER SUMMARY

This chapter tells you about many terms associated with vocabulary.

There are three ways we learn vocabulary:

1. From the **sound** of words
2. From the **structure** of words
3. From the **context** of words—how words are used in communication

Therefore, when you encounter unfamiliar words, you should ask yourself:

- Does this word sound like anything I've ever heard?
- Does any part of this word look familiar?
- How is this word used in the sentence I just read or heard?

Each lesson of this book presents a word list so you can try this process. As you read each word list, you'll find that you already recognize some of the words—maybe from your reading and listening vocabularies—and the ones you don't know you will learn as you proceed through the lesson.

Word Parts—Prefixes, Suffixes, and Roots

You use prefixes, suffixes, and word roots every day, whether you realize it or not. These parts of words make up almost all of the words we use in the English language, and you will find that the meanings of many unfamiliar words become much more clear when you understand the meanings of the most common of these word parts.

Prefixes

A prefix is the word part placed at the beginning of a word. It is usually only one syllable, but sometimes it is more. Its job is to change or add to the meaning of a word. For example, you probably use the word *review* on a regular basis. What does it mean? Let's break it down. First, we can break it down into syllables: re-view. *View* means to look at, and the prefix *re-* adds to the meaning of the word. *Re-* means back or again, so by putting together what you already know, you can figure out that the word *review* means to look back at, or to look at again. Other common prefixes include *in-*, *anti-*, *pre-*, *post-*, *un-*, *non-*, *con-*, and *dis-*. You will learn more about prefixes and their meanings in Chapter 4.

Suffixes

A suffix is a word part placed at the end of a word that signals how a word is being used in a sentence and identifies its part of speech. When you attach different suffixes onto the base of a word, they change the word's part of speech. For example, the word *sterilize* is a verb meaning to sanitize. As an adjective, it takes the suffix *-ile* and becomes *sterile*. As a noun, it takes the suffix *-tion* and becomes *sterilization*. The suffix changes the word's job in a sentence, and it also helps give you a clue as to the meaning of an unfamiliar word. You will learn more about suffixes and their meanings and jobs in Chapter 5.

Roots

The pieces of words that carry direct meaning are called roots. Many English words stem from ancient Greek and Latin words, and because so many English words have their source in certain recurring root words, knowing some of the most commonly used roots gives you access to many words at once. Thus, when you combine your knowledge of prefixes and suffixes with your knowledge of roots, you can figure out the meaning of many unfamiliar words. For example, the word root *cogn-* means *to know*. Words that include this root are *recognize*, meaning to identify as known, *incognito*, meaning unknown, and *cognition*, meaning knowledge. You can see how knowing the base of these three words, in addition to having knowledge of prefixes and suffixes, can really help you work out the meanings of unfamiliar words. You'll learn more about roots in Chapters 6 and 7.

> ## TIP
>
> As you are introduced to words throughout this book, take the time to break them down into prefixes, suffixes, and roots. It will help you remember them.

Syllables

When you were first learning to read, you learned about syllables, the parts of words that carry separate sounds. Breaking words into syllables is one of the best strategies for seeing if a word is in your listening or reading vocabularies. It also helps you break larger words into smaller, more manageable, and often more recognizable parts. This will be especially helpful in Chapters 4, 5, 6, and 7, when you are working with Vocabulary Lists that teach you about prefixes, suffixes, and roots. By breaking words down into syllables, you will be able to identify the meanings of unfamiliar words that contain these word parts.

Rules for Dividing Words into Syllables

Here are a couple of quick rules for dividing words by syllables:

1. Divide between double consonants: ham-mock.
2. Divide after prefixes and before suffixes: in-vest-ment.

If you already have some feel for how the word sounds, you can divide it according to the sound of the vowels:

3. Divide after the vowel if it has the long sound: so-lar.
4. Divide after the consonant if the vowel sound is short: pris-on.

Synonyms and Antonyms

Questions on standardized tests and civil service exams often ask you to find the synonym or antonym of a word. Therefore, as you learn the words in this book, you should try to think of or look up synonyms and antonyms of the words in the Vocabulary Lists. You will also be asked to complete exercises in this book to help you learn even more synonyms and antonyms.

Synonyms

A word is a synonym of another word if it has the same, or nearly the same, meaning as the word with which it is being compared. For example, the words *conceal* and *hide* are synonyms. They both mean the same thing: to keep out of sight.

Antonyms

An antonym is a word that means the opposite of the word with which it is being compared. A couple of obvious examples of antonym pairs are happy and sad, good and bad, and love and hate.

Denotation and Connotation

The denotation of a word is its dictionary definition, while the connotation of a word has to do with the tone of the word—the emotions it evokes in the reader. For example if you were to look up the word *joke* in the dictionary, you might get a definition similar to that of synonyms like *quip* or *prank*—something like "something said or done to provoke laughter"—but all three of these words have different connotations. In other words, they bring to mind different feelings—one positive, one negative, and one neutral. As you are learning the words in this book, try to think of other similar words that might be synonyms, but might also have slightly different connotations, or tones.

> **TIP**
>
> Most of the time, we simply "sense" the connotation of a word without giving it conscious thought, but if you are the one writing or speaking the word, take the time to choose carefully so that you are clearly understood.

Homonyms

Homonyms are words that sound the same, but aren't. They have the same pronunciation, but they are neither spelled the same way, nor do they have the same meaning. For example, *which* and *witch* are homonyms, and so are *their, there,* and *they're.* When you are listening to the words, or reading them in context, it is easy to work out their meaning; however, it is very important to know which definition corresponds to the correct spelling of the homonym. If you misspell a homonym, people will have a difficult time understanding what you are trying to communicate to them. You will learn more about homonyms in the next chapter.

Context Clues

Context is the surrounding text in which a word is used. Most people automatically use context to help them determine the meaning of an unknown word. When you encounter a word in its surroundings, it is much easier to figure out its meaning, or at least its connotation. The best way to take meaning from context is to search the surrounding text for key words in sentences or paragraphs that convey the meaning of the unfamiliar word.

Often, restatement and contrast clues will lead you right to the meaning of unfamiliar words. For example, read the following sentence and see if you can figure out the meaning of the italicized word from closely examining the surrounding text.

> Although when Hannah joined the company she was promised *perquisites* every six

months, she has been working at the company for two years and has never received any sort of bonus.

The words *although* and *bonus* should give you a clue as to the meaning of *perquisite.* You know that Hannah has never received a bonus in two years of work for the same company, and you know that she was promised something, so the word *although* gives you the final clue because it signals a contrast. You can conclude that a *perquisite* is a synonym for *bonus.*

> She was *exempt* from duty that day. She was excused because she had been injured.

In this sentence, the meaning of *exempt* is restated for you. *Exempt* is a synonym for *excused.*

You will get plenty of practice identifying the meanings of unfamiliar words in context throughout the rest of this book.

Good communication skills—including vocabulary and spelling—are essential. A good vocabulary increases your ability to understand reading material and to express yourself in speaking and in writing. Without a broad vocabulary, your ability to learn is limited. The good news is that vocabulary skills can be developed with practice, which is exactly what this book gives you.

3 ▶ SPELLING RULES

My spelling is wobbly. It's good spelling but it wobbles, and the letters get in the wrong places.

—A.A. MILNE, author of *Winnie the Pooh* (1882–1956)

CHAPTER SUMMARY

This chapter is designed to help you refresh your spelling skills by teaching you the rules you need to know to spell your best. You'll learn strategies to help you spell hyphenated and compound words and words with tricky letter combinations, unusual plurals, prefixes, suffixes, apostrophes, and abbreviations.

n the English language, if you simply wrote words the way they sound, you'd come up with some very peculiar spellings. If you tried to sound out every word and pronounce it exactly the way it's written, you'd come up with some pretty odd pronunciations too.

Here are some general multisensory tips for studying spelling:

- Use your eyes.
  - ✓ Look at words carefully. With a marker or pen, highlight the part of the word that is hard to remember.
  - ✓ Visualize the word with your eyes closed.
- Use your ears.
  - ✓ Listen for the sound of words you hear in conversation or on the radio or television.
  - ✓ Listen to the sound of the spelling of words. Ask someone to dictate the words and their spelling, and listen as the word is spelled out.

■ Use your hands.

   ✓ Write the word several times, spelling it in your head as you write.

There are two main stumbling blocks to spelling by sight and sound. One we have already identified—the fact that English is both phonetically inconsistent and visually confusing. Here are four strategies that can guide your way through a difficult system and give you some ways to make good spelling a part of your life.

1. Learn the rules, but expect some exceptions. The lessons that follow point out both spelling rules and their exceptions.

2. Use mnemonics (memory tricks) to help you remember how to spell unfamiliar or confusing words. The most common type of mnemonic is the *acronym*. An acronym is a word created from the first letters in a series of words. Another type of mnemonic is a silly sentence or phrase, known as an *acrostic*, which is made out of words that each begin with the letter or letters that start each item in a series that you want to remember.

3. Write it down. This book provides you with helpful exercises that require you to write your vocabulary words in a blank space. This act will help your hand and eye remember how to spell the word. Make sure to spell the word correctly as you go along so you don't have to relearn the word's spelling later on. After you are done with this book, you can teach yourself to spell new words in the same way. The simple act of writing words down several times will help you cement their spellings in your mind.

4. Referring to a pronunciation chart in any dictionary will help guide you through pronouncing the words in this book and also familiarize you with pronouncing other new words you encounter in everyday life. You can also access pronunciation charts online. The following is a list of a few online resources:

■ Merriam-Webster Dictionary: www.m-w.com/help/pronguide.htm

■ The Newbury House Online Dictionary: nhd.heinle.com/pronunciation.aspx

■ American Heritage Dictionary of the English Language Online at Bartleby.com: www. bartleby.com/61/12.html

There are many other online dictionaries such as www.dictionary.com; or just type "online dictionary" into any search engine, and get ready to pronounce.

Vowels

When to Use ie and ei

You probably learned this saying years ago in school:

> i before e except after c and when sound-
> ing like "ay" as in neighbor and weigh.

This saying should help you remember the basic principle of when to use *ie* and *ei* when spelling words. The following sections outline the specifics of when to spell a word with *ie* and when to spell a word with *ei* and their exceptions.

The ie Rule

Here are some examples of words that use *ie* to make the long *e* sound:

achieve	niece
belief	piece
cashier	retrieve
chief	series
fierce	wield

Exceptions

Sometimes, the *ie* combination has other sounds:

- It can sound like short *e*, as in *friend*
- It can sound like long *i*, as in *piety, fiery, quiet, notoriety, society, science*
- The only time the *ie* combination comes after *c* is when it sounds like *sh*, as in *ancient, deficient, conscience.*

The ei Rule

Here are some examples of words in which *ei* makes the long *a* sound:

deign	reign
eight	sleigh
feign	surveillance
freight	vein
heinous	weight

Exceptions

Sometimes, you will simply have to memorize words that use the *ei* combination because they don't follow the rule.

- In some words, *ei* is used even though it sounds like *ee*: *either, seize, weird, sheik, seizure, leisure*
- Sometimes, *ei* sounds like long *i*: *height, sleight, stein, seismology*
- Sometimes, *ei* sounds like short *e*: *heifer, their, foreign, forfeit*
- As you learned in the previous saying, after *c* you use *ei*, even if it sounds like *ee*: *ceiling, deceit, conceited, receive, receipt*

TIP

It can become overwhelming to try to remember all the exceptions to all the rules. Try making flash cards for each rule to separate them visually.

Spelling Practice 1

Circle the word in the parentheses that is spelled correctly. Check your answers at the end of the lesson.

1. My (**niece, neice**) was born on Thanksgiving Day.

2. The would-be criminal was prone to (**deciet, deceit**), but in the end his (**conscience, consceince**) got the better of him.

3. After (**acheiving, achieving**) his goal of winning the Super Bowl, the quarterback retired at the (**height, hieght**) of his career.

4. I was (**relieved, relieved**) when I realized I hadn't missed my flight.

5. The (**reign, riegn**) of a top-ranked tennis player is short-lived.

6. When I was in college, I worked as a (**casheir, cashier**) at the local grocery store.

7. There are (**surveillance, surviellance**) cameras in the lobby of my building.

8. I decided to go with a wallpaper (**frieze, freize**) along the upper wall in the family room.

9. I have always wanted to be a (**chief, cheif**) editor.

10. He is a (**feind, fiend**) with no conscience.

More Vowel Combinations

When two vowels are together, the first one is usually long, or says its own name, and the second one is silent. For example, in the word *reach*, you hear the long *e*, but not the short *a*. Similarly, if you know how to pronounce the word *caffeine* and know it has either an *ei* or *ie*, you stand a chance at spelling it correctly because you hear that the *e* sound comes first. If you know what sound you hear, that sound is likely to be the first of two vowels working together.

Here are some examples of words using *ai*, *ui*, and *ea* combinations in which the vowel you hear is the one that comes first.

Words with *ai*	Words with *ea*	Words with *ui*
abstain	cheap	juice
acquaint	conceal	nuisance
chaise	gear	ruin
paisley	heal	suit
prevail	lead	
refrain	reveal	
traipse	steal	

The Exceptions

There are several exceptions to this rule, which you will simply have to recognize by sight rather than by sound.

Exceptions
porcelain
beauty
healthy
hearse
hearty

In some cases, you still hear only the first of the two vowels, except the first vowel makes a different sound. For example, the word *healthy* is pronounced with a short *e* sound, but you still hear the *e* and not the *a*.

Words with ai or ia

When the vowel pair has one sound and says "uh" (e.g. *captain*), it uses *ai*. When the vowel pair has separate sounds (e.g. *genial*), it uses *ia*. However, there is an exception: When words combine *t* or *c* with *ia*, they make a "shuh" sound, for example, *martial*, *beneficial*,

glacial. The following are some examples of words that follow the *ai* and *ia* rules:

Words with *ai*	Words with *ia*
Britain	alleviate
captain	brilliant
certain	civilian
chieftain	familiar
curtain	guardian
fountain	median
villain	menial

Consonants

Silent Consonants

Many English words include silent consonants, ones that are written but not pronounced. Unfortunately, there is no rule governing silent consonants; you simply have to learn the words by sight. The following list includes some common examples, with the silent consonants highlighted.

answer	**g**naw	**p**seudonym
autum**n**	indic**t**	**p**sychology
blig**h**t	**k**neel	**rh**etorical
ca**l**m	**k**night	sub**t**le
deb**t**	**k**nowledge	throu**gh**
ghost	**p**salm	**w**rite

Memory Tricks

Use sound cues or sight cues, depending on which works better for you—or use both to reinforce your learning.

- Pronounce the silent consonants in your mind as you write them. Say **sub**tle, **oft**en, and so on.
- Write the words on index cards and highlight the missing consonant sounds with a marker.

Spelling Practice 2

Fill in the missing (silent) letters in the following words.

11. ___sychology

12. ans___er

13. de___t

14. ___narled

15. indi___t

16. ___nowledge

17. ca___m

18. g___ost

19. of___en

20. autum___

Doubling Consonants

Most of the time, a final consonant is doubled when you add an ending. For example, *drop* becomes *dropping*, *mop* becomes *mopping*, *stab* becomes *stabbing*. But what about *look/looking, rest/resting, counsel/counseled*?

The Rules

There are two sets of rules: one for when you're adding an ending that begins with a vowel (such as *-ed, -ing, -ance, -ence, -ant*) and another set for when the ending begins with a consonant (such as *-ness* or *-ly*).

1. When the ending begins with a vowel:

- Double the last consonant in a one-syllable word that ends with one vowel and one consonant. For example, *flip* becomes *flipper* or *flipping*, *quit* becomes *quitter* or *quitting*, and *clap* becomes *clapper* or *clapping*.
- Double the final consonant when the last syllable is accented and there is only one consonant in the accented syllable. For example, *acquit* becomes *acquitting*, *refer* becomes *referring*, and *commit* becomes *committing*.

You can remember a shorter version of the rules about doubling before an ending that begins with a vowel: one syllable or accented last syllable doubles the single consonant.

2. When the ending begins with a consonant:

- Keep a final *n* when you add *-ness*. You end up with a double *n: keenn*ess, leann*ess.
- Keep a final *l* when you add *-ly*. You end up with a double *l: formally, regally, legally*.

In other cases, then, you don't double the consonant.

The Exceptions

There are exceptions to the rules, but not many. Here are a few of them:

- *bus* becomes *buses*
- *chagrin* becomes *chagrined*
- *draw* becomes *drawing*

Spelling Practice 3

This exercise focuses on double consonants. Choose an appropriate ending for each word: *-ed, -ing, -ness,* or *-ly*. Rewrite the word on the line that follows it, doubling the consonant if necessary.

21. final _____

22. submit _____

23. think _____

24. stir _____

25. control _____

26. plain _____

27. rebel (v) _____

28. weak _____

29. legal _____

30. rain _____

The Special Challenges of c and g

The letters *c* and *g* can sound either soft or hard. When *c* is soft, it sounds like *s*; when it's hard, it sounds like *k*. When *g* is soft, it sounds like *j*; when it's hard, it sounds like *g* as in *guess*. But the difference isn't as confusing as it seems at first. The letters *c* and *g* are soft when followed by *e, i,* or *y*. Otherwise, they are hard. Thus, *c* sounds like *s* when it is followed by *e, i,* or *y,* as in *central, circle, cycle*. It sounds like *k* when followed by other vowels: *case, cousin, current*. The same rule also applies to the letter *g*: *g* sounds like *j* when followed by *e, i,* or *y,* as in *genius, giant, gym*. When followed by other vowels, *g* is hard: *gamble, go, gun*.

The following are examples of words in which *e, i,* or *y* makes a soft *c* or *g*.

centimeter	general
centrifuge	generous
circulate	genteel
circus	germ
cyclical	giraffe
cymbal	gyrate

One more thing to remember is that a *k* is added to a final *c* before an ending that begins with *e, i,* or *y*. If you didn't add the *k*, the *c* would become soft and sound like *s*. So in order to add *-ing* to panic, for example, you have to put a *k* first: *panicking*.

The following words are examples of words that have had a *k* added to *c* before an ending beginning with *e, i,* or *y*.

mimicking	picnicked
panicky	trafficking

There are virtually no exceptions to the rules about using *c* and *g*. Listen to the words as you spell them and let the rule guide your choice: *c, s,* or *k*; *g* or *j*.

Spelling Practice 4

Using the previous list, add the missing letters to the following words:

31. The crashing of the c___mbal made them all pay attention.

32. He was a g___nerous man who gave willingly of what he had.

33. He was arrested for traffic___ing in drugs.

34. The local c___rcus added a g___raffe to its main act.

35. The fan helped to c___rculate the air.

Homonyms

Homonyms are words that sound the same but are spelled differently. Many of these words have just one change in the vowel or vowel combination. There's no rule about these words, so you'll simply have to memorize them. Here are some examples of word pairs that can be troublesome. Sometimes, it helps to learn each word in terms of the job it will do in a sentence. Often, the two words in a homophone pair are a different part of speech. Take a look at the following examples:

affect/effect	led/lead
altar/alter	minor/miner

bare/bear	passed/past
bloc/block	peal/peel
cite/site	piece/peace
cord/chord	sheer/shear
coarse/course	stationery/stationary
descent/dissent	weak/week
dual/duel	which/witch
heal/heel	write/right

Since the meanings of these homonyms are different, context is probably the best way to differentiate between these words.

Examples in Context

- In the Middle Ages, many people used to shear (*verb*) sheep for a living.
  Since my curtains are **sheer** (*adjective*), I get a lot of light in the morning.
- We had to **alter** (*verb*) our plans because of the bad weather.
  The couple stood at the **altar** (*noun*) while they said their vows.
- I had to use **coarse** (*adjective*) sandpaper to strip the paint off of the wooden desk.
  When I was in college, drama was my favorite **course** (*noun*).

Try the following exercise to practice identifying the correct homonym in context.

Spelling Practice 5
Circle the word that fits correctly into the sentence.

36. I feel light-headed and (**week, weak**) if I skip lunch.

37. I can't (**bear, bare**) to leave my dog at the kennel.

38. My boss made a big deal out of a very (**miner, minor**) mistake.

39. I don't like to (**peal, peel**) onions because my eyes water.

40. I don't know (**witch, which**) decision is right for me.

41. Yesterday, I went to the (**stationary, stationery**) store to buy a red pen.

42. You have the (**right, write**) to request a promotion.

43. I like my new printer because it doesn't require a (**chord, cord**).

44. In the (**passed, past**), I used to run five miles a day.

45. When I fly, I always find the (**descent, dissent**) to be the most nerve-wracking part of the trip.

Endings

When to Drop a Final e
It's hard to remember when to drop letters and when to keep them. This lesson will nail down some simple rules to help you with those decisions.

Rule 1
Drop the final *e* when you add an ending that begins with a vowel.

- With *-ing*
  change + *-ing* = changing
- With *-able*
  argue + *-able* = arguable
- With *-ous*
  virtue + *-ous* = virtuous
- With *-ity*
  opportune + *-ity* = opportunity

The Exceptions

- Keep the final *e* after soft *c* or soft *g* in order to keep the soft sound.

    peace + *-able* = peaceable

    courage + *-ous* = courageous

- Keep the final *e* in other cases when you need to protect pronunciation.

    shoe + *-ing* = shoeing (not shoing)

    guarantee + *-ing* = guaranteeing (not guaranteing)

Rule 2

Keep the final *e* before endings that begin with consonants. Here are some examples of words that use this rule:

- With *-ment*

    advertise + *-ment* = advertisement

- With *-ness*

    appropriate + *-ness* = appropriateness

- With *-less*

    care + *-less* = careless

- With *-ful*

    grace + *-ful* = graceful

The Exception

There's one important exception to the rule about keeping the final *e* when you add an ending that begins with a consonant:

- Drop the final *e* when it occurs after the letters *u* or *w*.

    argue + *-ment* = argument

    awe + *-ful* = awful

    true + *-ly* = truly

Spelling Practice 6

Write the following combinations in the blanks provided, keeping or omitting the final *e* as necessary.

46. It was a (surprise + *-ing*) _____ ending.

47. The real estate agent said that the property would be very (desire + *-able*) _____ on the market.

48. The astronauts were remarkably (courage + *-ous*) _____ men and women.

49. (Fortunate + *ly*), she made it home right before the rain started.

50. The Quakers are a (peace + *-able*) _____ people.

51. He read a great (advertise + *-ment*) _____ in the paper today.

52. He had to learn not to be so (care + *-less*) _____ with his wallet.

53. He was known for his (polite + *-ness*) _____ and good manners.

54. They had an (argue + *-ment*) _____ on the phone.

55. He left the room in a (disgrace + *-ful*) _____ condition.

When to Keep a Final y or Change It to i

When you add a suffix to a word ending in *y*, keep the *y* if it follows a vowel. This time it doesn't matter whether the suffix begins with a vowel or a consonant. Always keep the *y* if it comes immediately after a vowel. The following are some examples.

- With *-s*

    attorney + *-s* = attorneys

- With *-ed*

    play + *-ed* = played

- With -ing
  relay + -ing = relaying
- With -ance
  annoy + -ance = annoyance
- With -able
  enjoy + -able = enjoyable

The Exceptions

Some words break this rule and change the *y* to *i*.

- *day* becomes *daily*
- *pay* becomes *paid*
- *say* becomes *said*

When you add a suffix to a word ending in *y*, change the *y* to *i* if it follows a consonant. Again, it doesn't matter whether the suffix begins with a vowel or a consonant. Here are some examples:

- With -ful
  beauty + -ful = beautiful
- With -ness
  lonely + -ness = loneliness
- With -ly
  angry + -ly = angrily
- With -es
  salary + -es = salaries

The Exception

There's one group of exceptions to the previous rule:

- When you add -ing, keep the final *y*.
  study + -ing = *studying*

Spelling Practice 7

Rewrite the words with their suffixes in the blanks.

56. We hired two (attorney + -s)
_____ to handle the case.

57. She insisted on (relay + -ing)
_____ the message to her
father.

58. I found the movie very (enjoy + -able)
_____.

59. The children were (play + -ing)
_____ outdoors.

60. The mosquitoes were a serious (annoy + -ance)
_____.

61. He always (hurry + -es) _____
to get to school early.

62. The lumberjack ate (hearty + -ly)
_____ through a stack of
pancakes.

63. She spent all her spare time (study + -ing)
_____ for the exam.

64. He (angry + -ly) _____
slammed the door.

65. The student is (worry + ed) _____
that she won't get her assignment turned
in on time.

Plurals

One of the difficulties of spelling in English is the making of plurals. Unfortunately, you can't always simply add the letter -s to the end of the word to signal more than one.

When to Use -s or -es to Form Plurals

There are two simple rules that govern most plurals.

Most nouns add -s to make plurals.
If a noun ends in a sibilant sound (*s, ss, z, ch, x, sh*), add -es.

The following are some examples of plurals:

books	computers	guesses
buzzes	dishes	indexes
cars	dresses	lunches
churches	faxes	skills

The Exception

Remember from the last lesson that when a word ends in a *y* preceded by a consonant, the *y* changes to *i* when you add *-es*.

Singular	Plural
fly	flies
rally	rallies

Plurals for Words That End in o

There's just one quick rule that governs a few words ending in *o*.

If a final *o* follows another vowel, it takes *-s*.

Here are some examples:

patios	radios
studios	videos

The Exceptions

When the final *o* follows a consonant rather than a vowel, there's no rule to guide you in choosing *-s* or *-es*. You just have to learn the individual words.

The following words form a plural with *-s* alone.

albinos	pianos
altos	silos
banjos	sopranos
logos	broncos

The following words take *-es*.

heroes	tomatoes
potatoes	vetoes

When in doubt about whether to add *-s* or *-es*, look it up in the dictionary.

Spelling Practice 8

Add *-s* or *-es* to the words in the following sentences.

66. The children created a game in which they pretended to be animal ___ .

67. There were flash ___ of lightning in the dark sky.

68. He struck several match ___ before one finally caught fire.

69. You have two guess ___ at the correct answer.

70. Spelling is one of the most helpful skill ___ you can develop.

71. He peeled so many potato ___ in the army that he wouldn't eat french fries for a year.

72. The two soprano ___ gave a wonderful performance.

73. He wished there were more hero ___ in the world today.

74. The piano ___ were out of tune.

75. The farmers harvest their tomato ___ in the summer months.

Plurals for Words That End in f

Some words that end in *f* or *fe* just take *-s* to form the plural. Others change the *f* to *v* and add *-es* or *-s*. Unfortunately, there are no rules that can apply to this category of plurals; you simply have to memorize them.

The following are some of the words that keep the final *f* and add *-s*:

beliefs	gulfs
chiefs	kerchiefs
cuffs	proofs

Here are some of the words that change the final *f* to *v* and take *-es*:

elves	loaves	thieves
knives	selves	wives
leaves	shelves	wolves

Plurals That Don't Use -s or -es

There are many words that don't use *-s* or *-es* to form plurals. These are usually words that still observe the rules of the languages from which they were adopted. Most of these plurals are part of your reading, speaking, and listening vocabularies. You can see that there are patterns that will help you. For instance, in Latin words, *-um* becomes *-a*, *-us* becomes *-i*, and, in Greek words, *-sis* becomes *-ses*. A good way to remember these plurals is by saying the words aloud, because for the most part, they do change form and you may remember them more easily if you listen to the sound of the spelling.

Singular	Plural	Singular	Plural
alumnus	alumni	man	men
analysis	analyses	medium	media
axis	axes	mouse	mice
basis	bases	oasis	oases
child	children	ox	oxen
curriculum	curricula	parenthesis	parentheses
datum	data	stratum	strata
deer	deer	thesis	theses
fungus	fungi	woman	women
goose	geese		

TIP

Have you ever written a word and then thought, *That looks like it's spelled wrong*? Trust your instincts. Take the time to look up the word to make sure you know how to spell it correctly. Plus, the act of looking it up will help you remember that word in the future!

Putting Words Together

Prefixes

Generally, when you add a prefix to a root word, neither the root nor the prefix changes spelling:

un- + prepared = unprepared
mal- + nutrition = malnutrition
sub- + traction = subtraction
mis- + informed = misinformed

This rule applies even when the root word begins with the same letter as the prefix. Generally, you use both consonants, but let your eye be your guide. If it looks odd, it's probably not spelled correctly. The following are some examples:

dissatisfied	irreverent
disservice	misspelled
illegible	misstep
irrational	unnatural

Spelling Practice 9

Circle the correctly spelled word in each of the following sentences.

76. The argument seemed (**ilogical, illogical**) to me.

77. He was busy (**collating, colating**) all the pages.

78. She was (**irreverent, ireverent**) in church today.

79. The (**comentator, commentator**) on TV summarized the news of the day.

80. They (**colaborated, collaborated**) on the project for school.

Hyphens

When you put words and word parts together, it's difficult to know when to leave the words separate, when to hyphenate, and when to put the words or word parts together into one new word. Do you write co-dependent or codependent? Do you have a son in law or a son-in-law? There are several rules for using hyphens to join words. Often, these words are joined so they can perform a new function in the sentence.

- Combine words with a hyphen to form an adjective when the adjective appears before a noun.
  > a well-heeled man
  > a first-rate hotel
  > a well-known actor
- When the combination of words that makes an adjective appears after the noun, the combination is not hyphenated.
  > It's a job ill suited to his talents.
  > She is well regarded in the community.
  > The hotel is first rate.
- Combine words with a hyphen when the words are used together as one part of speech. This includes family relationships.
  > editor-in-chief
  > jack-of-all-trades
  > maid-of-all-work
  > mother-in-law
  > runner-up
  > sister-in-law
- Use a hyphen before *elect* and after *vice*, *ex*, or *self* (except in the case of "vice president").

  > ex-president
  > ex-teacher
  > self-styled
  > senator-elect
  > vice-admiral

- Use a hyphen when joining a prefix to a capitalized word.
  > mid-Atlantic
  > pan-European
  > post-Civil War
  > trans-Siberian
  > un-American
- Use a hyphen to make compound numbers or fractions.
  > thirty-nine years
  > one and two-thirds cups of broth
  > one-half of the country
  > three-fourths of the electorate
- Also, use a hyphen when you combine numbers with nouns.
  > a class of six-year-olds
  > a two-year term
  > a twenty-five-cent fare
- Use a hyphen to form ethnic designations.
  > an African-American woman
  > the Sino-Russian War
  > the Austro-Hungarian Railroad

Except for the cases you just reviewed, prefixes are also joined directly to root words. The best rule of thumb is this: If the phrase acts like an adjective, it probably needs a hyphen. If you want to put two words together and they don't seem to fit into any of these rules, the best strategy is to consult a dictionary.

Apostrophes and Abbreviations

Apostrophes are often misused, and knowing when and when not to use them can be confusing. Of all the punctuation marks, the apostrophe is the one most likely to be misused. Fortunately, there are a few simple rules; if you follow them, you won't go wrong with apostrophes.

The Rules

1. Use an apostrophe to show possession: Jack's book.

2. Use an apostrophe to make a contraction: We don't like broccoli.

3. Do not use an apostrophe to make a plural: I have two apples (not apple's).

4. Do not use an apostrophe to make a number plural: the 1960s, ten 5s (five-dollar bills).

Possessives

The following rules show you how to use apostrophes to show possession.

- Singular noun: add *'s*
  the child's cap
- Singular noun ending in *ss*: add *'s*
  the hostess's home
- Plural noun ending in *s*: add *'*
  the lawyers' bills
- Plural noun not ending in *s*: add *'s*
  The Children's Museum, the men's clothes
- Proper noun (name): add *'s*
  Jenny's watch, Chris's car, the Jones's house
- Singular indefinite pronoun: add *'s*
  one's only hope
- Plural indefinite pronoun: add *'*
  all the others' votes
- Compound noun: add *'* or *'s* after the final word
  the men-at-arms' task, my mother-in-law's house
- Joint possession: add *'s* to the final name
  Jim and Fred's coffee house

- Separate possession: add *'s* after both names
  Betty's and Ching's menus

Contractions

A contraction is formed by putting two words together and omitting one or more letters. The idea is that you add an apostrophe to show that letters have been left out. For example, "We have decided to move to Alaska" becomes, "We've decided to move to Alaska."

Here's a list of some of the most common contractions:
he will = he'll
I will = I'll
we will = we'll
it is = it's
she is = she's
you are = you're
they are = they're
we are = we're
cannot = can't
1960 = '60
do not = don't
does not = doesn't
have not = haven't
should not = shouldn't
will not = won't

There are other ways in which an apostrophe can represent missing letters:

- In dialect: "I'm goin' down to the swimmin' hole," said the boy.
- When the letter *o* represents *of*: "Top o' the morning to you."

Spelling Practice 10

Practice using apostrophes by correcting the following sentences.

81. Mrs. Clarks' store had been built in the 1970s.

82. Everyones lawn chair's were stored in John and Marys backyard.

83. They had gone to the ladies room to powder their nose's.

84. Wed rather have dinner at my mother-in-laws house next door.

85. The Barnes' house has two garage door's.

Abbreviations

Many words and expressions in English are shortened by means of abbreviations. Though certain abbreviations are not usually used in formal writing, such as abbreviations for days of the week, they can be useful in less formal situations. Abbreviations are usually followed by periods.

The Exceptions

- Don't use periods with the two-letter postal code abbreviations for states: CA, FL, IL, NJ, NY, TX, and so on.
- Don't use periods for initials representing a company or agency: FBI, CBS, NFL.
- Don't use periods after the letters in acronyms.

Common Abbreviations

Type	Examples
Names of days	Sun., Mon., Tues., Wed., etc.
Names of months	Jan., Feb., Mar., Apr., etc.
Titles and degrees	Mr., Mrs., Ms., Esq., Dr., Hon., M.D., Ph.D., Ed.D.
Rank	Sgt., Capt., Maj., Col., Gen.
Business terms	C.O.D. (collect on delivery), Mfg. (Manufacturing), Inc. (Incorporated), Assn. (Association), Ltd. (Limited)

Spelling Practice 11

Circle the correct term in each sentence.

86. I will have two (**week's, weeks'**) vacation in (**N.O.V., Nov.**) this year.

87. Gen. (**Jone's, Jones's**) order was to leave on (**Sun., Sund.**)

88. My letter to my professor was addressed, "Mary Stevens, (**PHD., Ph.D.**)"

89. (**Les's and Larry's, Les and Larry's**) mopeds were parked outside.

90. My uncle moved to the state of (**M.D., MD**) when he became an (**M.D., MD**).

Answers

Spelling Practice 1
1. niece
2. deceit, conscience
3. achieving, height
4. relieved
5. reign
6. cashier
7. surveillance
8. frieze
9. chief
10. fiend

Spelling Practice 2
11. psychology
12. answer
13. debt
14. gnarled
15. indict
16. knowledge
17. calm
18. ghost
19. often
20. autumn

Spelling Practice 3
21. finally
22. submitting, submitted
23. thinking
24. stirred, stirring
25. controlling, controlled
26. plainness
27. rebelling, rebelled
28. weakness, weakly
29. legally
30. raining, rained

Spelling Practice 4
31. cymbal
32. generous
33. trafficking
34. circus, giraffe
35. circulate

Spelling Practice 5
36. weak
37. bear
38. minor
39. peel
40. which
41. stationery
42. right
43. cord
44. past
45. descent

Spelling Practice 6
46. surprising
47. desirable
48. courageous
49. fortunately
50. peaceable
51. advertisement
52. careless
53. politeness
54. argument
55. disgraceful

Spelling Practice 7
56. attorneys
57. relaying
58. enjoyable
59. playing
60. annoyance
61. hurries
62. heartily
63. studying
64. angrily
65. worried

Spelling Practice 8

66. animals
67. flashes
68. matches
69. guesses
70. skills
71. potatoes
72. sopranos
73. heroes
74. pianos
75. tomatoes

Spelling Practice 9

76. illogical
77. collating
78. irreverent
79. commentator
80. collaborated

Spelling Practice 10

81. Clark's
82. Everyone's, chairs, Mary's
83. ladies', noses
84. We'd, mother-in-law's
85. Barnes's, doors

Spelling Practice 11

86. weeks', Nov.
87. Jones's, Sun.
88. Ph.D.
89. Les's and Larry's
90. MD, M.D.

4 ▶ PREFIXES

First learn the meaning of what you say, and then speak.
—EPICTETUS, Greek philosopher (ca. 55–ca. 135)

CHAPTER SUMMARY

When actors analyze a character, they break the person's characteristics down into personality, mannerisms, and appearance in order to see what makes them tick. You do much the same thing when you analyze a word. Breaking a new word down into its parts can help you determine its meaning.

In order to be able to unlock the meaning of many words in the English language, it is useful for you to understand what a prefix is. A prefix is a word part at the beginning of a word that changes or adds to the meaning of the root word in some way. By learning some common prefixes, you will be able to decipher the meaning of many words that are unfamiliar to you. After you have completed the exercises in this chapter, you will be acquainted with the meanings of some common prefixes, which will improve your reading, speaking, and listening vocabularies.

Choose the word from the vocabulary list that best fits into the crossword puzzle. You can check your answers at the end of the chapter following the answers to the questions.

Vocabulary List 1: Prefixes

antecedent
antipathy
circumvent
consensus
controversy
decimate
demote
disinterested
euphemism
exorbitant
illegible
intermittent
malevolent
precursor
prognosis
retrospect
subordinate
synthesis
transcend
trivial

Across
4 medical "forecast"
5 unimportant
6 avoid, elude
8 occasional
9 preexistent, previous
11 the opposite of promote
12 excessive
13 integration
14 inferior
17 hindsight
18 predecessor
19 sinister, venomous

Down
1 destroy
2 to exceed
3 unreadable
6 dispute, argument
7 neutral, unprejudiced
10 general agreement
15 aversion, loathing
16 an expression for

antecedent   (an·ti·ˈsēd·ənt)
prefix: **ante** means before
(*adj.*)
going before in time
The VCR was a(n) _____ to the DVD player.

antipathy   (an·ˈtip·ə·thē)
prefix: **anti** means against
(*noun*)
revulsion, any object of strong dislike
I have a severe _____ toward cockroaches.

circumvent   (sər·kəm·ˈvent)
prefix: **circum** and **circ** mean around
(*verb*)
to go around; to catch in a trap; to gain superiority
    over; to prevent from happening
I tried to _____ any ill will between my two
    employees by giving them both a promotion.

consensus   (kən·ˈsen·səs)
prefix: **con** means with, together
(*noun*)
agreement, especially in opinion
The family finally reached a _____ and decided
    to adopt a dog from the pound.

controversy   (ˈkon·trə·ver·sē)
prefix: **contr** means against
(*noun*)
a discussion of a question in which opposing views
    clash
There is a _____ in my building about whether
    or not to implement a flip tax.

decimate   (ˈdes·i·māt)
prefix: **dec** means ten
(*verb*)
to destroy or kill a large portion of something, to take
    or destroy a tenth part of something
Humans continue to _____ the rainforest every
    day.

demote   (di·ˈmōt)
prefix: **de** means down, away from
(*verb*)
to lower in grade or position
The company had to _____ the vice president
    due to an economic downturn.

disinterested   (dis·ˈin·tər·est·ed)
prefix: **dis** means not, opposite of
(*adj.*)
not motivated by personal interest or selfish motives
He is the most _____ politician running for
    office this term.

euphemism   (ˈu·fə·mizm)
prefix: **eu** means good, well
(*noun*)
the use of a word or phrase that is considered less dis-
    tasteful or offensive than another
"Bachelorette" is a _____ for "spinster."

exorbitant   (ek·ˈzor·bi·tənt)
prefix: **ex** means out of, away from
(*adj.*)
going beyond what is reasonable and proper
The _____ cost of real estate in the big cities
    forces many people to move to the suburbs.

illegible   (i·ˈlej·ə·bəl)
prefix: **il** means not, opposite
(*adj.*)
not able to be read
Because my handwriting is _____, I always type
    my papers.

intermittent   (in·tər·ˈmit·ənt)
prefix: **inter** means between
(**adj.**)
stopping and starting again at intervals
_____ storms made for a turbulent flight.

malevolent   (mə·ˈlev·ə·lent)
prefix: **mal** means bad
(**adj.**)
having an evil disposition toward others
After losing her job, she became _____ toward
   those who became successful.

precursor   (pre·ˈkər·sər)
prefix: **pre** means before
(**noun**)
a forerunner, a harbinger, one who or that which
   goes before
My boss's _____ left the department in
   shambles.

prognosis   (prog·ˈnō·sis)
prefix: **pro** means before
(**noun**)
a forecast; especially in medicine
Even though my dog is old, her _____ for
   recovery is excellent.

retrospect   (ˈret·rō·spekt)
prefix: **retro** means back, again
(**verb**)
to think about the past
(**noun**)
looking back on or thinking about things past
In _____, I realized that perhaps I was too harsh
   with her.

subordinate   (sub·ˈor·din·it)
prefix: **sub** means under
(**adj.**)
inferior to or placed below another in rank, power, or
   importance

(**noun**)   (sub·ˈor·din·it)
a person or thing of lesser power or importance than
   another
(**verb**)   (sub·ˈor·din·āt)
to treat as inferior or less important
No one wanted to work for her because she treated
   those who were _____ to her without
   respect.

synthesis   (ˈsin·thə·sis)
prefix: **syn, sym** means with or together
(**noun**)
putting of two or more things together to form a
   whole
The _____ between the two elements created a
   poisonous mixture.

transcend   (tran·ˈsend)
prefix: **trans** means across
(**verb**)
to go beyond the limits of; to overstep; to exceed
Knowing him, he will _____ this setback and
   still win the marathon.

trivial   (ˈtriv·ē·əl)
prefix: **tri** means three
(**adj.**)
of little worth or importance
Although everyone was excited about the new
   development, it became clear that it was
   _____ and would not benefit the company
   in any way.

TIP

Make a list of some other words that use the
same prefixes. Look them up and make flash
cards!

Words in Context

The following exercise will help you figure out the meaning of some words from the vocabulary list by reading context clues. After you have read and understood the paragraph, explain the context clues that helped you with the meaning of the vocabulary word. Refer to the answer section at the end of this chapter for an explanation of the clues.

In our country, the use of nuclear power as a viable source of energy has been an ongoing *controversy.* During the gas and oil shortages of the 1970s, energy prices were *exorbitant.* The federal government supported nuclear power as a new energy source that would be cost effective. Now, the president's National Energy Policy Report lists nuclear power as a safe and affordable alternative. Today, however, as in the past, many people have voiced their *antipathy* toward nuclear power plants, especially in the wake of the 1979 partial meltdown of the Three Mile Island nuclear power plant. At that time, scientists scrambled to *circumvent* a total meltdown in a facility that was designed to be fail-safe. There was great fear that the meltdown would be complete and *decimate* the area. Now, the federal government is once again promoting this alternative energy source.

TIP

The next time you see a word you don't know, try to figure out its meaning based on the context in which it is used. Then, check to see if you're right.

Sentence Completion

Insert the correct word from the vocabulary list into the following sentences.

1. There has been a local _____ over the proposed plans for the renovation of a neighborhood park.

2. At the Cradle of Aviation Museum, a(n) _____ of man's first trip to the moon in 1969 will include a restored lunar module.

3. Soon after the war began in Bosnia in April 1992, the damaged buildings and burned homes reduced the country to ruins and _____ the landscape.

4. Scientists have discovered what could be the closest _____ to man, an upright apelike creature.

5. The stock market has on average declined over the past year, with _____ periods of growth.

6. Oprah Winfrey was able to _____ her humble roots to become one of the nation's most respected, wealthy, and powerful women.

7. The police department's crime stopper's unit placed a drawing and description of the _____ kidnapper in the newspaper.

8. Errors caused by physicians' _____ handwriting have sparked proposals to add handwriting courses to medical school curricula.

9. After the implantation of a heart pacemaker, the patient's _____ was good.

10. "Downsizing a company" is a(n) _____ for letting go or firing employees.

11. Different ethnic groups' _____ toward each other has resulted in many wars throughout the world.

12. Because of the _____ price and gas consumption of the sports utility vehicle, the first-time buyer selected a small, energy-efficient sedan.

13. After the _____ successfully increased the company's sales and production, the chief executive officer promoted her to regional sales manager.

14. Environmentalists and energy analysts have not reached a(n) _____ about how best to meet America's growing energy needs in a safe and financially sound manner.

15. Due to his mistreatment of fellow officers, the captain was _____ to the rank of sergeant.

16. The famous actor seemed _____ in fame and the constant media attention he received; he continued to live his life in the same way as before his rise to fame.

17. A patchwork quilt is the result of the _____ of many smaller pieces sewn together to make a unique design.

18. In order to _____ the impending storm, the pilot changed his flight plan to avoid turbulence and lightning.

19. My _____ were some of the first colonial activists in the United States; they took part in the Boston Tea Party.

20. What some may consider _____ or unimportant ideas sometimes blossom into good business ventures.

Synonyms

The following exercise lists vocabulary words from this chapter. Each word is followed by five answer choices. Four of them are synonyms of the vocabulary word in bold. Your task is to choose the one that is NOT a synonym.

21. controversy
  a. dispute
  b. quarrel
  c. consensus
  d. debate
  e. disputation

22. disinterested
  a. selfish
  b. impartial
  c. neutral
  d. objective
  e. unbiased

23. antipathy
  a. aversion
  b. dislike
  c. hatred
  d. sympathy
  e. abhorrence

24. exorbitant
  a. reasonable
  b. excessive
  c. overpriced
  d. inflated
  e. steep

25. intermittent
  a. sporadic
  b. alternating
  c. recurring
  d. occasional
  e. continual

26. malevolent
  a. malicious
  b. spiteful
  c. nasty
  d. disinterested
  e. wicked

27. transcend
  a. exceed
  b. descend
  c. excel
  d. surpass
  e. outdo

28. precursor
  a. successor
  b. forerunner
  c. ancestor
  d. antecedent
  e. predecessor

29. consensus
  a. agreement
  b. harmony
  c. disagreement
  d. consent
  e. unity

30. decimate
  a. demolish
  b. annihilate
  c. build
  d. slaughter
  e. kill

Antonyms

Choose the word from the vocabulary list that means the opposite, or most nearly the opposite, of the following groups of words.

31. descendant, successor, progeny, heir   _____

32. readable, decipherable, comprehensible, clear   _____

33. direct, face, aim, confront   _____

34. disorganization, chaos, decomposition, separation   _____

35. promote, encourage, sponsor, support   _____

36. benevolent, caring, compassionate, kindly   _____

37. leading, chief, primary, foremost   _____

38. trail, follow, tail, drag   _____

39. significant, major, important, noteworthy

_____

40. continuous, constant, nonstop, incessant

_____

Matching Questions

Match the word in the first column with the corresponding word in the second column.

41. circumvent   **a.** dispute

42. retrospect   **b.** combination

43. euphemism   **c.** excessive

44. precursor   **d.** destroy

45. synthesis   **e.** skirt

46. antipathy   **f.** predecessor

47. disinterested   **g.** hindsight

48. exorbitant   **h.** pleasant substitute words

49. controversy   **i.** hatred

50. decimate   **j.** neutral

Practice Activities

Write ten words that begin with the same prefixes as the words in this unit. Write your definition of each word based on what you already know about each prefix. Be sure to check your answers with a dictionary definition of each word.

Example: _preactivity_ means a warm-up activity that comes before the main activity.

Create a personal "pictionary" prefix book. List common prefixes along with their definitions and create drawings that remind you of their meanings.

Example:

Prefix	Definition	Illustration
anti	against	(draw a no-smoking sign) 🚭 to show you are **against** smoking

Answers

Words in Context

We learn that nuclear energy has its supporters and opponents who continually debate each other; therefore, *controversy* means a public dispute. We read that energy prices were *exorbitant* and the government began to promote nuclear power as a *financially reasonable alternative*. The implication is that *exorbitant* is excessive. After reading what has gone wrong with one particular power plant, we can infer that *antipathy* refers to the *negative feelings* of a significant portion of the population who oppose and intensely *dislike the idea* of nuclear power plants. After the disaster, we learn that scientists tried to *circumvent*, or *prevent*, a total meltdown. Finally, it was necessary for the scientists to stop a complete meltdown because it would *decimate*, or totally destroy, the area. The partial meltdown of the reactor was disastrous enough, so the result of a total meltdown would be unimaginable destruction.

Sentence Completion

1. *controversy.* If you got this question wrong, refer back to the word's definition.
2. *retrospect.* If you got this question wrong, refer back to the word's definition.
3. *decimated.* If you got this question wrong, refer back to the word's definition.
4. *precursor.* If you got this question wrong, refer back to the word's definition.
5. *intermittent.* If you got this question wrong, refer back to the word's definition.
6. *transcend.* If you got this question wrong, refer back to the word's definition.
7. *malevolent.* If you got this question wrong, refer back to the word's definition.
8. *illegible.* If you got this question wrong, refer back to the word's definition.
9. *prognosis.* If you got this question wrong, refer back to the word's definition.
10. *euphemism.* If you got this question wrong, refer back to the word's definition.
11. *antipathy.* If you got this question wrong, refer back to the word's definition.
12. *exorbitant.* If you got this question wrong, refer back to the word's definition.
13. *subordinate.* If you got this question wrong, refer back to the word's definition.
14. *consensus.* If you got this question wrong, refer back to the word's definition.
15. *demoted.* If you got this question wrong, refer back to the word's definition.
16. *disinterested.* If you got this question wrong, refer back to the word's definition.
17. *synthesis.* If you got this question wrong, refer back to the word's definition.
18. *circumvent.* If you got this question wrong, refer back to the word's definition.
19. *antecedents.* If you got this question wrong, refer back to the word's definition.
20. *trivial.* If you got this question wrong, refer back to the word's definition.

Synonyms

21. c. *consensus.* Controversy is a discussion where opposing views clash. Therefore, consensus would not be a synonym of the word because it means to come to an agreement.
22. a. *selfish.* Disinterested means not motivated by personal interest. Therefore, selfish would not be a synonym of the word because it means the opposite—to have a personal interest.
23. d. *sympathy.* Antipathy means to have a feeling of hatred toward someone or something. Since sympathy means to have feelings of compassion for someone or something, it cannot be a synonym of the word.
24. a. *reasonable.* Exorbitant means excessive; thus, reasonable is the opposite in meaning and cannot be a synonym.

25. e. *continual.* Intermittent means to happen at regular intervals, whereas continual means without stopping; therefore, it cannot be the synonym of the word.

26. d. *disinterested.* Malevolent means to have evil feelings and intentions toward someone or something. Disinterested means to be neutral about someone or something; thus, it cannot be the synonym of the word.

27. b. *descend.* Transcend means to go beyond, whereas descend means to go below and cannot be a synonym of the word.

28. a. *successor.* A precursor is something that comes before. Successor cannot be a synonym because it means something that comes after.

29. c. *disagreement.* Consensus is an agreement, so disagreement cannot be a synonym.

30. c. *build.* Decimate means to destroy; therefore, build cannot be a synonym of the word.

Antonyms

31. *antecedent.* Antecedent means ancestors, the opposite of the meaning of the words in the group.

32. *illegible.* Illegible means unreadable, the opposite of the words in the group.

33. *circumvent.* Circumvent means to go around, the opposite of the words in the group.

34. *synthesis.* Synthesis means the combination of two or more items to become a whole, the opposite of the meaning of the words in the group.

35. *demote.* Demote means to downgrade, the opposite of the meaning of the words in the group.

36. *malevolent.* Malevolent means evil, the opposite of the meaning of the words in the group.

37. *subordinate.* Subordinate means secondary, the opposite of the meaning of the words group.

38. *transcend.* Transcend means exceed, the opposite of the meaning of the words in the group.

39. *trivial.* Trivial means unimportant, the opposite of the meaning of the words in the group.

40. *intermittent.* Intermittent means interrupted, the opposite of the meaning of the words in the group.

Matching Questions

41. e

42. g

43. h

44. f

45. b

46. i

47. j

48. c

49. a

50. d

Across

4 prognosis
5 trivial
6 circumvent
8 intermittent
9 antecedent
11 demote
12 exorbitant
13 synthesis
14 subordinate
17 retrospect
18 precursor
19 malevolent

Down

1 decimate
2 transcend
3 illegible
6 controversy
7 disinterested
10 consensus
15 antipathy
16 euphemism

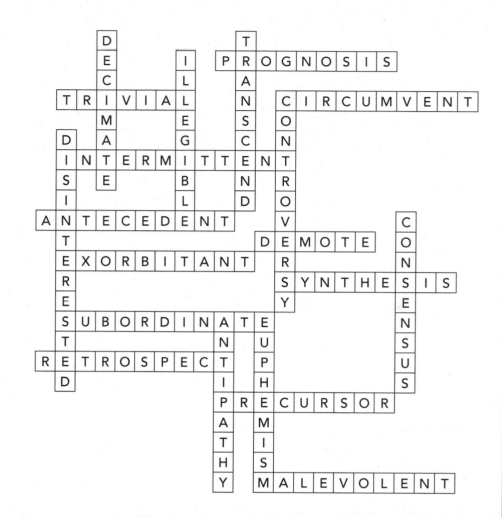

5 ▶ SUFFIXES

To handle a language skillfully is to practice a kind of evocative sorcery.

—CHARLES BAUDELAIRE, French poet (1821–1867)

CHAPTER SUMMARY

Just as a movie director must check each part of a movie set in order to make sure it's functioning correctly, readers must check each part of a word in order to analyze its meaning. And similarly, just as the end of a movie is as important as its beginning, a word ending plays an important role in determining its part of speech.

Word endings that are added to the main part, or root, of words are called suffixes. Suffixes are word parts that signal how a word is being used in a sentence. Suffixes often change the part of speech of a word.

For example, take a look at the word *deferment* from this chapter's vocabulary list. *Deferment* is a noun that means a postponement. If the suffix (*-ment*) is removed, the word becomes *defer,* and it is used as a verb that means to postpone.

As a *verb,* it appears as *defer*:
I will *defer* the payment until next month.

As a *noun,* it appears as it is:
The bank gave him a *deferment.*

As an *adjective,* it appears as *deferred*:
The *deferred* payment is due in one month.

Choose the word from the vocabulary list that best fits into the crossword puzzle. You will use 17 of the words from the vocabulary list to solve the puzzle. You can check your answers at the end of the chapter following the answers to the questions.

Vocabulary List 2: Suffixes

bigotry
consummate
copious
cryptic
deferment
etymology
exacerbate
furtive
laudable
mutation
obsolescence
parity
pragmatism
protagonist
provocative
puerile
rectify
relentless
satirize
venerate

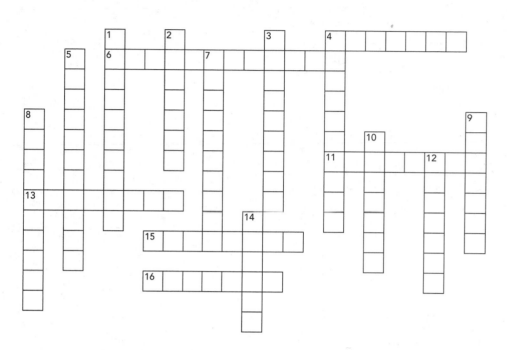

Across

4 to correct, make right
6 uselessness
11 praiseworthy
13 change, variation
15 to honor
16 obscure, secret

Down

1 perfect, complete, accomplished
2 bountiful
3 delay
4 unceasing
5 irritating, stirring into action
7 to make worse
8 practicality
9 childish
10 stealthy
12 prejudice, intolerance
14 equality

NOUN ENDINGS

SUFFIX	MEANING	EXAMPLES
-tion	act or state of	benefaction, conservation
-ment	quality	comportment, indictment
-ist	one who	archaeologist, biologist
-ism	state or doctrine of	absolutism, altruism
-ity	state of being	sanity, scarcity
-ology	study of	theology
-escence	state of	acquiescence
-y, -ary	act or state of	flattery, commentary

ADJECTIVE ENDINGS

SUFFIX	MEANING	EXAMPLES
-able	capable	dependable, believable
-ic	causing, making	eccentric, optimistic
-ian	one who is or does	politician, statistician
-ile	pertaining to	reptile, fertile
-ious	having the quality of	delicious, superstitious
-ive	having the nature of	decisive, incisive
-less	without	senseless, painless

VERB ENDINGS

SUFFIX	MEANING	EXAMPLES
-ize	to bring about	aggrandize, monopolize
-ate	to make	operate, translate
-ify	to make	verify, magnify

TIP

Before you flip the page, go back to the list next to the crossword and see if you can identify each word's part of speech based on its suffix. Then, check the definitions to see if you are right.

The previous table shows the suffixes that are used in this vocabulary list. They are divided into the parts of speech, or the "jobs" they suggest for the words. Other words that contain those suffixes are listed. In the last column, add at least one other word that uses the suffix, besides the one in today's vocabulary list.

agrarian   (ə·ˈgrer·ē·ən)
suffix: **-ian** means one who is or does
(*adj.*)
having to do with agriculture or farming
The farmer loved his _____ life.

antagonist   (an·ˈta·gə·nist)
suffix: **-ist** means one who
(*noun*)
one that contends with or opposes another
In the movie *Batman*, the Joker is Batman's
    _____.

bigotry   (ˈbig·ə·trē)
suffix: **-ry** means state of
(*noun*)
unreasonable zeal in favor of a party, sect, or
    opinion; excessive prejudice
_____ can lead to malevolent actions.

consummate   (ˈkon·səm·māt)
suffix: **-ate** means to make
(*verb*)
to complete, to carry to the utmost degree
The business woman needed to _____ the deal
    quickly.

copious   (ˈcōp·ē·əs)
suffix: **-ious** means having the quality of
(*adj.*)
abundant; plentiful; in great quantities
A _____ amount of sunshine is predicted for the
    summer.

cryptic   (ˈkrip·tik)
suffix: **-ic** means causing
(*adj.*)
hidden; secret; having a hidden or ambiguous
    meaning
The detective uncovered the meaning of the
    _____ message.

deferment   (di·ˈfər·mənt)
suffix: **-ment** means quality of
(*noun*)
the act of putting off or delaying; postponement
The bank offered the struggling college graduate a
    _____ on his student loan payment.

exacerbate   (ig·ˈza·ser·ˈbāt)
suffix: **-ate** means to make
(*verb*)
to make more violent, bitter, or severe
The cold weather _____ her dry skin.

furtive   (ˈfər·tiv)
suffix: **-ive** means having the nature of
(*adj.*)
done in a stealthy manner; sly and underhanded
The two criminals who were in cahoots gave each
    other _____ looks behind the detective's
    back.

laudable   (ˈlaw·də·bəl)
suffix: **-able** means capable of
(*adj.*)
praiseworthy
Her dedication and ability to rehabilitate the injured
    is _____.

geology   (jē·ˈä·lə·jē)
suffix: **-ology** means study of
(*noun*)
the study of the history of the earth and its life,
    especially as recorded in rocks
The _____ major traveled to Mt. Etna to
    examine the effects of the volcano's most recent
    eruption.

minimize   (ˈmi·nə·mīz)
suffix: **-ize** means to subject to an action
(*verb*)
to play down; to keep to a minimum
The president tried to _____ his involvement in
    the trial so that he would not be implicated in
    the scandal.

mutation   (mū·ˈtā·shən)

suffix: **-tion** means action of, state of

(*noun*)

the act or process of changing

Scientists research gene _____ in fruit flies to see how genes change from one generation to the next.

obsolescence   (äb·sə·ˈles·ens)

suffix: **-escence** means state of

(*noun*)

the state of being outdated

With the advent of the personal computer, the typewriter has been in _____ for many years.

parity   (ˈpar·i·tē)

suffix: **-ity** means state of being

(*noun*)

the state or condition of being the same in power, value, or rank; equality

Women and minorities continue to fight for _____ in the workplace.

pragmatism   (ˈprag·mə·tizm)

suffix: **-ism** means state or doctrine of

(*noun*)

faith in the practical approach

Her _____ has helped her start her own business and maintain it for many years.

provocative   (prō·ˈvok·ə·tiv)

suffix: **-ive** means having the nature of

(*adj.*)

something that stirs up an action

His _____ speech caused many to support his campaign.

puerile   (ˈpyoor·əl)

suffix: **-ile** means pertaining to

(*adj.*)

childish, silly, immature

Based on Jared's _____ behavior, one would think he is a teenager rather than a father of two.

rectify   (ˈrek·ti·fī)

suffix: **-ify** means to make

(*verb*)

to make right; to correct

I tried to _____ the situation by seating the two employees in different departments.

relentless   (re·ˈl ənt·les)

suffix: **-less** means without

(*adj.*)

harsh; unmoved by pity; unstoppable

I was _____ with my athletic training when I was preparing for the Regionals.

venerate   (ˈven·ə·rāt)

suffix: **-ate** means to make

(*verb*)

to look upon with deep respect and reverence

My parents taught me to _____ my teachers.

Words in Context

The following exercise will help you figure out the meaning of some words from the vocabulary list by reading context clues. After you have read and understood the paragraph, explain the context clues that helped you with the meaning of the vocabulary word. Refer to the answer section at the end of this chapter for an explantion of the clues.

The latest remake of *Planet of the Apes* develops the theme of *bigotry* in a world where apes are the dominant culture and humans are enslaved. *Parity* between the two species is unthinkable because the simians regard humans as inferior creatures. Leo, the central character, is the story's protagonist. He is a human astronaut who lands on a strange planet where apes *venerate* their own kind by offering praise and promotions for negative actions taken against humans. Leo's *antagonist*, General Thade, is the leader of the apes in this bizarre culture, and encourages the mistreatment of humans by apes. In General Thade's opinion, extermination of the humans is a *laudable* cause, and he mounts a full-scale campaign to exterminate humans from the planet.

Sentence Completion

Insert the word from the vocabulary list that best completes the sentences.

1. Pulitzer Prize–winning novelist Eudora Welty was _____ in her obituary.

2. You would never accuse Mark of _____; he's the most open-minded person I know.

3. It took several months to _____ the merger, but after tough negotiation, the two companies became one.

4. The young boy's removal from the Little League game was due to his _____ behavior of throwing the bat when he was angry.

5. Rainforests are known for their _____ amounts of rainfalls, which supply the fauna with many nutrients.

6. During WWII, Native Americans worked to develop a(n) _____ code that could not be deciphered by the enemy.

7. Because of the family's _____ search, they were quickly reunited with their lost dog.

8. My little brother is the _____ in the family; he constantly provokes fights with my sister and me.

9. Sally wore sunscreen at the beach to _____ her chances of getting a sunburn.

10. Due to the _____ of the budget director's financial policies, the economy grew stronger.

11. In order to _____ the wrongdoing of the internment of innocent Japanese Americans during WWII, the U.S. government has agreed to pay reparations to victims.

12. A(n) _____ in certain strains of powerful bacteria has turned them into drug-resistant menaces.

13. The actions of a few skittish animals _____ the majority of horses to stampede.

14. Union officials continuously fight for _____ in pay and working conditions.

15. The horse and buggy reached its _____ in the early 1900s with the production of the automobile.

16. In order to entice the consumer, companies will offer a short-term _____ on payments for buying merchandise.

17. I loved studying _____ because I enjoyed looking at interesting rocks and how they came to be on Earth.

18. The young teen's heroic effort to save the family from the sinking car was _____.

19. The spy's disguise and _____ actions were undetected by foreign government officials.

20. The haying season is my favorite part of _____ life.

Synonyms

The following exercise lists vocabulary words from this chapter. Each word is followed by five answer choices. Four of them are synonyms of the vocabulary word in bold. Your task is choose the one that is NOT a synonym.

21. relentless
- **a.** unstoppable
- **b.** persistent
- **c.** unyielding
- **d.** capitulate
- **e.** inexorable

22. laudable
- **a.** praiseworthy
- **b.** worthy
- **c.** commendable
- **d.** creditable
- **e.** furtive

23. parity
- **d.** equity
- **b.** inequality
- **c.** par
- **d.** fairness
- **e.** evenhandedness

24. venerate
- **a.** respect
- **b.** honor
- **c.** minimize
- **d.** revere
- **e.** worship

25. puerile
- **a.** childish
- **b.** juvenile
- **c.** mature
- **d.** infantile
- **e.** babyish

26. furtive
- **a.** stealthy
- **b.** secret
- **c.** sly
- **d.** honest
- **e.** surreptitious

27. copious
- **a.** scarce
- **b.** abundant
- **c.** numerous
- **d.** plentiful
- **e.** profuse

28. rectify
- **a.** revise
- **b.** correct
- **c.** fix
- **d.** destroy
- **e.** remedy

29. provocative
- **a.** challenging
- **b.** inciting
- **c.** stimulating
- **d.** confrontational
- **e.** conciliatory

30. mutation
- **a.** static
- **b.** changing
- **c.** transformation
- **d.** metamorphosis
- **e.** alteration

TIP

Sometimes associating a word with a synonym can help you remember its meaning.

Antonyms

Choose the word from the vocabulary list that means the opposite, or most nearly the opposite, of the following groups of words.

31. curtail, shorten, curb, limit _____

32. tolerance, broadmindedness, open-mindedness, acceptance _____

33. impracticality, uselessness, fruitlessness, pointlessness _____

34. clear, obvious, apparent, straightforward _____

35. scarce, limited, inadequate, scant _____

36. protagonist, leader, hero, supporter _____

37. inequality, inequity, discrimination, disparity _____

38. urban, city, metropolitan, cosmopolitan _____

39. despise, loathe, scorn, hate _____

40. magnify, intensify, enhance, overplay _____

Choosing the Right Word

Circle the word in bold that best completes the sentence.

41. Since I grew up on a ranch in Montana, I appreciate the constant struggle of the (**antagonist, agrarian**) lifestyle.

42. She filled an entire notebook with the (**copious, laudable**) notes that she took during the class.

43. The car salesman wanted to (**consummate, rectify**) the car deal before the customers changed their minds.

44. Her (**cryptic, puerile**) behavior made her seem childish and immature.

45. The automotive industry builds a certain amount of (**pragmatism, obsolescence**) into cars so that they will need to be replaced in a few years.

46. Language interpreters can even decipher (**provocative, cryptic**) phrases that most people wouldn't understand.

47. In order to eliminate (**bigotry, geology**) many schools have included programs to reduce hatred of others and increase tolerance.

48. The Coast Guard's (**relentless, furtive**) search for any survivors of the airplane crash lasted three weeks.

49. In some cultures, people (**minimize, venerate**) their elders by seeking their wisdom.

50. Scientists can monitor the (**mutation, deferment**) of certain bacteria by watching them change form over time.

Practice Activities

List all the words in this chapter and try changing the part of speech of each word by changing its suffix. For instance, change *deferment* to *deferred* or *defer*. Be sure to check the definition of the altered word.

> Example: **Venerate** changed to **veneration** means a feeling of deep respect.

Find words in the newspaper that have the same suffixes as the words in this unit. Write them next to the chapter words and take a guess at their meanings. Check your definition with a dictionary definition.

For example, one of the suffixes in the vocabulary list is *-tion*, which means state of or action of. You might find in the newspaper the word *evolution*, meaning the act of changing over a period of time.

Answers

Words in Context

After reading the paragraph, we learn that the movie *Planet of the Apes* is an upside-down world where apes rule over humans and believe them to be inferior creatures whose only use are to be slaves; thus, we may conclude that *bigotry* means intolerance. Since the humans are slaves, their ape owners would **not** want them to achieve *parity*; therefore, the inference is that *parity* means equality. Leo, the central character, is the protagonist. Therefore, we know that *antagonist* must mean someone who is opposing him, because Thade mounts an attempt to exterminate humans, and we know that Leo is a human. The story shows the *antipathy*, the hatred, between apes and humans. The apes *venerate*, show respect, and honor their leaders. They respect their species and reward *laudable* deeds such as capturing escaped humans. We can infer that *laudable* means praiseworthy.

Sentence Completion

1. *venerated*. If you got this question wrong, refer back to the word's definition.
2. *bigotry*. If you got this question wrong, refer back to the word's definition.
3. *consummate*. If you got this question wrong, refer back to the word's definition.
4. *puerile*. If you got this question wrong, refer back to the word's definition.
5. *copious*. If you got this question wrong, refer back to the word's definition.
6. *cryptic*. If you got this question wrong, refer back to the word's definition.
7. *relentless*. If you got this question wrong, refer back to the word's definition.
8. *antagonist*. If you got this question wrong, refer back to the word's definition.
9. *minimize*. If you got this question wrong, refer back to the word's definition.
10. *pragmatism*. If you got this question wrong, refer back to the word's definition.
11. *rectify*. If you got this question wrong, refer back to the word's definition.
12. *mutation*. If you got this question wrong, refer back to the word's definition.
13. *provoked*. If you got this question wrong, refer back to the word's definition.
14. *parity*. If you got this question wrong, refer back to the word's definition.
15. *obsolescence*. If you got this question wrong, refer back to the word's definition.
16. *deferment*. If you got this question wrong, refer back to the word's definition.
17. *geology*. If you got this question wrong, refer back to the word's definition.
18. *laudable*. If you got this question wrong, refer back to the word's definition.
19. *furtive*. If you got this question wrong, refer back to the word's definition.
20. *agrarian*. If you got this question wrong, refer back to the word's definition.

Synonyms

21. d. *capitulate*. Relentless means to never give up, so capitulate would not be a synonym of the word, since it means to surrender.
22. e. *furtive*. Laudable means worthy of praise, so furtive would not be a synonym of the word, since it means sneaky.
23. b. *inequality*. Parity means equality, thus inequality would not be a synonym of the word because it means to not be equal.
24. c. *minimize*. Venerate means to hold in the highest regard, so minimize would not be a synonym of the word, since it means to play down or keep to a minimum.
25. c. *mature*. Puerile means childish, so mature would not be a synonym of the word, since it means grown-up.

26. d. *honest.* Furtive means sneaky and under-handed, so honest would not be a synonym of the word, since it means open.

27. a. *scarce.* Copious means plentiful, so scarce would not be a synonym of the word, since it means in short supply.

28. d. *destroy.* Rectify means to make right or correct, so destroy is not a synonym.

29. e. *conciliatory.* Provocative means inciting to action, so conciliatory would not be a synonym of the word, since it means appeasing.

30. a. *static.* Mutation means to change in form, so static would not be a synonym of the word, since it means unchanging.

Antonyms

31. *consummate.* Consummate means to complete, the opposite of the meaning of the words in the group.

32. *bigotry.* Bigotry means narrow-mindedness, the opposite of the meaning of the words in the group.

33. *pragmatism.* Pragmatism means common sense, the opposite of the meaning of the words in the group.

34. *cryptic.* Cryptic means hidden, the opposite of the meaning of the words in the group.

35. *copious.* Copious means plentiful, the opposite of the meaning of the words in the group.

36. *antagonist.* An antagonist is opposition or an adversary, the opposite of the meaning of the words in the group.

37. *parity.* Parity means equality, the opposite of the meaning of the words in the group.

38. *agrarian.* Agrarian means having to do with farming and agriculture, the opposite of the words in the group.

39. *venerate.* Venerate means to honor, the opposite of the meaning of the words in the group.

40. *minimize.* Minimize means to play down or keep to a minimum, the opposite of the meaning of the words in the group.

Choosing the Right Word

41. *agrarian.* Context clue is the ranch in Montana; life on a ranch would have to do with agriculture and farming.

42. *copious.* Context clue is that she filled a notebook with her notes.

43. *consummate.* Context clue is that the car salesman wanted the customers to finish the transaction by buying a car.

44. *puerile.* Context clue is that her behavior appeared childish and immature.

45. *obsolescence.* Context clue is that the car industry makes cars that eventually must be replaced.

46. *cryptic.* Context clue is that most people wouldn't understand the phrase.

47. *bigotry.* Context clue is that many schools have programs to reduce hatred.

48. *relentless.* Context clue is that the Coast Guard searched for three weeks.

49. *venerate.* Context clue is that people in some cultures seek their elders' wisdom.

50. *mutation.* Context clue is that the bacteria change over time.

Across

4 rectify
6 obsolescence
11 laudable
13 mutation
15 venerate
16 cryptic

Down

1 consummate
2 copious
3 deferment
4 relentless
5 provocative
7 exacerbate
8 pragmatism
9 puerile
10 furtive
12 bigotry
14 parity

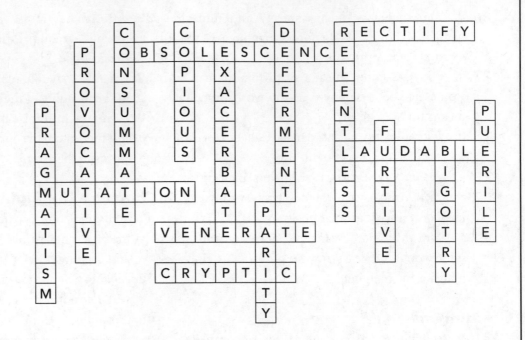

6 ▶ LEARNING ROOTS

One forgets words as one forgets names. One's vocabulary needs constant fertilizing or it will die.

—Evelyn Waugh, author (1903–1966)

CHAPTER SUMMARY

Becoming familiar with Greek and Latin roots will help you build your vocabulary by helping you recognize the base of many words.

Just as a good gardener builds a lovely garden by having its plants maintain strong, healthy roots, you will see your vocabulary grow by recognizing common roots in words. Although it is the main part of a word, a root is not necessarily a complete word by itself. It is the base to which a prefix and/or suffix might be added.

In this chapter, you will become familiar with 20 common roots. Connected to these roots are various suffixes that you have already become acquainted with in Chapter 5. You are on your way toward building a strong vocabulary by making the connections between these word parts and their meanings.

Choose the word from the vocabulary list that best fits into the crossword puzzle. You can check your answers at the end of the chapter following the answers to the questions.

Vocabulary List 3: Learning Roots

agonize
audible
belligerent
chronic
demographic
fidelity
fluctuate
genocide
incognito
inducement
interrogate
loquacious
nominal
pathos
protracted
rejected
sophisticated
tenacious
verify
vivacious

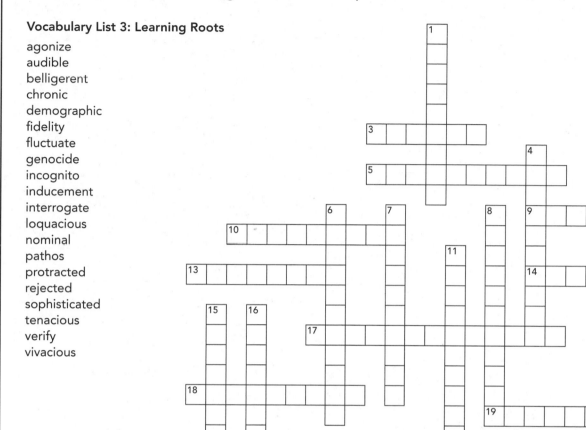

Across

3 confirm
5 incentive
9 able to be heard
10 undercover
13 intentional destruction of an entire group of people
14 small amount
17 experienced and aware
18 change often
19 constant, continuous
20 drawn out

Down

1 persistent
2 discarded
4 to provoke
6 question, investigate
7 talkative, garrulous
8 statistical characteristics of human populations
11 hostile, aggressive
12 pathetic quality
15 faithfulness
16 lively, ebullient

agonize   ('a·gə·nīz)
root: **agon** means struggle, contest
(*verb*)
to suffer intense pain, to struggle over something
As a teacher, I _____ over how to reprimand my
    students.

audible   ('ô·də·bəl)
root: **aud** means hear
(*adj.*)
able to be heard
Something was wrong with the sound system, so the
    lead singer's voice was barely _____.

belligerent   (bəl·'lij·ər·ənt)
root: **bell** means war
(*adj.*)
warlike, hostile
I don't know what got into Margo; she became
    _____ when they told her that the class
    was full.

chronic   ('kron·ik)
root: **chron** means time
(*adj.*)
constant, habitual
Living with _____ pain can be exhausting.

demographic   (dem·ə·'graf·ik)
root: **dem** means people
(*noun*)
statistical characteristics of human population, such
    as age or income
The _____ information we received helped us
    create a marketing plan.

fidelity   (fi·'del·i·tē)
root: **fid** means faith
(*noun*)
faithfulness
One thing I will never question is her _____; she
    is one of the most loyal people I know.

fluctuate   ('flək·chu·āt)
root: **flux, flu** means to flow
(*verb*)
to move up and down, constantly changing
My weight tends to _____ according to the
    seasons.

genocide   ('jen·ə·sīd)
root: **gen** means race or kind
(*noun*)
the deliberate extermination of an entire group of
    people
Mass _____ is an atrocity that many times
    happens during civil war.

incognito   (in·kog·'nē·tō)
root: **cog, gno** means to know
(*noun*)
disguised, unrecognizable
I had to go to the party _____ in order to
    supervise my daughter and her friends.

inducement   (in·'düs·mənt)
root: **duc** means lead
(*noun*)
motive, leading to an action, incentive
As an _____, they offered free appetizers to
    anyone arriving between 9 and 10.

interrogate   (in·'ter·rə·gāt)
root: **rog** means to ask
(*verb*)
to question
Customs agents have the right to _____
    passengers.

loquacious   (lō·ˈkwā·shəs)
root: **loq** means speak
(***adj.***)
talkative
The _____ guest monopolized the conversation.

nominal   (ˈnom·ən·əl)
root: **nom** means name
(***adj.***)
in name only, small amount
She expended only _____ energy during the
    heat wave so that she wouldn't collapse.

pathos   (ˈpaˉ·thoˉs)
root: **path** means feelings
(***noun***)
suffering; feeling of sympathy or pity
Children who are raised to feel _____ are not
    usually bullies.

protracted   (prō·ˈtrak·ted)
root: **tract** means draw; pull
(***adj.***)
drawn out in time, prolonged
The union and the city could not agree on
    contractual terms, which led to a _____
    settlement.

rejected   (ri·ˈjek·ted)
root: **ject** means to throw or send
(***verb***)
sent back, refused, discarded
She _____ his offer of marriage, so he took the
    ring back to the jeweler.

sophisticated   (sə·ˈfis·ti·kā·ted)
root: **soph** means wisdom
(***adj.***)
knowledgeable; refined, experienced, and aware
The dance couple mastered the _____ jazz step.

tenacious   (tə·ˈnā·shəs)
root: **ten** means hold
(***adj.***)

unwilling to let go, stubborn
The _____ grip of the pit bull is what makes it
    so dangerous.

verify   (ˈver·ə·fī)
root: **ver** means truth
(***verb***)
to establish as truth, confirm
Scientists have not been able to _____ the
    existence of UFOs.

vivacious   (vi·ˈvā·shəs)
root: **viv** means life
(***adj.***)
lively in manner
The _____ teen became captain of the
    cheerleading team.

TIP

If you are a visual learner, it might help you to rewrite this list and use a different color pen to write the root of each word, in order to highlight it visually.

Words in Context

The following exercise will help you figure out the meaning of some words from the vocabulary list by reading context clues. After you have read and understood the paragraph, explain the context clues that helped you with the meaning of the vocabulary word. Refer to the answer section at the end of this chapter for an explanation of the clues.

Medical researchers can now *verify* that college freshman living in dormitories are at a greater risk of contracting meningitis than other college students. Meningococcal meningitis is a *tenacious* bacterial infection of membranes around the brain and spinal chord that, if left untreated, can be fatal.

Symptoms include fever, neck stiffness, and constant pain from a *chronic* headache. College officials are using this information as an *inducement* for vaccinating incoming freshman. Many universities are now offering this vaccine either free or for a *nominal* fee. The vaccination's *protracted* effectiveness is three to five years.

Sentence Completion

Insert the correct word from the vocabulary list into the following sentences.

1. Cambodian government officials are preparing to prosecute those leaders most responsible for the Khmer Rouge's _____ of one-fifth of the total population of the country.

2. Almost every area of our lives will be affected by our country's _____ changes as the baby boomers age.

3. Some infomercials promise rock-hard abdominals as a(n) _____ to buy a variety of exercise machines.

4. Janice is awfully quiet and pale tonight; it's such a contrast to her normally _____ personality.

5. Because of the _____ they feel for people, studies show that dogs in hospitals treat human patients with unconditional love.

6. During the annual San Fermin running of the bulls festival, spectators try to avoid the path of _____ bulls.

7. After the car collision, the passenger suffered from _____ back pain for the rest of his life.

8. Health fitness experts now _____ that walking ranks as America's most popular activity.

9. Temperatures in the desert can _____ greatly from brutally hot during the day to freezing temperatures at night.

10. Because of their known _____ toward their human companions, over one thousand dogs were sent overseas to protect American soldiers during the Vietnam War.

11. It's hard for my grandfather not to _____ over having to go into a retirement home, as he wants to remain independent as long as possible.

12. Famous sports and movie personalities often travel _____ in order to avoid being hounded by the media.

13. In order to _____ the alleged thief, proper police procedures must be followed.

14. The celebrity guest was known for his exciting storytelling; the talk-show host asked her _____ guest to tell the story of his youth.

15. After placing their home for sale, the homeowners _____ the first offer for their house because it was too low.

16. Even after being treated with strong antibiotics, the _____ ear infection would not ease its grip on its victim.

17. The radio was turned down so low that it was barely _____.

18. The _____ dispute between management and the team players lasted several years.

19. Since there was only a(n) _____ fee to enter the bike race, everyone could participate.

20. Animal cloning begins with a(n) _____ procedure in which scientists remove the DNA-containing nucleus of a female animal's egg and replace it with the genetic material from a body cell of an adult animal's donor.

Synonyms

The following exercise lists vocabulary words from this chapter. Each word is followed by five answer choices. Four of them are synonyms of the vocabulary word in bold. Your task is to choose the one that is NOT a synonym.

21. vivacious
   a. cheerful
   b. bubbly
   c. animated
   d. tenacious
   e. spirited

22. interrogate
   a. grill
   b. verify
   c. ask
   d. cross-examine
   e. interview

23. tenacious
   a. steadfast
   b. lazy
   c. stubborn
   d. strong
   e. hardworking

24. chronic
   a. continuing
   b. constant
   c. intermittent
   d. unceasing
   e. never-ending

25. incognito
   a. disguised
   b. undercover
   c. anonymously
   d. secretly
   e. open

26. illegible
   a. indecipherable
   b. scrawled
   c. scribbled
   d. audible
   e. unreadable

27. fluctuate
   a. vary
   b. steady
   c. vacillate
   d. oscillate
   e. ebb and flow

28. agonize
   a. struggle
   b. torment
   c. contend
   d. upset
   e. endure

29. nominal
   a. supposed
   b. small amount
   c. actual
   d. in name only
   e. so-called

30. **pathos**
   a. sorrow
   b. joy
   c. suffering
   d. pity
   e. grief

Antonyms

Choose the word from the vocabulary list that means the opposite, or most nearly the opposite, of the following groups of words.

31. passive, peaceful, nonviolent, diplomatic   _____

32. silent, reserved, reticent, taciturn   _____

33. disloyalty, betrayal, unfaithfulness, treachery   _____

34. accepted, agreed to, assented, wanted   _____

35. primitive, unrefined, uncultured, naïve   _____

36. agreeable, amenable, easygoing, flexible   _____

37. disprove, refute, invalidate, contradict   _____

38. candidly, openly, honestly, frankly   _____

39. languid, unenergetic, unhurried, lethargic   _____

40. occasional, intermittent, discontinued, rarely   _____

Matching Questions

Match the word in the first column with the corresponding word in the second column.

41. genocide   **a.** sent back

42. audible   **b.** sympathy

43. verify   **c.** destruction of a race

44. tenacious   **d.** disguised

45. rejected   **e.** talkative

46. fidelity   **f.** to suffer anguish

47. loquacious   **g.** can be heard

48. agonize   **h.** loyalty

49. incognito   **i.** stubborn

50. pathos   **j.** prove

TIP

Using a new word throughout the day will help you to remember it. Choose a word in the morning and try to use it before you go to bed at night.

Practice Activities

The following are words that have the same roots as the words in this chapter. Divide each word into its parts: prefix, root, suffix. See if you can recognize the meaning of the new words and check your answers using a dictionary.

agony, audit, antebellum, chronicle, democracy, infidel, influx, progeny, diagnosis, surrogate, soliloquy, anonymous, apathy, distracted, interjected, philosopher, tenable, voracious, vivid

Select any five words from the list and create your own sentences.

Answers

Words in Context

After reading the paragraph, we learn that a study has been done that shows that college freshmen living in dormitories have a higher risk of getting meningitis; therefore, we can conclude that *verify* means confirm. Because this disease can be fatal, we can understand that once contracted, it is not easily wiped out; thus, we can infer that *tenacious* means persistent and not easily stopped. Since the symptoms include constant pain from a headache, we can deduce that *chronic* means continual. It makes sense that college officials are concerned about the possible outbreak of such a disease on campus and would take measures to prevent its occurrence, so we can infer that *inducement* means encouragement. Students would be encouraged to take the vaccine if it were free or inexpensive; therefore, we can see that *nominal* means a small amount. Finally, we can gather that *protracted* means drawn out by the mention that the vaccine will last from three to five years.

Sentence Completion

1. *genocide.* If you got this question wrong, refer back to the word's definition.
2. *demographic.* If you got this question wrong, refer back to the word's definition.
3. *inducement.* If you got this question wrong, refer back to the word's definition.
4. *vivacious.* If you got this question wrong, refer back to the word's definition.
5. *pathos.* If you got this question wrong, refer back to the word's definition.
6. *belligerent.* If you got this question wrong, refer back to the word's definition.
7. *chronic.* If you got this question wrong, refer back to the word's definition.
8. *verify.* If you got this question wrong, refer back to the word's definition.
9. *fluctuate.* If you got this question wrong, refer back to the word's definition.
10. *fidelity.* If you got this question wrong, refer back to the word's definition.
11. *agonize.* If you got this question wrong, refer back to the word's definition.
12. *incognito.* If you got this question wrong, refer back to the word's definition.
13. *interrogate.* If you got this question wrong, refer back to the word's definition.
14. *loquacious.* If you got this question wrong, refer back to the word's definition.
15. *rejected.* If you got this question wrong, refer back to the word's definition.
16. *tenacious.* If you got this question wrong, refer back to the word's definition.
17. *audible.* If you got this question wrong, refer back to the word's definition.
18. *protracted.* If you got this question wrong, refer back to the word's definition.
19. *nominal.* If you got this question wrong, refer back to the word's definition.
20. *sophisticated.* If you got this question wrong, refer back to the word's definition.

Synonyms

21. **d.** *tenacious.* Vivacious means lively, so tenacious would not be a synonym of the word, since it means stubborn.
22. **b.** *verify.* Interrogate means to question, so verify would not be a synonym of the word, since it means confirm.
23. **b.** *lazy.* Tenacious means stubborn, so lazy would not be a synonym.

24. c. *intermittent.* Chronic means recurring, so intermittent would not be a synonym of the word, since it means alternating.

25. e. *open.* Incognito means in disguise, so open would not be synonym of the word, since it means visible.

26. d. *audible.* Illegible means hard to read, so audible would not be a synonym of the word, since it means easy to hear.

27. b. *steady.* Fluctuate means to change, so steady would not be a synonym of the word, since it means unchanging.

28. e. *endure.* Agonize means to struggle, so endure would not be a synonym of the word, since it means to bear, or to accept.

29. c. *actual.* Nominal means supposed, so actual would not be a synonym of the word, since it means real.

30. b. *joy.* Pathos means sadness, so joy would not be a synonym of the word, since it means delight.

Antonyms

31. *belligerent.* Belligerent means aggressive, the opposite of the meaning of the words in the group.

32. *loquacious.* Loquacious means talkative, the opposite of the meaning of the words in the group.

33. *fidelity.* Fidelity means loyalty, the opposite of the meaning of the words in the group.

34. *rejected.* Rejected means not wanted, the opposite of the meaning of the words in the group.

35. *sophisticated.* Sophisticated means urbane, the opposite of the meaning of the words in the group.

36. *tenacious.* Tenacious means stubborn, the opposite of the meaning of the words in the group.

37. *verify.* Verify means to prove, the opposite of the meaning of the words in the group.

38. *incognito.* Incognito means in disguise, the opposite of the meaning of the words in the group.

39. *vivacious.* Vivacious means energetic, the opposite of the meaning of the words in the group.

40. *chronic.* Chronic means constant or habitual, the opposite of the meaning of the words in the group.

Matching Questions

41. c

42. g

43. j

44. i

45. a

46. h

47. e

48. f

49. d

50. b

Across

3 verify
5 inducement
9 audible
10 incognito
13 genocide
14 nominal
17 sophisticated
18 fluctuate
19 chronic
20 protracted

Down

1 tenacious
2 rejected
4 antagonize
6 interrogate
7 loquacious
8 demographic
11 belligerent
12 pathos
15 fidelity
16 vivacious

7 ▶ MORE ROOTS

If you wish to know the mind of a man, listen to his words.
—JOHANN WOLFGANG VON GOETHE, German writer (1749–1832)

CHAPTER SUMMARY

Just as many people in our culture have their roots in other countries, roots of English words, too, come from other languages. The words of the English language have been borrowed from other languages over the course of history. The history of a word is called its etymology. Many of the roots in Chapter 6 come from Greek and Latin languages. We have included 20 more words with important roots in this chapter, because the more roots and origins with which you are familiar, the more you will be able to recognize related words.

For example, in this chapter, you will be introduced to the root *phobe,* which means fear. You can then guess that any word that contains this root has to do with the fear of something. For instance, *claustrophobia* means an abnormal fear of small spaces.

Choose the word from the vocabulary list that best fits into the crossword puzzle. You can check your answers at the end of the chapter following the answers to the questions.

Vocabulary List 4: More Roots

agoraphobic
assimilate
attribute
benevolent
biodegradable
conspicious
contradiction
credence
evident
gregarious
impediment
incisive
inference
mediocre
philanthropy
precedent
recapitulate
remittance
tangential
urbane

Across

1 average
6 able to be broken down by living things
8 payment
9 to credit
10 relating to
13 hindrance
14 easily noticed
17 social

Down

2 summarize
3 goodwill toward men
4 denial
5 fear of open or public spaces
6 bighearted, good
7 to fit in
11 obvious
12 deduction
13 clear cut
14 belief
15 preceding
16 suave

agoraphobic (ag·ə·rə·′fō·bik)
root: **phobe** means fear
(**adj.**)
fear of open or public spaces
My neighbor is _____, so I do his grocery
shopping for him.

assimilate (əs·′sim·ə·lāt)
root: **simul** means copy
(**verb**)
to fit in
It is very difficult to _____ to another culture as
an adult.

attribute (′at·tri·būt)
root: **trib** means to give
(**noun**)
a special quality
(**verb**) (at·trib·′ūt)
to credit
I _____ much of my success to my education.

benevolent (bə·′nev·ə·lent)
root: **ben** means good
(**adj.**)
kind, having goodwill
The _____ counselor always seemed to
understand her students' problems.

biodegradable (bī·ō·dē·′grād·ə·bəl)
root: **bio** means life
(**adj.**)
able to be broken down by living things
Ella is a staunch environmentalist, so she buys only
_____ products.

conspicuous (con·′spic·ū·əs)
root: **spic, spec** mean see
(**adj.**)
highly visible
Nikolai's _____ Halloween costume made it
hard not to notice him.

contradiction (con·trə·′dik·shən)
root: **contra** means against, **dict** means say
(**noun**)
the act or state of disagreeing
My teacher made a direct _____ to her earlier
instructions by allowing us to turn in a
handwritten report.

credence (′krē·dəns)
root: **cred** means believe
(**noun**)
belief, believability
Marty gave _____ to the gossip because it came
from a reliable source.

evident (′ev·i·dent)
root: **vid** means see
(**adj.**)
obvious
The effects of the drought will be _____ to
anyone who comes to visit the area.

gregarious (gre·′gair·ē·əs)
root: **greg** means crowd
(**adj.**)
sociable
People want to be around Eva because of her
_____ nature.

impediment (im·′ped·ə·mənt)
root: **pod** means foot, **ped** means child
(**noun**)
a barrier or hindrance
I had to work with a therapist to overcome my
speech _____.

incisive (in·′sī·siv)
root: **cis, cid** mean to cut
(**adj.**)
penetrating, clear cut
Journalistic writing should be _____ and
factual.

inference   ('in·fər·ens)
root: **fer** means bear or carry
(**noun**)
guess or surmise
Using his technical expertise, he was able to make an
_____ about his findings.

mediocre   (mēd·ē·'ō·kər)
root: **med** means middle
(**adj.**)
of medium quality, neither good nor bad, average
The movie was _____ at best, but I watched the
whole thing anyway.

philanthropy   (fi·'lan·thrə·pē)
root: **phil** means love
(**noun**)
giving generously to worthy causes
The Stark family is very wealthy and known for its
_____; last year, they donated one million
dollars to help build a new community arts
center.

precedent   ('pres·i·dənt)
root: **ced** means go
(**noun**)
a prior ruling or experience
There is no _____ for this case, so it will be
difficult to win in court.

recapitulate   (rē·ka·'pitch·ū·lāt)
root: **cap** means head
(**verb**)
to review in detail
Before the final exam, the professor always likes to
_____ key points for the students.

remittance   (re·'mit·əns)
root: **mit, mis** means to send
(**noun**)
payment, transmittal of money
I forgot to enclose my _____, so I had to pay a
late fee the following month.

tangential   (tan·'jen·shəl)
root: **tang, tac, tig** mean touch
(**adj.**)
touching slightly, relating to
When giving a speech, Jeanine makes so many
_____ remarks that it is hard to grasp her
message.

urbane   (ər·'bān)
root: **urb** means city
(**adj.**)
polished, sophisticated
Her _____ manner is a result of many years in
the public eye.

TIP

Go through the list and circle each word's suffix.
Review their meanings. Now that you know about
prefixes, suffixes, and roots, you can successfully
dissect a word to discover its meaning.

Words in Context

The following exercise will help you figure out the
meaning of some words from the vocabulary list by
reading context clues. After you have read and understood the paragraph, explain the context clues that
helped you with the meaning of the vocabulary word.
Refer to the answer section at the end of this chapter
for an explanation of the clues.

Scientists at the New York Aquarium in
Brooklyn have discovered that bottle-nosed
dolphins may have self-awareness. They
attribute this belief to the result of experiments by Dr. Diane Reiss at the Osborn Lab
of Marine Science. She and her team gave
further *credence* to this notion by marking
dolphins' noses with an *x* and an *o*. Sometimes the mark was done with just water,
sometimes with colored waterproof dye.

Each time a dolphin was marked, it would check itself in the mirror. If it had a *conspicuous* colored mark, it would swim to the side of the pool and try to rub it off. As a result of these experiments, scientists made an *inference* that because these dolphins recognized their image in a mirror, they were self-aware. Before these experiments, gorillas had set the *precedent* of being the only mammals other than humans who could recognize their images.

Sentence Completion

Insert the correct word from the vocabulary list into the following sentences.

1. Reaching heights of 310 feet, the Millennium Force roller coaster is the most _____ ride at the Cedar Point Amusement Park.

2. In only one generation, the immigrant family was able to _____ to its new surroundings.

3. Recent ocean-floor discoveries have made it _____ that the huge part of our planet hidden underwater still holds surprises that are waiting to be uncovered.

4. Some pest-control companies guarantee that their _____ products will not leave any traces in either air or soil.

5. The _____ couple founded *Out of Africa* rehabilitation and learning center for abandoned or injured wild cats.

6. In order to become more _____, the shy young woman enrolled in a public speaking course.

7. The largest _____ to advancing in society is a lack of education.

8. Despite recent attacks, it is no _____ that humans are much more dangerous to sharks than sharks are to humans.

9. The restaurant got four stars in the newspaper review, but I thought it was only _____.

10. Lance Armstrong's recovery from cancer and comeback as world-champion cyclist gives _____ to his positive attitude and perseverance.

11. As a result of the administration's tax rebate policy, most U.S. taxpayers received a(n) _____ of $300–$600.

12. The multimillion-dollar cultural arts center was built due to the _____ of wealthy patrons.

13. Scientists made _____ predictions about the damage from Europe's most active volcano, Mt. Etna in Sicily.

14. In her warm and funny short stories, Eudora Welty preferred to talk about simple, humble characters rather than _____, high-society people.

15. Her local association was _____ to the worldwide environmental organization.

16. The writer _____ from his publisher's e-mail that his book was approved for publishing.

17. The elderly woman became increasingly
_____ and refused to leave her
apartment.

18. He used the first chapter of his novel to
_____ the historical back-
ground of the special air force unit in WWII.

19. Research has shown that as adults, even twins
who are separated at birth have similar
_____.

20. Before Sandra Day O'Connor's appointment,
there was no _____ set for a
federally appointed female Supreme Court Justice.

Synonyms

The following exercise lists vocabulary words from this
chapter. Each word is followed by five answer choices.
Four of them are synonyms of the vocabulary word in
bold. Your task is to choose the one that is NOT a
synonym.

21. benevolent
   a. compassionate
   b. caring
   c. malevolent
   d. kind
   e. generous

22. recapitulate
   a. repeat
   b. summarize
   c. reiterate
   d. decimate
   e. review

23. urbane
   a. sophisticated
   b. advanced
   c. complicated
   d. polished
   e. puerile

24. conspicuous
   a. cryptic
   b. evident
   c. visible
   d. prominent
   e. noticeable

25. incisive
   a. keen
   b. insightful
   c. unclear
   d. intuitive
   e. penetrating

26. gregarious
   a. sociable
   b. companionable
   c. outgoing
   d. extroverted
   e. shy

27. assimilate
   a. incorporate
   b. reject
   c. absorb
   d. digest
   e. understand

28. impediment
   a. hindrance
   b. obstacle
   c. obstruction
   d. aid
   e. barrier

29. inference
   a. deduction
   b. assumption
   c. obsolescence
   d. suggestion
   e. supposition

30. evident
   a. obvious
   b. clear
   c. apparent
   d. foggy
   e. blatant

Antonyms

Choose the word from the vocabulary list that means the opposite, or most nearly the opposite, of the following groups of words.

31. aid, assistance, support, backing _____

32. bill, cost, charge _____

33. central, vital, innermost, crucial _____

34. nastiness, greed, selfishness, gluttony _____

35. unsophisticated, simple, crude, unrefined _____

36. disbelief, incredulity, doubt, mistrust _____

37. agreement, consensus, accord, harmony _____

38. mean, nasty, unkind, malevolent _____

39. outstanding, exceptional, superior, first-rate _____

40. unclear, murky, indistinct, doubtful _____

TIP

The thing about roots is that you probably know more than you think. Pay attention to words you already know and use, and notice how many roots you've already learned along the way.

Choosing the Right Word

Circle the word in bold that best completes the sentence.

41. Because she was fearful of wide-open spaces, she was diagnosed as being (**agoraphobic, gregarious**).

42. During the scavenger hunt, the easily seen clue was left under a (**conspicuous, incisive**) rock.

43. The quickly dissolving fertilizer was (**mediocre, biodegradable**).

44. (**Benevolent, Urbane**) Peace Corps volunteers selflessly devote their time to help others in need.

45. In order to receive high marks, Olympic ice skaters' performances cannot be (**conspicuous, mediocre**).

46. His blindness did not stop him from becoming a Grammy winner, nor was it an (**impediment, precedent**) to him becoming a singing sensation.

47. In the Preamble of the Constitution, it clearly states, "We hold these truths to be self-(**evident, benevolent**), that all men are created equal."

48. To sum up the important events, the producer had the narrator (**attribute, recapitulate**) those events at the movie's finale.

49. It's always a good idea to send your (**inference, remittance**) to the phone company immediately after you receive your bill.

50. Because of their clarity and logic, no one questioned the (**incisive, mediocre**) orders of the captain.

Practice Activities

The following is a list of words that contain the same roots as the words in this chapter. See if you can determine the words' meanings. Check your definitions with the dictionary definitions.

xenophobia, facsimile, contribution, beneficiary, bionic, introspection, dictate, credulous, video, egregious, pedestrian, precise, interfere, media, bibliophile, intercede, commission, contiguous, suburban

Select any five words from the list and create your own sentences.

Answers

Words in Context

After reading the paragraph, we learn that scientists have made a discovery about bottle-nosed dolphins. Because of their experiments using mirrors, they believe that the dolphins can recognize themselves in a reflection. Therefore, they credit these experiments with proving this to be true. We can deduce that *attribute* means giving credit to the results that support this finding. The next word we see is *credence*. Further experiments of placing marks on the noses of these dolphins cause them to seek out their reflection to check their noses for marks that they try to wipe off. We can presume that *credence* means it makes these findings more believable. Because the dolphins tried to rub off *conspicuous* colored marks on their noses, we can infer that *conspicuous* marks were highly visible. Because of the results of these experiments, the scientists *inferred* that dolphins could recognize their own images. We can tell that the *inference* was their conclusion. The last vocabulary word we see is *precedent*. Since there have been no other examples of mammals being aware of their own image, other than gorillas setting a *precedent*, we can infer that the discovery of gorillas' self-awareness came before the dolphin discovery.

Sentence Completion

1. *conspicuous*. If you got this question wrong, refer back to the word's definition.
2. *assimilate*. If you got this question wrong, refer back to the word's definition.
3. *evident*. If you got this question wrong, refer back to the word's definition.
4. *biodegradable*. If you got this question wrong, refer back to the word's definition.
5. *benevolent*. If you got this question wrong, refer back to the word's definition.
6. *gregarious*. If you got this question wrong, refer back to the word's definition.
7. *impediment*. If you got this question wrong, refer back to the word's definition.
8. *contradiction*. If you got this question wrong, refer back to the word's definition.
9. *mediocre*. If you got this question wrong, refer back to the word's definition.
10. *credence*. If you got this question wrong, refer back to the word's definition.
11. *remittance*. If you got this question wrong, refer back to the word's definition.
12. *philanthropy*. If you got this question wrong, refer back to the word's definition.
13. *incisive*. If you got this question wrong, refer back to the word's definition.
14. *urbane*. If you got this question wrong, refer back to the word's definition.
15. *tangential*. If you got this question wrong, refer back to the word's definition.
16. *inferred*. If you got this question wrong, refer back to the word's definition.
17. *agoraphobic*. If you got this question wrong, refer back to the word's definition.
18. *recapitulate*. If you got this question wrong, refer back to the word's definition.
19. *attributes*. If you got this question wrong, refer back to the word's definition.
20. *precedent*. If you got this question wrong, refer back to the word's definition.

Synonyms

21. **c.** *malevolent*. Benevolent means giving and kind, so malevolent would not be a synonym of the word because it means evil.
22. **d.** *decimate*. Recapitulate means to recap, so decimate would not be a synonym of the word because it means destroy.
23. **e.** *puerile*. Urbane means refined, so puerile would not be a synonym of the word because it means childish.
24. **a.** *cryptic*. Conspicuous means obvious, so cryptic would not be a synonym of the word because it means hidden.

25. **c.** *unclear.* Incisive means perceptive, so unclear would not be the synonym of the word because it means wishy-washy.

26. **e.** *shy.* Gregarious means outgoing, so shy would not be a synonym of the word because it means timid.

27. **b.** *reject.* Assimilate means to take in, so reject would not be a synonym of the word because it means to discard or throw out.

28. **d.** *aid.* Impediment means an obstacle, so aid would not be a synonym of the word because it means to help.

29. **c.** *obsolescence.* Inference means a presumption, so obsolescence would not be a synonym of the word because it means outdated.

30. **d.** *foggy.* Evident means obvious, so foggy cannot be a synonym.

Antonyms

31. *impediment.* Impediment means hindrance, the opposite of the meaning of the words in the group.

32. *remittance.* Remittance means payment, the opposite of the meaning of the words in the group.

33. *tangential.* Tangential means secondary or unimportant, the opposite of the meaning of the words in the group.

34. *philanthropy.* Philanthropy means generosity, the opposite of the meaning of the words in the group.

35. *urbane.* Urbane means sophisticated and cultured, the opposite of the meaning of the words in the group.

36. *credence.* Credence means belief, the opposite of the meaning of the words in the group.

37. *contradiction.* Contradiction means disagreement, the opposite of the meaning of the words in the group.

38. *benevolent.* Benevolent means kind, having good-will, the opposite of the meaning of the words in the group.

39. *mediocre.* Mediocre means commonplace, the opposite of the meaning of the words in the group.

40. *evident.* Evident means obvious, the opposite of the meaning of the words in the group.

Choosing the Right Word

41. *agoraphobic.* Context clue is that she was fearful of wide-open spaces.

42. *conspicuous.* Context clue is the easily seen clue.

43. *biodegradable.* Context clue is quickly dissolving fertilizer.

44. *benevolent.* Context clue is volunteers selflessly devote their time.

45. *mediocre.* Context clue is that Olympic skaters must "receive high marks."

46. *impediment.* Context clue is the man's blindness did not stop him from becoming a Grammy winner.

47. *evident.* Context clue is "the Constitution clearly states."

48. *recapitulate.* Context clue is that the important events were summarized.

49. *remittance.* Context clue is that the customers need to pay the bill.

50. *incisive.* Context clue is that the captain's orders had clarity and logic.

Across

1 mediocre
6 biodegradable
8 remittance
9 attribute
10 tangential
13 impediment
14 conspicuous
17 gregarious

Down

2 recapitulate
3 philanthropy
4 contradiction
5 agoraphobic
6 benevolent
7 assimilate
11 evident
12 inference
13 incisive
14 credence
15 precedent
16 urbane

CHAPTER 8 ▶ FOREIGN LANGUAGE TERMS USED IN ENGLISH

We don't just borrow words; on occasion, English has pursued other languages down alleyways to beat them unconscious and rifle their pockets for new vocabulary.

—BOOKER T. WASHINGTON,
American educator and author (1856–1915)

CHAPTER SUMMARY

In this chapter, you will learn words from other languages, such as French and Italian, that are used in everyday English. Many of these words have been adopted into the English language because there is not an English word that means exactly the same thing. For example, the word *naïve* is used frequently to describe someone who is young, innocent, simple, and sometimes gullible. In English, we would have to use three or four words to express the same thing that the word *naïve* does. Some of these words are used frequently in articles about the arts. Others are used in writing about history or politics. All of these words are used frequently in everyday speech and writing, so it is important to be familiar with them.

In this chapter, you will practice using these "foreign" words and learn the meaning and spelling of each one by completing the exercises. You may recognize many of these words when you hear them, but they may appear foreign to you when you see them written. This is because the pronunciation of each word follows the rules of the original language it is from and not necessarily traditional English pronunciation. Practice saying each word out loud as you read through the list.

Choose the word from the vocabulary list that best fits into the crossword puzzle. You can check your answers at the end of the chapter following the answers to the questions.

Vocabulary List 5: Foreign Language Terms Used in English

aficionado
avant-garde
blasé
bourgeois
cliché
debut
élan
entrepeneur
epitome
fait accompli
gauche
imbroglio
ingenue
laissez-faire
malaise
naïve
non sequitur
rendezvous
vendetta
vignette

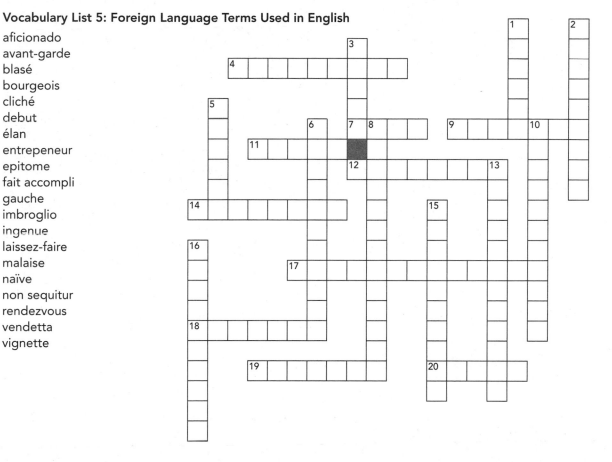

Across

4 a complicated or embarrassing situation
7 animation, spirit, life
9 a naïve young woman
11 unsophisticated and gullible
12 a short, descriptive piece of writing
14 grudge, feud
17 something finished and irreversible
18 quintessence
19 vague feeling of illness
20 first appearance

Down

1 an overly familiar, overused phrase
2 middle class
3 apathetic, uninterested
5 bumbling, crude
6 cutting edge
8 hands-off
10 a statement that has no connection to the previous statement or idea
13 someone who takes on a new business challenge or risk
15 a buff or devotee
16 to meet at an appointed place and time

aficionado   (ə·fi·shē·ˈnä·dō)

(*noun*)

a person who likes, knows about, and is devoted to a
    particular activity or thing

Jonelle has been a baseball _____ ever since she
    went to her first game with her dad.

avant-garde   (ˈa·vänt·ˈgärd)

(*noun*)

a group of people who develop innovative and
    experimental concepts, especially in the arts

(*adj.*)

relating to a group of people who develop innovative
    and experimental concepts, especially in the
    arts

As part of the _____, Abe's paintings have
    always been on the cutting edge.

Ted's art has become increasingly _____; he now
    is building sculptures in his loft in Brooklyn.

blasé   (blä·ˈzā)

(*adj.*)

apathetic to pleasure or excitement as a result of
    excessive indulgence in something

Because Jon works in the music industry, going to
    concerts has become _____, as they are no
    longer a novelty.

bourgeois   (ˈbŭrzh·wä)

(*adj.*)

having the attributes and beliefs of the middle class,
    marked by materialistic concerns

Pete has never succumbed to _____ values—he
    is comfortable living a simple life.

cliché   (klē·ˈshā)

(*noun*)

a phrase or saying that has been overused and, as a
    result, has little significance or meaning

Try to avoid using _____ in your writing, as they
    arc not as powerful as vivid, fresh language.

debut   (ˈdā·byü)

(*noun*)

a first appearance

The tennis player was nervous about her _____
    as a professional.

élan   (ā·län)

(*noun*)

spirit, enthusiasm, or excitement

The medical resident showed great _____ for
    medicine; she was always prepared and asked a
    lot of questions.

entrepreneur   (ann·trə·prə·ˈnər)

(*noun*)

a person who takes on the challenge and risk of
    starting his or her own business

Being an _____ is nerve-wracking because you
    can never be certain that your idca will be a hit.

epitome   (i·ˈpi·tə·mē)

(*noun*)

an exact example of something; someone or
    something that embodies the essence of a
    concept or type

He is the _____ of a scientist with his wire-
    rimmed glasses and absentminded attitude.

fait accompli   ('fā·tə·käm·'plē)

(*noun*)

something that is complete and seemingly
    irreversible

When she signed the one-year lease for her new
    apartment, it was a _____.

gauche   ('gōsh)

(*adj.*)

lacking social graces or sophistication

The teenager felt _____ in the company of a
    more sophisticated crowd.

imbroglio   (im·'brō⁻l·yō)

(*noun*)

a complicated or embarrassing situation due to a
    misunderstanding

When David thought that Sally was my girlfriend
    instead of my sister, it created an _____
    until I cleared up the misunderstanding.

ingenue   ('an·jə·nü)

(*noun*)

a young girl or woman, an actress playing such a role

She was an _____; she was young and innocent.

laissez-faire   (le·sā·'far)

(*noun*)

a doctrine opposing government control of
    economic matters except in the case of
    maintaining peace and the concept of property

He believed in a _____ policy because he
    thought that the government should not
    interfere with economic matters.

malaise   (mə·'lāz)

(*noun*)

the vague feeling of illness

She went to the doctor because she felt a general
    _____ and thought she was coming down
    with something.

naïve   (nä·'ēv)

(*adj.*)

innocent, simple, lacking knowledge of the world

I told him he was _____ to think that his
    landlord would offer to fix his sink without a
    written or verbal request.

non sequitur   ('nän·'se·kwə·tər)

(*noun*)

a statement that has no connection to the previous
    statement or idea

My grandmother made such a _____ yesterday.
    She was telling me about her wedding and then
    in the next breath said her car needed to be
    fixed.

rendezvous   ('rän·dā·vü)

(*noun*)

a meeting place

(*verb*)

to meet at a meeting place

They decided the school would be their _____,
    and then they would go to the park.

vendetta   (ven·'de·tə)

(*noun*)

a grudge or feud characterized by acts of retaliation

He had a _____ against the man who killed his
    father and vowed he would seek revenge.

vignette   (vin·'yet)

(*noun*)

a short descriptive written piece

The teacher asked the class to write a _____
    about their home so they could practice writing
    short but clear, descriptive pieces.

TIP

Many languages, including English, have roots in
Latin, so a knowledge of Latin would be an extra
boost to your vocabulary skills.

Words in Context

The following exercise will help you figure out the meaning of some words from the vocabulary list by reading context clues. After you have read and understood the paragraph, explain the context clues that helped you with the meaning of the vocabulary word. Refer to the answer section at the end of this chapter for an explanation of the clues.

At the party, I watched as a young man introduced himself as an entrepreneur to a *naïve* young woman, and then continued to brag about the business he recently opened. The young woman was so innocent that she didn't even realize that the man was flirting with her. For her sake, I joined the conversation rather abruptly by making a political comment about our government's *laissez-faire* policy regarding economic regulation. I explained that it was ridiculous that our government did not see itself as responsible for regulating economic relations in our country because many low-income people suffered as a result. The young entrepreneur seemed confused at first by my apparent *non sequitur* because it had absolutely nothing to do with his previous statement regarding his business. Yet he did not want to appear *gauche* in front of the young woman so he smiled and politely asked me to explain my view on laissez-faire policies. At that point, the young woman excused herself and said that she was feeling a slight *malaise* and thought she should go home to rest. The young entrepreneur quickly suggested that they *rendezvous* at the park the following day, but the young woman politely declined.

Sentence Completion

Insert the correct word from the vocabulary list into the following sentences.

1. She couldn't pinpoint exactly what was bothering her, but she felt a general _____ .

2. In my favorite movie, the main character, Ray, has a _____ against the mob boss who bankrupted his father.

3. The college graduate was too _____ to realize that his boss wouldn't give him a vacation unless he asked for it.

4. The prospective college freshman was so nervous during her interview that she answered her first question with a(n) _____; it was irrelevant to what the admissions officer had asked.

5. We arranged that if we got lost, we would _____ in the lobby of the hotel.

6. On the first day of class, he wrote a(n) _____ about his house to practice his descriptive writing.

7. The young actress hated playing a(n) _____, but she always got those parts because she was young and attractive.

8. She went to dinner with some friends at a very fancy restaurant and felt _____ because she didn't know which fork to use for her salad.

9. My dad always speaks in _____ when he gives me advice. For example, the other day, he told me not to count my chickens before they hatch.

10. My mother is a car _____; she knows everything there is to know about cars and loves to test drive different models.

11. Her art teacher said her sculpture was _____ because she used both metal and plastic in a way he had never seen before.

12. When Kathy asked Sylvia if she wanted to go to the World Series with her, she was surprised that Sylvia was _____ about it, but Sylvia explained that she had been to the World Series five years in a row, and it was starting to get boring.

13. The young musician showed such _____ when he played the guitar; he played very difficult pieces without missing a note and seemed to enjoy himself immensely.

14. The _____ was very proud when he opened the doors of his new pet-supply store on the first day of business.

15. She had just graduated from law school, but she already looked like the _____ of a lawyer with her expression, briefcase, and no-nonsense professional suit.

16. The politician argued against the _____ policy because she felt that if economic matters were not regulated in the country, large companies would take advantage of consumers.

17. The plot of many TV sitcoms seems to revolve around a(n) _____; there is some big misunderstanding, which results in an embarrassing situation, but it is usually resolved by the end of the show.

18. When she graduated from high school, it was a(n) _____; she had completed all of the requirements.

19. At the ballet, the young dancer made her _____ in the second act.

20. Most advertisements seem to include _____ values because middle-class people are able to buy the items being advertised.

Synonyms

The following exercise lists vocabulary words from this chapter. Each word is followed by four answer choices. Three of them are synonyms of the vocabulary word in bold. Your task is to choose the one that is NOT a synonym.

21. blasé
   a. bored
   b. enthusiastic
   c. apathetic
   d. neutral

22. avant-garde
   a. creative
   b. cutting edge
   c. conventional
   d. innovative

23. naïve
   a. innocent
   b. simple
   c. knowledgeable
   d. trusting

24. élan
   a. disinterest
   b. excitement
   c. spirit
   d. enthusiasm

25. aficionado
   a. fan
   b. novice
   c. devotee
   d. expert

26. non sequitur
   a. unrelated
   b. disconnected
   c. clear line of thought
   d. disjointed

27. debut
   a. premier
   b. opening
   c. appearance
   d. retirement

28. vignette
   a. novel
   b. short piece
   c. description
   d. literary piece

29. cliché
   a. truism
   b. commonplace
   c. original statement
   d. familiar

30. malaise
   a. sickness
   b. illness
   c. healthy
   d. unwell

TIP

Knowing a word's language of origin will help you spell and pronounce it correctly.

Antonyms

Choose the word from the vocabulary list that means the opposite, or most nearly the opposite, of the following groups of words.

31. sophisticated, graceful, classy, worldly _____

32. wise, mature, complicated, sophisticated _____

33. poor, not materialistic, working class _____

34. incomplete, reversible, disputable _____

35. old, wise, masculine _____

36. boredom, disinterest, despondent _____

37. clear, comfortable, easily understand situation _____

38. excitement, enthusiasm, wide-eyed, naïve _____

39. friendship, peaceful relationship, reconciliation _____

40. novice, uninformed, first-timer _____

Matching Questions

Match the word in the first column with the corresponding word in the second column.

41. debut   **a.** a young girl

42. aficionado   **b.** lacking social graces

43. avant-garde   **c.** a meeting place

44. élan   **d.** apathetic

45. gauche   **e.** spirit

46. naïve   **f.** a complicated misunderstanding

47. vendetta   **g.** a statement that does not relate to the previous statement

48. vignette   **h.** a completed fact

49. cliché   **i.** a feeling of sickness

50. malaise   **j.** an overused statement

51. entrepreneur   **k.** a short descriptive piece

52. epitome   **l.** a feud characterized by acts of retaliation

53. fait accompli   **m.** a fan or devotee

54. rendezvous   **n.** artistically innovative

55. ingenue   **o.** having middle-class values

56. laissez-faire   **p.** first appearance

57. imbroglio   **q.** one who starts his/her own business

58. bourgeois   **r.** an example or the embodiment of something

59. non sequitur   **s.** a political doctrine, which supports government deregulation of economic matters

60. blasé   **t.** innocent, simple

Practice Activities

Many of the words from this chapter are used in articles about art, politics, and history. Read a newspaper or magazine article about art or architecture, and an article about contemporary or historical politics, and write down all of the foreign words you come across. How do you know if a word is a foreign word? How is it being used in the article? Add these words to your vocabulary list and look up the definition.

Now that you know these words, make a note when and where you see them. Think about the following questions: When do people use these words? What effect does it have on the piece of writing you are reading? Why have these particular words become such a regular part of our vocabulary?

Answers

Words in Context

In the first sentence, we learn that the young man is an *entrepreneur* and that he is talking about a business he started, so we can conclude that being an *entrepreneur* has something to do with starting one's own business. The young woman is described as *naïve* and then in the next sentence described as very innocent. The narrator also explains that she enters this conversation "for her sake," so we can conclude that naïve means young and innocent and possibly in need of help. The next word we encounter is *laissez-faire,* which is used to describe our government's economic policy, so we know that it refers to something political and relates to economics. In the next sentence, it becomes clearer that the narrator is using the word to mean that our government is not regulating economic matters. *Non sequitur* is used to refer to the narrator's comment and the fact that it is completely unrelated to the entrepreneur's previous statement, so we can deduce that *non sequitur* means an unrelated statement. The entrepreneur does not want to appear *gauche,* so he is polite even though he is confused by the comment. We can conclude that *gauche* must mean impolite or lacking social graces. We can deduce that *malaise* must mean feeling ill or tired because the young woman needs to go home and rest. Finally, the entrepreneur asks the young woman to "*rendezvous* at the park the next day," so we can conclude that *rendezvous* must mean meet.

Sentence Completion

1. *malaise.* If you got this question wrong, refer back to the word's definition.
2. *vendetta.* If you got this question wrong, refer back to the word's definition.
3. *naïve.* If you got this question wrong, refer back to the word's definition.
4. *non sequitur.* If you got this question wrong, refer back to the word's definition.
5. *rendezvous.* If you got this question wrong, refer back to the word's definition.

6. *vignette.* If you got this question wrong, refer back to the word's definition.
7. *ingenue.* If you got this question wrong, refer back to the word's definition.
8. *gauche.* If you got this question wrong, refer back to the word's definition.
9. *clichés.* If you got this question wrong, refer back to the word's definition.
10. *aficionado.* If you got this question wrong, refer back to the word's definition.
11. *avant-garde.* If you got this question wrong, refer back to the word's definition.
12. *blasé.* If you got this question wrong, refer back to the word's definition.
13. *élan.* If you got this question wrong, refer back to the word's definition.
14. *entrepreneur.* If you got this question wrong, refer back to the word's definition.
15. *epitome.* If you got this question wrong, refer back to the word's definition.
16. *laissez-faire.* If you got this question wrong, refer back to the word's definition.
17. *imbroglio.* If you got this question wrong, refer back to the word's definition.
18. *fait accompli.* If you got this question wrong, refer back to the word's definition.
19. *debut.* If you got this question wrong, refer back to the word's definition.
20. *bourgeois.* If you got this question wrong, refer back to the word's definition.

Synonyms

21. **b.** *enthusiastic.* Blasé means apathetic about something due to over indulgence. Enthusiastic would not be a synonym because it means to be excited about something.
22. **c.** *conventional.* Avant-garde means original and creative, so conventional is not a synonym because it means lacking originality.

23. c. *knowledgeable.* Naïve means simple and innocent, so knowledgeable is not a synonym because it means having knowledge.

24. a. *disinterest.* Élan means spirit or enthusiasm, so disinterest is not a synonym because it means lacking interest.

25. b. *novice.* An aficionado is an expert or devotee to something. A novice is someone who is new to something, so it is not a synonym.

26. c. *clear line of thought.* A non sequitur is a statement that is not connected to the previous statement. A clear line of thought refers to several statements that follow each other, so it is not a synonym.

27. d. *retirement.* A debut is a first appearance. Retirement means the end of a career, so it would not be a synonym of debut.

28. a. *novel.* A vignette is a short descriptive piece, but a novel is a long written story, so it is not a synonym.

29. c. *original statement.* A cliché is a statement or saying that has been so overused that it lacks meaning. An original statement is not a synonym because it means a statement that is new and has not been used before.

30. c. *healthy.* Malaise means a feeling of sickness, but healthy means to feel well, so it is not a synonym.

Antonyms

31. *gauche.* Gauche means lacking social grace or sophistication, the opposite of the meaning of the words in the group.

32. *naïve.* Naïve means simple and innocent, the opposite of the meaning of the words in the group.

33. *bourgeois.* Bourgeois means characteristics of the middle class and materialistic, the opposite of the words in the group.

34. *fait accompli.* Fait accompli means a completed fact that is irreversible, the opposite of the words in the group.

35. *ingenue.* An ingenue is a young naïve girl, the opposite of the words in the group.

36. *élan.* Élan means spirit, enthusiasm, the opposite of the words in the group.

37. *imbroglio.* An imbroglio is a complicated situation or an embarrassing misunderstanding, the opposite of the words in the group.

38. *blasé.* Blasé means apathetic due to overindulgence in something, the opposite of the words in the group.

39. *vendetta.* Vendetta means a feud of grudge characterized by retaliation, the opposite of the words in the group.

40. *aficionado.* An aficionado is an expert, the opposite of the words in the group.

Matching Questions

41. p
42. m
43. n
44. e
45. b
46. t
47. l
48. k
49. j
50. i
51. q
52. r
53. h
54. c
55. a
56. s
57. f
58. o
59. g
60. d

Across

4 imbroglio
7 élan
9 ingenue
11 naïve
12 vignette
14 vendetta
17 fait accompli
18 epitome
19 malaise
20 debut

Down

1 cliché
2 bourgeois
3 blasé
5 gauche
6 avant-garde
8 laissez-faire
10 non sequitur
13 entrepreneur
15 aficionado
16 rendezvous

9 ▶ BUSINESS TERMS

Language is the dress of thought.

—SAMUEL JOHNSON, English author (1709–1784)

CHAPTER SUMMARY

In this chapter, you will learn words frequently used in business. Many of the words in this chapter may be familiar to you, but it is important to become comfortable using these words in your day-to-day life. You will see these words in articles about business and economic matters, as well as in the written policies and procedures found in most work environments. You may also see some of the words on your tax return and other work-related forms. Think about when and where you have seen these words before and how they were used. Once you know these words, you will find that many business-related articles and policies that you encounter at work or in your day-to-day life are easier to understand. As you go through the list, say each word aloud to yourself and practice spelling it. This will help you to become more comfortable using each word. Think about other words you know that may have similar prefixes, suffixes, or roots, and see if you can use this knowledge to help you remember the meaning of the new words found in this chapter.

Choose the word from the vocabulary list that best fits into the crossword puzzle. You can check your answers at the end of the chapter following the answers to the questions.

Vocabulary List 6: Business Terms

arbitrage
arbitration
beneficiary
capital
collusion
consortium
deduction
discrimination
entitlement
equity
exempt
fiscal
franchise
harassment
jargon
nepotism
perquisite
prospectus
subsidy
tenure

Across

4 someone who benefits from something
5 annoy or irritate persistently
6 a joining of two or more businesses for a specific purpose
8 conspiracy
11 special privilege or benefit
15 the process by which disputes are settled by a third party
16 accumulated wealth
17 fairness of treatment
18 the state or period of holding a particular position, or a guarantee of employment to teachers who have particular standards
19 a grant

Down

1 prejudiced actions or treatment
2 favoring relatives
3 terminology
7 a business that is owned by a parent company but run by independent operators under rules set by the parent company
9 the subtraction of a cost from income
10 buying stocks, bonds, and securities to resell for a quick profit
12 bonus
13 a published report of a business and its plans
14 pertaining to money
17 excused

arbitrage (ˈär·bə·träzh)
(*noun*)
the buying of "paper"—stocks, bonds, and
    securities—to resell for a quick profit
_____, the buying of bonds and other securities
    to sell at a higher price, is a risky business.

arbitration (är·bə·ˈtrā·shən)
(*noun*)
the process by which disputes are settled by a third
    party
They decided to resolve the matter through
    _____; that is, they gave the decision-
    making power to an independent person.

beneficiary (ben·nə·fi·shē·er·ē)
(*noun*)
one who will benefit from something
He is the sole _____ of her estate. He will be
    given all the property when the old woman
    dies.

capital (ˈka·pə·təl)
(*noun*)
accumulated wealth, used to gain more wealth
She put some money in the bank and would only
    spend the interest she earned on the initial
    investment or _____.

collusion (kə·ˈlü·zhen)
(*noun*)
a secret agreement for a deceitful or fraudulent
    purpose, conspiracy
At the poker game, Sarah and Tom made a
    _____ to cheat together so Sarah would
    win the game and then they could share the
    winnings.

consortium (kən·ˈsor·shē·em)
(*noun*)
a joining of two or more businesses for a specific
    purpose
The joining of the three companies into one made
    for a powerful _____ that would dominate
    the industry.

deduction (di·ˈdək·shən)
(*noun*)
the subtraction of a cost from income
He took his children as a tax _____ so that he
    could subtract the cost of their care from his
    taxes.

discrimination (dis·kri·mə·ˈnā·shən)
(*noun*)
the act of making distinctions, the act of
    distinguishing between one group of people
    and another and treating people differently as a
    result, prejudiced actions or treatment
Many workers still face _____ in workplaces that
    choose not to hire or promote employees based
    on their sex, skin color, or ethnic background.

entitlement (in·ˈtī·təl·mənt)
(*noun*)
special privilege or benefit allowed to a group of
    people
In our society, the elderly have an _____ to
    health care and money for food and shelter.

equity (ˈe-kwə·tē)
(*noun*)
fairness or evenness of treatment, or the value of
    property after all claims have been made
    against it
Though she was accused of being unfair in her
    demands, she claimed she only wanted
    _____ in what was owed her.

exempt (ig·ˈzem(p)t)
(*adj.*)
excused from some rule or job
She was _____ from duty that day; she was
    excused because she had been injured.

fiscal (ˈfis·kəl)
(*adj.*)
pertaining to money or finance
At the end of a company's _____, or financial, year, the company usually announces the amount it earned in that year.

franchise (ˈfran·chīz)
(*noun*)
a business that is owned by a parent company but run by independent operators under rules set by the parent company
McDonald's is a _____ because each outlet is independently owned but still operates under rules set out by the parent company.

harassment (hə·ˈras·mənt)
(*noun*)
the act of irritating or annoying persistently; sexual harassment
(*noun*)
unwelcome physical or verbal conduct directed at an employee because of his or her sex
There are many laws today that protect workers from sexual _____ by their employer.

jargon (ˈjär·gən)
(*noun*)
the specialized vocabulary of an industry or interest group
Learning the _____, or language, of a particular interest or job is an important part of learning about the workplace.

nepotism (ˈne·pə·ti·zəm)
(*noun*)
the employment or promotion of friends and family members
Many public employment arenas have been accused of _____, because workers related to persons in authority are given preference in hiring.

perquisite (ˈpər·kwə·zet)
(*noun*)
a privilege or bonus given in addition to regular salary
Many companies give stock options as a _____ in addition to an employee's salary.

prospectus (prə·ˈspek·təs)
(*noun*)
a published report of a business and its plans for a program or offering
The company published a _____ to offer details of its plan for expansion. This plan offers potential investors pertinent information about the plan and the company.

subsidy (ˈsəb·sə·dē)
(*noun*)
a grant of money for a particular purpose
The state gave several school districts a _____ to rebuild the schools in those districts.

tenure (ˈten·yər)
(*noun*)
the state or period of holding a particular position, or a guarantee of employment to teachers who have met particular standards
Even faculty with _____ at colleges and universities are losing the security promised by their guarantee of permanent employment.

TIP

Do you know any jargon? Brainstorm your own vocabulary list of words you use in a particular area of your life.

Words in Context

The following exercise will help you figure out the meaning of some words from the vocabulary list by reading context clues. After you have read and understood the paragraph, explain the context clues that helped you with the meaning of the vocabulary word.

Refer to the answer section at the end of this chapter for an explanation of the clues.

When she took the job as the manager of a Wendy's *franchise,* Sarah quickly learned many things about the business world. On her first day of work, she read the *discrimination* policy, which stated that Wendy's does not discriminate against race, ethnicity, gender, sexual preference, or people with disabilities when hiring employees. Then she read Wendy's policy on sexual *harassment* and was glad to see that they were very strict about creating a comfortable working environment for all of the employees. Her boss explained that flirting of any kind was not tolerated at work. Next she was asked to fill out many forms, including a life insurance policy. She had to pick someone to be the *beneficiary* on the policy in the event of her death, so she picked her son, Michael. After she was done with all of the paperwork, Sarah followed her boss into the back room and he showed her the various systems they used and began to teach her the *jargon* used in the fast food industry. It was important to understand these terms because many vendors and members of the Wendy's company use this shorthand language. Sarah mentioned that her sister really wanted to work at Wendy's as well, but her boss cautioned her against committing an act of *nepotism.* He explained that it was important that every potential employee had a fair chance of employment and that, as store manager, it was her responsibility to ensure that she did not give preferential treatment to her family members. At the end of the meeting, her boss told her that as a *perquisite* in addition to her salary, she and her family were allowed one free meal a week at Wendy's.

TIP

Read a financial periodical to see many of these words in context. Seeing them in context will help you remember their meanings.

Sentence Completion

Insert the correct word from the vocabulary list into the following sentences.

1. Beware of those two; they are always in _____ with each other to sell defective products at a hefty sum.

2. They decided to settle the dispute through _____ because they couldn't agree on anything amongst themselves.

3. I would love to start my own magazine, but I don't know where I am going to get the _____ to fund it.

4. When employees refer to their company's _____ year, they are talking about the 12-month period that the organization plans to use its funds.

5. Some industries have such a unique _____ that it can be difficult for an outsider to understand what people are saying.

6. I was thinking of opening a(n) _____ of my favorite ice cream store, but the parent company's rules and regulations are too strict.

7. I was _____ from taking Spanish 101 in college because I placed out of it with an exam that I took in high school.

8. The _____ of this job are not too great; you have to work here four years before they give you a third week of vacation.

9. Even though he is not a good teacher, he will never be fired because he has _____.

10. Now that I own a home, I can take many _____ on my taxes, which means I get to keep more of my income.

11. Before I bought my apartment, I read everything about the building in its _____.

12. Because she was wrongfully accused of _____, she didn't lose her job.

13. My daughter is the only _____ to my life insurance policy.

14. This company is guilty of _____; only the president's immediate family holds a supervisory role.

15. The three companies joined together to form a _____, making their presence in the industry even stronger.

16. There is much debate about what to do with Social Security, a(n) _____ that many people depend on upon retirement.

17. As a child, my favorite game was Monoply, so it is no surprise that I ended up working in _____.

18. One thing I can say about the management here is that they treat all employees with _____, which makes it a very pleasant place to work.

19. The development company depleted the _____ that the city had donated to build a new park, so construction has halted.

20. I can't prove it, but I think I have been a victim of _____; I am almost sure I was let go because I am a woman.

Synonyms

The following exercise lists vocabulary words from this chapter. Each word is followed by four answer choices. Three of them are synonyms of the vocabulary word in bold. Your task is to choose the one that is NOT a synonym.

21. **deduction**
    a. subtraction
    b. to take away
    c. addition
    d. the cost of children on your tax forms

22. **perquisite**
    a. privilege
    b. bonus
    c. reward
    d. punishment

23. **tenure**
    a. termination of employment
    b. guarantee of employment
    c. length of employment
    d. period of employment

24. **exempt**
    a. excused
    b. forced
    c. pardoned
    d. set apart

25. equity
   a. fairness
   b. evenness
   c. value of property
   d. special privilege

26. beneficiary
   a. one who gives
   b. heir
   c. one who benefits
   d. one who inherits

27. entitlement
   a. penalty
   b. advantage
   c. privilege
   d. benefit

28. discrimination
   a. discernment
   b. the act of making distinctions
   c. prejudiced treatment
   d. fair

29. subsidy
   a. tax
   b. money
   c. gift of money
   d. grant

30. fiscal
   a. financial
   b. economic
   c. monetary
   d. franchise

Antonyms

Choose the word that means the opposite, or most nearly the opposite, of the following groups of words.

31. addition, income, give   _____

32. favoritism, prejudiced, unfair, unjust   _____

33. giver, bestower, donor   _____

34. debt, poverty, insufficient resources   _____

35. forced, duty-bound, liable   _____

36. fairness, unprejudiced, equity   _____

37. friendly, unthreatening, not provocative   _____

38. unemployed, fired, lack of job security   _____

39. separation, liquidation, singular company _____

40. slang, proper English, clichés   _____

Matching Questions

Match the word in the first column with the corresponding word in the second column.

41. beneficiary   **a.** privilege in addition to salary

42. deduction   **b.** grant of money

43. arbitrage   **c.** period of holding a job

44. fiscal   **d.** published report

45. jargon   **e.** pertaining to money

46. exempt   **f.** fairness or evenness of treatment

47. franchise   **g.** the buying of stocks to resell for profit

48. consortium   **h.** one who benefits

49. discrimination   **i.** special privilege enjoyed by a group

50. equity   **j.** accumulated wealth

51. tenure   **k.** the employment of friends or family

52. arbitration   **l.** terms specific to an industry

53. perquisite   **m.** the subtraction of cost from income

54. collusion   **n.** annoying persistently

55. capital   **o.** a deceitful agreement

56. entitlement   **p.** process of a dispute settled by third party

57. prospectus   **q.** independently run business owned by parent company

58. subsidy   **r.** excused from duty or job

59. nepotism   **s.** joining of two or more companies

60. harassment   **t.** the act of unfairly distinguishing between two groups of people

Practice Activities

Find a copy of a work-related memo, letter, or policy and see if the words you have learned in this chapter are used in the piece of writing. See if you can find five more business-related words that you can add to your vocabulary list.

Find an article in the business section of the paper or a magazine dedicated to business and see how many of these words are used in the publication. What are the articles about? Are there other words you can add to your vocabulary list? Try to determine the definition of the new words from the context of the article and then check the definition in your dictionary.

Answers

Words in Context

The first word we encounter is *franchise*, and we know from the context that it must be a Wendy's restaurant, so franchise could refer to the individual store or restaurant in a chain. Sarah reads the *discrimination* policy, which explains that Wendy's does not discriminate against people in their hiring practices, so *discrimination* must mean judging or treating someone differently. The sexual *harassment* policy does not allow flirting at work, so harassment must mean bothering someone or pressuring someone. Sarah makes her son the *beneficiary* of her life insurance policy, so we can conclude that her son will receive the money, or be the one to benefit from the policy if Sarah were to pass away. Her boss teaches her the *jargon* of the industry because she must know the terms used in the fast-food industry, so *jargon* must mean language used in a particular industry. Sarah is cautioned against an act of *nepotism* and in the next sentence, we can deduce that *nepotism* must mean giving your family preferential treatment. Finally, we see the word *perquisite* used to explain an extra benefit Sarah receives in addition to her salary.

Sentence Completion

1. *collusion.* If you got this question wrong, refer back to the word's definition.
2. *arbitration.* If you got this question wrong, refer back to the word's definition.
3. *capital.* If you got this question wrong, refer back to the word's definition.
4. *fiscal.* If you got this question wrong, refer back to the word's definition.
5. *jargon.* If you got this question wrong, refer back to the word's definition.
6. *franchise.* If you got this question wrong, refer back to the word's definition.
7. *exempt.* If you got this question wrong, refer back to the word's definition.
8. *perquisites.* If you got this question wrong, refer back to the word's definition.

9. *tenure.* If you got this question wrong, refer back to the word's definition.
10. *deductions.* If you got this question wrong, refer back to the word's definition.
11. *prospectus.* If you got this question wrong, refer back to the word's definition.
12. *harassment.* If you got this question wrong, refer back to the word's definition.
13. *beneficiary.* If you got this question wrong, refer back to the word's definition.
14. *nepotism.* If you got this question wrong, refer back to the word's definition.
15. *consortium.* If you got this question wrong, refer back to the word's definition.
16. *entitlement.* If you got this question wrong, refer back to the word's definition.
17. *arbitrage.* If you got this question wrong, refer back to the word's definition.
18. *equity.* If you got this question wrong, refer back to the word's definition.
19. *subsidy.* If you got this question wrong, refer back to the word's definition.
20. *discrimination.* If you got this question wrong, refer back to the word's definition.

Synonyms

21. **c.** *addition.* Deduction means the act of subtracting; since **c** is addition, it is not a synonym.
22. **d.** *punishment.* Perquisite means a bonus or privilege given in addition to salary; since punishment means a penalty, it is not a synonym.
23. **a.** *termination of employment.* Tenure means the state of holding a particular job or the guarantee of employment. Termination of employment is not a synonym because it means the end of one's employment.
24. **b.** *force.* Exempt means to be excused from some rule or job; because force means to make someone do something, it is not a synonym.

25. d. *special privilege.* Equity means fairness or evenness of treatment, or the value of property after all claims have been have been made against it. Special privilege is not a synonym because it is not an even or fair arrangement. If you got this one wrong, you may have confused equity with entitlement.

26. a. *one who gives.* Beneficiary means one who will benefit from receiving something. Because one who gives is a person who gives something, it is not a synonym.

27. a. *penalty.* Entitlement is a special privilege or benefit, so penalty is not a synonym.

28. d. *fair.* Discrimination means the act of making distinctions and it is often used to refer to making distinctions between different groups of people in an unfair way. Because fair means even or just, it is not a synonym.

29. a. *tax.* Subsidy means a grant of money for a particular purpose. Tax is money paid to the government by citizens, so it is not a synonym.

30. d. *franchise.* Fiscal means pertaining to money or finance. Because franchise means a business owned by a parent company but run independently, it is not a synonym.

Antonyms

31. *deduction.* Deduction means the subtraction of cost from income, the opposite of the words in the group.

32. *equity.* Equity means fairness or evenness of treatment, the opposite of the words in the group.

33. *beneficiary.* A beneficiary is one who will benefit from something, the opposite of the words in the group.

34. *capital.* Capital means accumulated wealth used to earn more money, the opposite of the words in the group.

35. *exempt.* Exempt means excused from a duty or job, the opposite of the words in the group.

36. *discrimination.* Discrimination means the act of making distinctions in treatment of people, the opposite of the words in the group.

37. *harassment.* Harassment means to harass or bother someone persistently in a threatening way, the opposite of the words in the group.

38. *tenure.* Tenure means a period of holding a job or a guarantee of employment, the opposite of the words in the group.

39. *consortium.* Consortium means a joining together of two or more businesses for a specific purpose, the opposite of the words in the group.

40. *jargon.* Jargon means the language used in a particular industry, the opposite of the words in the group.

Matching Questions

41. h
42. m
43. g
44. e
45. l
46. r
47. q
48. s
49. t
50. f
51. c
52. p
53. a
54. o
55. j
56. i
57. d
58. b
59. k
60. n

Across

4 beneficiary
5 harassment
6 consortium
8 collusion
11 entitlement
15 arbitration
16 capital
17 equity
18 tenure
19 subsidy

Down

1 discrimination
2 nepotism
3 jargon
7 franchise
9 deduction
10 arbitrage
12 perquisite
13 prospectus
14 fiscal
17 exempt

10 ▶ TECHNOLOGY TERMS

It's none of their business that you have to learn how to write. Let them think you were born that way.

—ERNEST HEMINGWAY, American author (1899–1961)

CHAPTER SUMMARY

The technology terms found in this chapter are words commonly used by technology experts and people who use a computer. No matter what your computer knowledge is, learning these words will be extremely useful because they are used frequently in advertisements, newspaper articles, computer manuals, and in many work places. Technology is such a huge part of our daily lives that it is important to feel comfortable with the terminology, or *jargon* (see Vocabulary List 6 if you are unfamiliar with this word), used in this industry. Technology jargon can be intimidating because many of the words, such as *cookie*, have other meanings or seem odd in the context of technology. Have fun with these words and think about how the definition of each word influenced how the word is used.

Many of these words were coined very recently and are intentionally similar to other commonly used words. For instance, a *motherboard* is the main circuit board of the computer. Why do you think it is called a motherboard instead of a sisterboard or brotherboard? As you read through these words and their definitions, underline parts of the words that may serve as useful memory tricks. For example, what is the difference between *uploading* and *downloading* a file? Since these words are all very new, be sure to use a current dictionary or look at an online technology dictionary, such as www.webopedia.com, when you hear or read new technology words.

Choose the word from the vocabulary list that best fits into the crossword puzzle. You will use 19 words from the vocabulary list to solve the puzzle. You can check your answers at the end of the chapter following the answers to the questions.

Vocabulary List 7: Technology Terms

application
bandwidth
bitmap
cache
cookie
cursor
database
download
encryption
Ethernet
firewall
information technology
keyword
motherboard
network
plug-in
search engine
server
upload
workstation

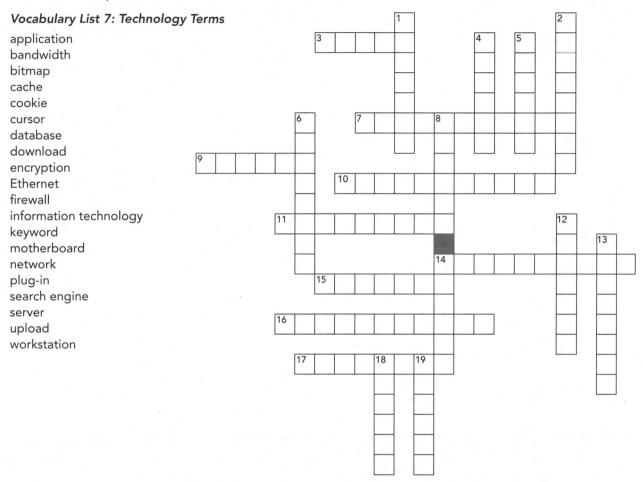

Across

3 high-speed computer storage to help you access frequently accessed information locally
7 any computer connected to a local area network (LAN)
9 blinking line that shows where your mouse is on a computer screen
10 the main circuit board of a computer
11 transfer capacity in kilobits per second
14 translation of information into a secret code
15 allows a Web browser to run multimedia files
16 software program
17 information stored and organized so that a computer can quickly retrieve selected pieces of information

Down

1 a representative word that specifies a particular record or file

2 a network that allows a wide variety of computers to communicate
4 to transmit documents from your computer to a network or an online source
5 a message given to a Web browser by a Web server that is stored in the browser and sent back to the server every time the browser contacts the server for a Web page
6 a system to prevent unauthorized access to and from a private network
8 a program that searches documents for a keyword and then provides a list of those documents
12 a group of two or more computers linked together
13 to copy a file from an online source to your own computer
18 binary data that represents an image or display
19 a computer on a network that manages network resources

application ('a·plə·kā·shən)
(*noun*)
a software program that lets you complete a task on your computer, such as word processing, listening to music, or viewing a Web page
The computer _____ I use for word processing is really easy to learn.

bandwidth ('band·with)
(*noun*)
the amount of information that one can send through a connection at a given time, usually measured in kilobits per second
At work, I can download files from the Internet a lot faster because I have more _____.

bitmap ('bit·map)
(*noun*)
the representation in rows and columns of dots of an image in computer memory
I downloaded the _____ so I could keep the picture on my computer.

cache ('kash)
(*noun*)
a high-speed storage mechanism that allows a computer to store frequently accessed information locally
I had to download the Web page again because it wasn't saved in my computer's _____.

cookie ('kŭ ·kē)
(*noun*)
a message given to a Web browser by a Web server that is stored in the browser and sent back to the server every time the browser contacts the server for a Web page
A _____ enables a Web page to recognize your computer when you log on to it so the page may say something like, "Welcome back, Jessie!"

cursor ('kər·sər)
(*noun*)
a symbol, usually a blinking line that shows where the next letter will be typed on a computer screen
I bought the 12-inch laptop, and because the monitor is so small, I have a hard time seeing the _____.

database ('dā·tə·bās)
(*noun*)
information stored and organized so that a computer can quickly retrieve selected pieces of information
Our _____ hasn't been updated in six months, so I am not sure whether we have this item in stock.

download ('daŭ n·lōd)
(*verb*)
the process of copying a document or file from an online source to your own computer
I had to _____ the application form from the university's website before I could print it.

encryption   (in·ˈkrip·shən)
(*noun*)
the translation of information into a secret code
When entering my credit card number on a website, I am always worried that the _____ is not as secure as it should be and a hacker can easily get my personal information.

Ethernet   (ˈē·thər·net)
(*noun*)
a common method of enabling computers in the same local area network (LAN—see Chapter 15: Acronyms) to communicate with each other
Before _____, computers in the same office could not communicate with each other.

firewall   (fīr·ˈwŏ l)
(*noun*)
a system (using either hardware or software) that prevents unauthorized access to and from a private network
My company's _____ is ironclad; no one could ever hack into our computer system.

information technology (IT)   (in·fər·ˈmā·shən tek·ˈnä·lō·jē)
(*noun*)
the broad subject of anything concerning processing or managing information, especially in a large company
Because Alison is such a whiz with computers, she was recruited to head the _____ department here.

keyword   (ˈkē·wərd)
(*noun*)
a word that specifies a particular record or file in programming a specific command
I entered the _____ Byzantine when I had to write a report on that era for school.

motherboard   (mə·thər·bōrd)
(*noun*)
the main circuit board of a computer
She opened the computer and showed me the _____, a thin piece of plastic with many different wires running through it.

network   (ˈnet·wərk)
(*noun*)
a group of two or more computers linked together
At work, we have 20 computers on our _____.

plug-in   (ˈpləg·in)
(*noun*)
a piece of hardware or software that adds a specific feature to a larger, already existing system
Once I downloaded the _____, I was able to see and listen to movie clips on my computer.

search engine   (ˈsərch·ˈen·jən)
(*noun*)
a program that searches documents, websites, and databases for a keyword and then provides a list of those documents
For some reason, this _____ is more efficient than the other one I was using; no matter what I am researching, I can find a slew of information.

server   (ˈsər·vər)
(*noun*)
a computer on a network that manages network resources
At my last company, the _____ was down so often it was hard to get anything accomplished on the computer.

upload   (əp·ˈlōd)
(*verb*)
the opposite of download; to transmit documents from your computer to an online source
When I built my Web page, I had to _____ the final page to our network to add it to the website.

workstation   ('wərk·stā·shən)

(*noun*)

a type of computer that has enough power to run applications used in work environments, such as graphic design programs and software design programs; also refers to any computer connected to a LAN, whether a personal computer or workstation

At home, I have a personal computer, but at work, I have a much faster _____ because I use it to develop video games.

TIP

These terms tend to change as technology changes, so be sure to keep up to date on new technology in order to keep your vocabulary current.

Words in Context

The following exercise will help you figure out the meaning of some words from the vocabulary list by reading context clues. After you have read and understood the paragraph, explain the context clues that helped you with the meaning of the vocabulary word. Refer to the answer section at the end of this chapter for an explanation of the clues.

On Tom's first day of work as a computer programmer, he had to set up his *workstation*. He was really excited because his computer was really fast and many of the *applications* he would use for work were already installed. First he connected his *workstation* to the *network* by using the *Ethernet* cord at his desk. This enabled him to communicate with all of the other computers in the office. Once he was connected to the *network*, he opened his Internet program and went immediately to his favorite

search engine. He wanted to see how his favorite baseball team did in their game, so he typed the keyword "baseball" in the search engine, and it gave him a list of several baseball-related websites. He quickly checked the score of the game and then got back to work.

TIP

As you may have noticed, many of these terms have other meanings (for example, *server*, *cookie*, *network*), so pay very close attention to context.

Sentence Completion

Insert the correct word from the vocabulary list into the following sentences.

1. At work, I can communicate with the other computers in the office as long as they are connected on our _____.

2. The _____ prevents people without authorization from accessing our system and potentially damaging it.

3. When the _____ goes down, we cannot access the Internet, save files, or communicate with other computers on the network.

4. I was surprised when the Web page said, "Welcome back, Margaret!" But then my friend explained how _____ work.

5. The clerk said that they were out of the sofa we wanted to buy, but said she would check the _____ to see if one of their other stores had it in stock.

6. In my computer class, I learned how to use several different graphic design _____(s).

7. When I first open my Internet program, the last Web page I went to appears in my browser window because it is saved in my computer's _____.

8. My friend e-mailed me a funny animated cartoon, but I couldn't watch it because I didn't have the right _____.

9. I needed information for my school report on various weather systems, so I used "meteorology" as a(n) _____ on an Internet search engine.

10. I would like to work in the _____ department at a company because I like to work with computers and help people use them more effectively.

11. When you press RETURN on your keyboard, the _____ moves to the next line.

12. It took me a long time to download the file because I didn't have enough _____.

13. I opened the _____ in a graphic design program so I could edit the image.

14. At work, our network is connected via _____.

15. He studied _____, the translation of information into a secret code.

16. Before I left for my camping trip, I used a(n) _____ to search for information about the campsite.

17. I like to _____ songs from the Internet so that I can listen to them on my computer.

18. I _____(ed) my resume from my computer to an online job board.

19. My _____ has a lot more memory than my computer at home.

20. I thought it would be really hard to add more memory to my computer, but I followed the directions and all I had to do was put it in the slot located on the _____ of my computer.

True/False

In the space provided, write a *T* if the sentence is true or an *F* if the sentence is false. If the sentence is false, cross out the word that makes the sentence false, and write the correct word from the vocabulary list above it.

21. _____ When I want to put a picture on my blog, I *download* it from my computer onto the Internet.

22. _____ A *cookie* is a high-speed storage mechanism that allows my computer to store information I frequently use.

23. _____ I used a *server* to do research on my new car by typing in the model and year. It then gave me a list of websites relating to my car.

24. _____ I just installed this new *application* on my computer that enables me to balance my checkbook and keep track of my expenses on my computer.

25. _____ Our office recently added five more computers to our *network*.

26. _____ Our computers are all connected via *encryption* so my computer can communicate with all of the others in the office.

27. _____ When you *upload* a file, you transmit it from your computer to an online bulletin board or network.

28. _____ The *database* is the main circuit board of the computer.

29. _____ At work, I can download files from the Internet much faster than at home because I have more *bitmap*.

30. _____ A *firewall* is used to protect a private network from unauthorized access.

Choosing the Right Word

Circle the word in bold that best completes the sentence.

31. At work, I have a(n) (**application, workstation**) that is much faster than my computer at home.

32. I saved the image I created in my design program as a (**bitmap, cookie**) so I could open it again in a different program.

33. When my mother first used a computer, she had difficulty seeing the (**cache, cursor**), but now that she is used to it, she knows to look for a blinking line.

34. He studied (**encryption, information technology**) and became an expert at deciphering secret codes used to protect hidden information.

35. When doing research, it is useful to come up with several (**keywords, plug-ins**) you can use to find articles and websites about your topic.

36. I wasn't able to view the video on the website because I didn't have the necessary (**plug-in, bitmap**) on my computer.

37. My boss asked me to create a (**server, database**) of all of our business contacts and clients so all of the contact information would be organized and easy to retrieve.

38. My friend sent me a funny animated cartoon, but when I opened it, a window popped up on the screen. It said I didn't have the right (**plug-in, cookie**) to play the cartoon, but that I could download it for free from another website.

39. My sister got a job in the (**Ethernet, information technology**) department at a financial services company, so now she helps fix computer problems in the office and helps people use their computers more effectively for their work.

40. The (**motherboard, server**) is the computer at work that manages all of our network resources, so when there is a problem with it, we can't share files with other computers or work on the website.

Matching Questions

Match the word in the first column with the corresponding word in the second column.

41. search engine   **a.** process of copying files from an online source to your computer

42. motherboard   **b.** process of copying files from your computer to an online or network location

43. workstation   **c.** word used to specify particular file or record

44. application   **d.** a system to protect a private network from outside access

45. cache   **e.** main circuit board of a computer

46. database   **f.** a group of computers linked together

47. upload   **g.** a representation in rows and columns of dots of an image in computer memory

48. server   **h.** stored and organized information that is easily retrievable

49. firewall   **i.** information stored in a Web browser and sent to a server when the browser contacts that server

50. bandwidth   **j.** translation of information into a secret code

51. cursor   **k.** program used to search for websites or documents containing a given keyword

52. Ethernet   **l.** a high-speed computer used in work environments

53. plug-in   **m.** protocol used to connect two or more computers to each other

54. network   **n.** a module that adds a specific feature to a larger system

55. information technology   **o.** subject of anything concerning processing or managing information

56. bitmap   **p.** the capacity for data transfer at a given time

57. cookie   **q.** a program that performs a certain task on a computer

58. download   **r.** a computer on a network that manages all of the network resources

59. encryption   **s.** a high-speed storage mechanism used to store frequently accessed information

60. keyword   **t.** blinking line on computer screen

Practice Activities

Find an article about technology in the technology section of your local newspaper or in a magazine. Add at least five new technology words to your vocabulary list and write down the definition of your new words based on the context clues in the article. Look up your new words and write down the dictionary definition. Go back and reread the article with your vocabulary list handy and note how the new words are used in the article.

Go to your local library or computer center and use a computer to search on a search engine using some of your new vocabulary words as keywords. See if you can find articles or websites that refer to your new vocabulary words. Does knowing these new vocabulary words make using a computer easier? Can you find any online dictionaries or other tools to help you develop your vocabulary?

Answers

Words in Context

The first word we encounter is *workstation*. Just from dissecting the word, we can determine that it is a station where one does work. Tom is a computer programmer, so it must refer to the computer he will use for work. The context clues tell us that the *applications* are on his computer and are things that he will use for work, so we can conclude that *application* must mean programs on a computer. He connects to the *network* via the *Ethernet* so he can communicate with the other computers. The *network* is what he is connecting to, so *network* must mean the group of computers in the office. *Ethernet* is the type of cord he is using to connect to the network, so it must be a means of connecting several computers to each other. Finally, he uses a *search engine* to find information about baseball. The *keyword* is the word he uses to search, and the *search engine* is a program that provides search results about baseball.

Sentence Completion

1. *network.* If you got this answer wrong, refer back to the word's definition.
2. *firewall.* If you got this answer wrong, refer back to the word's definition.
3. *server.* If you got this answer wrong, refer back to the word's definition.
4. *cookies.* If you got this answer wrong, refer back to the word's definition.
5. *database.* If you got this answer wrong, refer back to the word's definition.
6. *application.* If you got this answer wrong, refer back to the word's definition.
7. *cache.* If you got this answer wrong, refer back to the word's definition.
8. *plug-in.* If you got this answer wrong, refer back to the word's definition.
9. *keyword.* If you got this answer wrong, refer back to the word's definition.
10. *information technology.* If you got this answer wrong, refer back to the word's definition.
11. *cursor.* If you got this answer wrong, refer back to the word's definition.
12. *bandwidth.* If you got this answer wrong, refer back to the word's definition.
13. *bitmap.* If you got this answer wrong, refer back to the word's definition.
14. *Ethernet.* If you got this answer wrong, refer back to the word's definition.
15. *encryption.* If you got this answer wrong, refer back to the word's definition.
16. *search engine.* If you got this answer wrong, refer back to the word's definition.
17. *download.* If you got this answer wrong, refer back to the word's definition.
18. *upload.* If you got this answer wrong, refer back to the word's definition.
19. *workstation.* If you got this answer wrong, refer back to the word's definition.
20. *motherboard.* If you got this answer wrong, refer back to the word's definition.

True/False

21. False, correct word is upload
22. False, correct word is cache
23. False, correct word is search engine
24. True
25. True
26. False, correct word is Ethernet
27. True
28. False, correct word is motherboard
29. False, correct word is bandwidth
30. True

Choosing the Right Word

31. workstation

32. bitmap

33. cursor

34. encryption

35. keywords

36. plug-in

37. database

38. plug-in

39. information technology

40. server

Matching Questions

41. k

42. e

43. l

44. q

45. s

46. h

47. b

48. r

49. d

50. p

51. t

52. m

53. n

54. f

55. o

56. g

57. i

58. a

59. j

60. c

Across

3 cache
7 workstation
9 cursor
10 motherboard
11 bandwidth
14 encryption
15 plug-in
16 application
17 database

Down

1 keyword
2 Ethernet
4 upload
5 cookie
6 firewall
8 search engine
12 network
13 download
18 bitmap
19 server

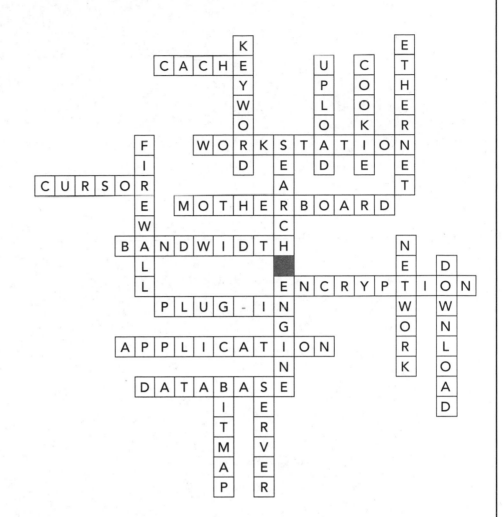

11 ▶ LEGAL TERMS

Study lends a kind of enchantment to all our surroundings.
—HONORÉ DE BALZAC, French author (1799–1850)

CHAPTER SUMMARY

Legal terms are important to know but often seem intimidating. The law governs every aspect of our lives, so it is important to understand the legal documents with which we may come into contact. You have most likely already signed a legal contract if you have a credit card, rent an apartment, have bought or sold a car, or have car insurance. Legal documents such as these are meant to protect citizens' rights, but because most legal terms are not used in everyday speech, legal documents can be confusing.

In this chapter, you will learn many terms commonly used in the legal profession. Read through the list and see which words are familiar to you. Where have you seen or heard them before? Look at the prefix, root, and suffix of each word and see if there are any similarities between these new words and other words you already know that may serve as useful memory tricks. Once you are comfortable with these words, continue to build your legal vocabulary by reading articles about courtroom cases and watching the news.

Choose the word from the vocabulary list that best fits into the crossword puzzle. You will use 20 words from the vocabulary list to solve the puzzle. You can check your answers at the end of the chapter following the answers to the questions.

Vocabulary List 8: Legal Terms

abrogate
adjudicate
affidavit
appellate
bequest
contraband
deposition
exhume
extradite
intestate
ipso facto
jurisprudence
larceny
lien
litigious
malfeasance
perjury
plagiarism
sanction
tort

Across

3 wrongdoing or misconduct especially by a public official
7 to dig up, to unbury
8 the science or philosophy of law
11 a sworn statement in writing made under oath
12 a wrongful act for which you can get damages or an injunction
14 to surrender an alleged criminal to the state or country in which he or she can be tried
16 theft, purloining
17 contentious, argumentative
20 to abolish

Down

1 the act of giving or leaving by will
2 having the power to review the judgment of another court
4 a charge upon real or personal property for the satisfaction of some debt
5 to act as a judge
6 testimony taken down in writing under oath
9 by that very fact or act
10 prohibited by law
13 the voluntary violation of an oath; false swearing
15 the act of stealing and passing off the ideas or words of another as one's own
18 having made no valid will
19 to approve or authorize

abrogate ('a·brə·gāt)
(*verb*)
to abolish by authoritative action
During the U.S. Civil War, the North fought the
South and wanted the American government to
_____ slavery.

adjudicate (ə·'jü·di·kāt)
(*verb*)
to act as a judge, to settle judicially
"You are not going to _____ this case. I am," the
judge said to the attorney.

affidavit (a·fə·'dā·vət)
(*noun*)
a sworn statement in writing made under oath
He was not asked to testify; instead, the attorney
asked him to sign a written _____ that
described what he knew about the case.

appellate (ə·'pe·lət)
(*adj.*)
having the power to review the judgment of another
court
When a case is appealed, it is tried in an _____
court.

bequest (bi·'kwest)
(*noun*)
the act of bequeathing, the act of leaving someone
something in a will, something that is
bequeathed
When my grandmother died, she gave me her house
as a _____.

contraband ('kän·trə·band)
(*noun*)
illegal or prohibited exporting or importing of goods
Cuban cigars are _____ in this country; it is
against the law to import them into the United
States.

deposition (de·pə·'zi·shən)
(*noun*)
testimony under oath, taken down in writing
In his _____, he said that he saw a gun, but
under cross-examination in court, he said that
he didn't remember seeing a gun.

exhume (ig·'züm)
(*verb*)
to remove from a grave; to bring back from neglect
or obscurity
When archeologists excavate ancient tombs, they
frequently _____ the remains of the people
who are buried there.

extradite ('ek·strə·dīt)
(*verb*)
to surrender an alleged criminal to the state or
country in which he or she can be tried
After ten years of hiding, he was _____(ed) to
the United States to stand trial for murder.

intestate (in·'tes·tāt)
(*adj.*)
one who dies without a will
My grandfather died _____, so we didn't know
who in the family should inherit his house.

ipso facto   (ˈip·sō·ˈfak·tō)
(*adverb*)
by the very fact or act, an inevitable act
In bankruptcy, an _____ provision is a provision
    that automatically comes into play when a
    company files for bankruptcy.

jurisprudence   (jur·əs·ˈprü·dən̦țs)
(*noun*)
a system of laws, the science or philosophy of the law
In law school, people study _____.

larceny   (ˈlärs·nē)
(*noun*)
the unlawful taking of someone else's property with
    the intention of not giving it back
He was accused of _____ when he was found
    driving the stolen car.

lien   (ˈlēn)
(*noun*)
a charge against real or personal property for the
    satisfaction of a debt or duty originally arising
    from the law
Before the bank would lend me the money, I had to
    prove that there were no previous _____(s)
    on my property.

litigious   (lə·ˈti·jəs)
(*adj.*)
contentious situation, prone to litigation
When my landlord did not give us our security
    deposit back after we moved out, it turned into
    a _____ situation.

malfeasance   (mal·ˈfē·zən̦țs)
(*noun*)
wrongdoing or misconduct especially by a public
    official
When a government official embezzles money, it is
    an act of _____.

perjury   (pər·jə·rē)
(*noun*)
lying or intentionally omitting information under
    oath
When she lied under oath, she committed _____.

plagiarism   (ˈplā·jə·ri·zəm)
(*noun*)
the act of passing off someone else's work as your
    own
In college, you can be expelled if you commit

    _____.

sanction   (ˈsan̦k̦·shən)
(*noun*)
authoritative permission or approval that makes a
    course of action valid, a law or decree
(*verb*)
to give permission or approval, to encourage or
    tolerate by indicating approval
The ruling was a _____; it made it clear that the
    court approved of the defendant's behavior.
When the judge gave his ruling, he turned to the
    defendant and said, "I find you guilty as charged.
    This court does not _____ your behavior."

tort   (ˈtŏrt)
(*noun*)
wrongdoing for which damages can be claimed; an
    unintentional violation of someone's rights,
    which can result in civil action but not criminal
    proceedings
A _____ is an unintentional violation of another
    person's rights.

TIP

When signing a contract of any kind, it's important to know what you're agreeing to, so get to
know these words and then read carefully before
signing.

Words in Context

The following exercise will help you figure out the meaning of some words from the vocabulary list by reading context clues. After you have read and understood the paragraph, explain the context clues that helped you with the meaning of the vocabulary word. Refer to the answer section at the end of this chapter for an explanation of the clues.

The attorney explained that if I gave a *deposition*, then I probably would not have to testify in court. I would still be under oath, but my testimony would be given and transcribed into written form before the trial actually began. I was glad I didn't have to testify because the case seemed pretty ridiculous to me. My Aunt Sally died *intestate* and without children, so the family did not know what she wanted us to do with her possessions. I was sure that she meant for her house to be a *bequest* for my mother, who is her sister; yet my aunt's ex-husband, Tom, said the house should be his. He said he had a signed *affidavit* stating that my aunt told him she would leave him the house. Initially, my mom and I thought we could keep this from becoming a *litigious* matter, but Tom wasn't willing to discuss the situation with us and come to a compromise. He wanted a third party to *adjudicate* this dispute, so he hired an attorney, and we were forced to do the same.

Sentence Completion

Insert the correct word from the vocabulary list into the following sentences.

1. The mayor issued a(n) _____ approving the city's subway-improvement plans.

2. When I clerked for a judge, I was lucky to be able get to work in a(n) _____ court, where I saw many cases appealed.

3. Since it was a small case, I didn't have to go to court; instead, I had to give a(n) _____ under oath while a stenographer recorded everything I said.

4. Many types of fur are considered _____ and cannot be imported into the country.

5. I am leaving my antiques to my children as a(n) _____.

6. I had to sign a(n) _____ that stated the house was in perfect condition and that the leak had been fixed.

7. It would be nice if the federal government would _____ the use of nuclear weapons.

8. When my brother and I were children and got into petty fights, sometimes my father would act as a judge and _____ our dispute.

9. In the medical community, many doctors are leading a(n) _____ reform movement, as patients have begun to sue for malpractice even when the doctor is not at fault.

10. She was charged with grand theft _____ when she was only sixteen, and since then, has been in and out of juvenile detention centers.

11. A(n) _____ clause is a statement that says a contract or agreement will automatically terminate on the expiration date of the agreement unless otherwise amended.

12. I do not want to die _____, so I plan to draft a will that clearly states who should inherit my possessions.

13. When public officials engage in _____, many citizens feel betrayed.

14. Committing _____ in a court of law is a very serious offense.

15. The teacher accused the student of _____ when she handed in a paper she found on the Internet.

16. _____, the philosophy of the law, is an interesting but complicated topic.

17. When the criminal escaped to Mexico, we hoped Mexico would _____ him so we could make him stand trial in the United States for his crime.

18. We have a(n) _____ on our house, because we were not able to pay off our debt, so now the bank from which we borrowed the money may take our house to satisfy the loan.

19. Scientists sometimes study ancient remains that have been _____(ed) from very old burial grounds.

20. When the attorney called, I knew that the matter had become _____ and we were no longer going to try and settle our disagreement out of court.

True/False

In the space provided, write a *T* if the sentence is true or an *F* if it is false. If the sentence is false, cross out the word that makes it false and write the correct word from the vocabulary list above it.

21. _____ When the mayor embezzled money from the city, it was an act of *jurisprudence*.

22. _____ Cases are appealed in *appellate* court.

23. _____ In a court of law, the judge is the person who will *abrogate* the case.

24. _____ Lying under oath is an act of *plagiarism*.

25. _____ When the cops found him with the stolen diamond ring, they charged him with *larceny*.

26. _____ When the witness gave her *affidavit*, she was asked many questions under oath while a stenographer wrote down both the questions and her responses.

27. _____ When I went through customs at the airport, they asked me if I was carrying any *contraband* items.

28. _____ After her death, her family realized that she had died *intestate*, so they were not sure what to do with her estate.

29. _____ If you run to another country after committing a crime, there is a very good chance that the country will *exhume* you to your homeland to be prosecuted.

30. _____ Trying to pass off someone else's work as your own is an act of *deposition*.

Choosing the Right Word

Circle the word in bold that best completes the sentence.

31. Her father died (**ipso facto, intestate**), so she and her siblings had difficulty dividing his estate.

32. Before we could close the deal, the borrower had to provide evidence to the lender that there were no (**liens, larcenies**) against the borrower's property.

33. In our town, our water became contaminated because a local factory was not disposing of dangerous chemicals properly, so we brought a (**sanction, tort**) claim against them and won.

34. I am very interested in studying (**jurisprudence, malfeasance**), because I am fascinated by the different systems of law and the philosophical tenets on which they are based.

35. In our country, child labor was (**extradited, abrogated**) a long time ago; however, in some countries, people are still fighting to end it.

36. When my grandfather died, he left me his piano as a (**contraband, bequest**), which touched me deeply because he was the one who taught me how to play.

37. After they found the tomb, the explorers wanted to (**extradite, exhume**) the remains to see if they could determine the date it was buried.

38. The contract stated that the parties must give written notification of intent to extend the contract, or the contract (**ipso facto, adjudicate**) terminated on the expiration.

39. Before the bank would give us our loan, the attorney prepared a(n) (**deposition, affidavit**) that stated that our property was debt-free and environmentally sound and asked me to sign it under oath.

40. The woman who snatched the other woman's purse was eventually charged with (**plagiarism, larceny**).

TIP

Don't be afraid to ask questions. In a legal situation, ask someone to explain unfamiliar terms. It will give you a better understanding, and you might learn a new word or two in the process.

Matching Questions

Match the word in the first column with the corresponding word in the second column.

41. lien

a. the very fact

42. extradite

b. testimony under oath

43. adjudicate

c. the act of passing someone else's writing off as your own

44. bequest

d. to abolish

45. contraband

e. a violation of someone's rights

46. perjury

f. one who dies without a will

47. jurisprudence

g. the act of bequeathing

48. ipso facto

h. charge against real property to satisfy a debt

49. exhume

i. to act as judge

50. abrogate

j. contentious

51. appellate

k. misconduct, especially of a public official

52. larceny

l. to surrender a criminal to a country where he or she can be tried

53. tort

m. lying under oath

54. sanction

n. to remove from a grave

55. affidavit

o. stealing

56. litigious

p. sworn written statement

57. malfeasance

q. illegal import or export of goods

58. plagiarism

r. authoritative approval

59. intestate

s. the philosophy of the law

60. deposition

t. having the power to review the judgment of another court

Practice Activities

Read an article about a current or historical court case and see how many of the vocabulary words from this chapter appear in the article. Write down any additional legal words you find in the article and their definitions based on the context clues. Be sure to look up each word in your dictionary and to write down its definition as well.

Find a legal document such as the lease for your apartment, the back of a credit card application, a letter from a lawyer, the agreement with your car insurance company, or any other contract. Read through the document, add any new legal words to your vocabulary list, and look them up. As you read, think about the following questions: How is the document written? Is it easy to understand? Why or why not? How are legal words used in the document?

Answers

Words in Context

The first word we encounter is *deposition.* The context tells us that it is an alternative to testifying in court, but that you are still under oath. We can conclude that it means a written testimony under oath prior to a trial. Sally died *intestate,* leaving the family unsure of how she wanted them to split up her belongings, so *intestate* must mean without a will. The narrator says he thinks Sally meant the house to be a *bequest,* or meant the narrator's mother to inherit the house. So *bequest* must mean something that is left to someone in a will. Tom has a signed *affidavit,* so an *affidavit* must mean a written statement. The narrator didn't want this to become *litigious* but it has, so we can conclude that *litigious* must mean contentious and prone to litigation. Finally, Tom wants someone else to *adjudicate,* or settle, this dispute. So *adjudicate* must mean to act as a judge or to settle judicially.

Sentence Completion

1. *sanction.* If you got this question wrong, go back and review the word's definition.
2. *appellate.* If you got this question wrong, go back and review the word's definition.
3. *deposition.* If you got this question wrong, go back and review the word's definition.
4. *contraband.* If you got this question wrong, go back and review the word's definition.
5. *bequest.* If you got this question wrong, go back and review the word's definition.
6. *affidavit.* If you got this question wrong, go back and review the word's definition.
7. *abrogate.* If you got this question wrong, go back and review the word's definition.
8. *adjudicate.* If you got this question wrong, go back and review the word's definition.
9. *tort.* If you got this question wrong, go back and review the word's definition.
10. *larceny.* If you got this question wrong, go back and review the word's definition.
11. *ipso facto.* If you got this question wrong, go back and review the word's definition.
12. *intestate.* If you got this question wrong, go back and review the word's definition.
13. *malfeasance.* If you got this question wrong, go back and review the word's definition.
14. *perjury.* If you got this question wrong, go back and review the word's definition.
15. *plagiarism.* If you got this question wrong, go back and review the word's definition.
16. *jurisprudence.* If you got this question wrong, go back and review the word's definition.
17. *extradite.* If you got this question wrong, go back and review the word's definition.
18. *lien.* If you got this question wrong, go back and review the word's definition.
19. *exhume.* If you got this question wrong, go back and review the word's definition.
20. *litigious.* If you got this question wrong, go back and review the word's definition.

True/False

21. False, correct word is malfeasance
22. True
23. False, correct word is adjudicate
24. False, correct word is perjury
25. True
26. False, correct word is deposition
27. True
28. True
29. False, correct word is extradite
30. False, correct word is plagiarism

Choosing the Right Word

31. intestate

32. liens

33. tort

34. jurisprudence

35. abrogated

36. bequest

37. exhume

38. ipso facto

39. affidavit

40. larceny

Matching Questions

41. h

42. l

43. i

44. g

45. q

46. m

47. s

48. a

49. n

50. d

51. t

52. o

53. e

54. r

55. p

56. j

57. k

58. c

59. f

60. b

Across

3 malfeasance
7 exhume
8 jurisprudence
11 affidavit
12 tort
14 extradite
16 larceny
17 litigious
20 abrogate

Down

1 bequest
2 appellate
4 lien
5 adjudicate
6 deposition
9 ipso facto
10 contraband
13 perjury
15 plagiarism
18 intestate
19 sanction

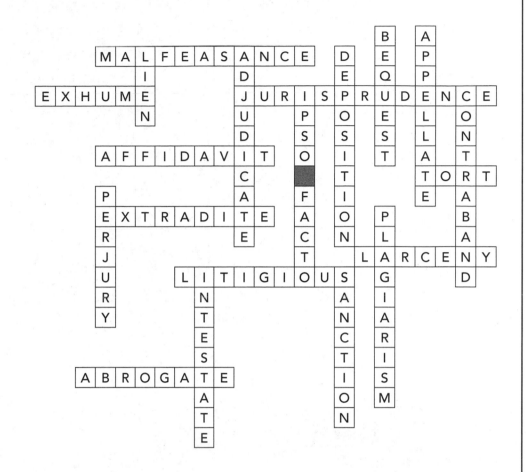

12 ▶ TERMS RELATING TO LANGUAGE AND LITERATURE

Don't use words too big for the subject. Don't say 'infinitely' when you mean 'very'; otherwise you'll have no word left when you want to talk about something really infinite.

—C.S. LEWIS, novelist and literary critic (1898–1963)

CHAPTER SUMMARY

This chapter will introduce you to a number of widely used literary terms, or words used to talk about language and literature. When we say *literary terms*, we mean ideas that are useful when discussing or analyzing a piece of literature such as a novel, short story, or poem. Yet literary terms are also applicable when we wish to describe situations that come up in everyday life.

That is, it is not only in the context of an English class or a sophisticated conversation about the fine points of literature that we use such terminology. For example, we encounter *irony* not only in Joseph Heller's famous novel, *Catch-22*, but also when the math teacher makes more computation errors than all her students combined!

Try to consider the following vocabulary words both in terms of how they may appear in literary texts and in the more general fabric of our lives.

Choose the word from the vocabulary list that best fits into the crossword puzzle. You can check your answers at the end of the chapter following the answers to the questions.

Vocabulary List 9: Terms Relating to Language and Literature

anecdote
anthropomorphism
aphorism
archetype
construe
deduce
epigram
etymology
infer
irony
onomatopoeia
personification
perspective
prose
protagonist
pun
rhetoric
satire
soliloquy
trite

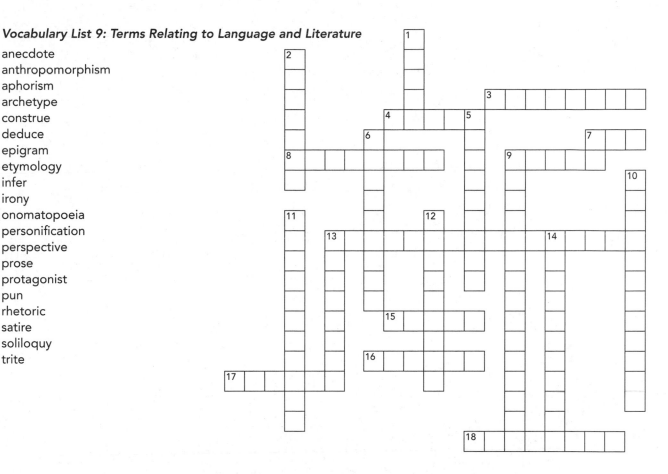

Across

3 using language effectively and persuasively
4 banal, ordinary, common
7 play on words
8 maxim, adage
9 ordinary writing
13 humanization
15 incongruity, or expressing something other than, or opposite to, the literal meaning
16 infer
17 the use of ridicule, usually to criticize
18 explain, interpret

Down

1 deduce, judge
2 a poem or paragraph dealing with a single thought
5 word origins
6 model, exemplar
9 embodiment
10 using words whose sounds suggest the meaning
11 outlook, point of view
12 talking to oneself, usually in drama, to reveal thoughts without actually addressing the listener
13 short tale relating an incident
14 main character

anecdote　(ˈa·nik·dōt)

(*noun*)

a short account of an interesting or humorous
　　incident

In order to capture classroom life for the visiting
　　parents at Back to School Night, the teacher
　　shared a number of comical _____(s)
　　about her kindergarten students.

anthropomorphism　(anˌt̩·thrə·pə·ˈmȯr·fi·zəm)

(*noun*)

attribution of human motivation, characteristics, or
　　behavior to inanimate objects, animals, or
　　natural phenomena

The Native American legend exhibited elements of
　　_____, as it was a bear who emotionally
　　narrated the tale of loss on the reservation.

aphorism　(ˈa·fə·ri·zəm)

(*noun*)

a brief statement of a truth or opinion; a saying or an
　　adage

The old _____, "Good things come to those who
　　wait," proved true when after many years, the
　　patient boy got his wish.

archetype　(ˈär·ki·tīp)

(*noun*)

an original model or type after which other similar
　　things are patterned; an ideal example of a type

Shakespeare's dramas provide a literary _____
　　that has influenced many subsequent authors
　　who follow the pattern his work provides.

construe　(kən·ˈstrü)

(*verb*)

to explain the meaning of; interpret; to analyze the
　　grammatical structure of (a sentence)

The boy _____(d) his mother's silence as
　　disappointment in his behavior.

deduce　(di·ˈdüs)

(*verb*)

to reach a conclusion by reasoning; to infer from a
　　general principle; to trace the origin of

Are you able to _____ the meaning of a word
　　once you are given ample context clues?

epigram　(ˈe·pə̃·gram)

(*noun*)

a short, witty poem expressing a single thought or
　　observation; a concise, clever, often paradoxical
　　statement or saying

The novelist began her text with a short _____
　　on the first page that truly captured the
　　complexity of the story that followed.

etymology　(e·tə·ˈmä·lə·jē)

(*noun*)

the origin and historical development of a word's
　　forms, meanings, and usages

Students were asked to trace the _____ of the
　　word, looking in particular for its earliest usage.

infer　(ˈin·fər)

(*verb*)

to conclude or reason from evidence, premises, or
　　circumstance; to hint or imply

Given the circumstances, we may _____ that the
　　young mother's motive for putting her baby up
　　for adoption was indeed honorable.

irony　(ˈī·rə·nē)

(*noun*)

the use of words to express something different from,
　　and often opposite to, their literal meaning; a
　　literary style employing such contrasts for witty
　　effect; incongruity between what might be
　　expected and what actually occurs

The _____ of his name, Tiny, became apparent
　　when I saw the seven-foot-tall man for the first
　　time.

onomatopoeia   (ä·nə·mä·tə·ˈpē·ə)

(*noun*)

the formation or use of words that imitate the
    sounds associated with the objects or actions to
    which they refer

The author of this musical review uses _____ to
    describe the sounds of the musical instruments
    at yesterday's concert.

personification   (pər·sä·nə·fə·ˈkā·shən)

(*noun*)

a person or thing typifying a certain quality or idea;
    an embodiment or exemplification; a figure of
    speech in which inanimate objects or
    abstractions are endowed with human qualities
    or are represented as possessing human form

The puppy was a true _____ of playfulness as he
    went to fetch the stick every time his owner
    threw it.

perspective   (pər·ˈspek·tiv)

(*noun*)

a mental view or outlook; a point of view; the ability
    to perceive things in their actual interrelations
    or comparative importance

I didn't have a good _____ on Abby's current
    situation until I learned that she had grown up an
    only child.

prose   (ˈprōz)

(*noun*)

ordinary speech or writing, without metrical
    structure (as in poetry)

I prefer to read _____ instead of poetry.

protagonist   (prō·ˈta·gə·nist)

(*noun*)

the main character in a drama or other literary work

The _____ of the story, Bridget, is a young
    woman that many women in their 30s can
    easily relate to, as she struggles with common
    issues such as dating, dieting, and work.

pun   (ˈpən)

(*noun*)

play on words

Mark is always making a _____, or a play on
    words, to make people laugh.

rhetoric   (ˈre·tə·rik)

(*noun*)

the art or study of using language effectively and
    persuasively

Because he is such a good speaker, his _____ is
    very convincing, even if what he says doesn't
    make a lot of sense.

satire   (ˈsa·tīr)

(*noun*)

a literary work in which human vice or folly is
    attacked through irony or wit

I love late-night television talk shows because the
    hosts always make a _____ of current
    politics.

soliloquy   (sə·ˈli·lə·kwē)

(*noun*)

a dramatic or literary form of discourse in which a
    character talks to himself or herself or reveals
    his or her thoughts without addressing a listener

As I get older, I find that I talk out loud to myself,
    just like a character in a drama who performs a
    _____.

trite   (ˈtrīt)

(*adj.*)

lacking power to evoke interest through overuse or
    repetition; hackneyed

Because he kept repeating the same joke over and
    over again, it became _____.

Words in Context

The following exercise will help you figure out the meaning of some words from the vocabulary list by reading context clues. After you have read and understood the paragraph, explain the context clues that helped you with the meaning of the vocabulary word. Refer to the answer section at the end of this chapter for an explanation of the clues.

When asked why the *prose* of the new novelist, Jane Jackson, appealed to me, I immediately thought of what makes any good novel. Considering the standard *archetype*, I think the successful novel should include mastery of a range of literary elements. In Jackson's case, she indeed effectively employs the device of *anthropomorphism*, in particular, when she writes of the "angry storm" waiting to take her revenge. It is as if the storm itself is the novel's *protagonist*: its central and most dynamic character. An *anecdote* I would like to share regarding the popularity of Jackson's writing takes place on the New York City subway. I noticed a young woman reading Jackson's latest novel, a *satire* that exposes and pokes fun of dating in the big city. When I, instinctively as a literary critic, approached the reader to ask her opinion, I realized it was Jackson herself! The *irony* of the situation was that the novelist still wished to critique the text she had authored; she was her own worst critic!

TIP

Some people learn best by doing. Try writing a short story or poem using some of the concepts defined in this list. Seeing them in action will help you commit the words to memory.

Sentence Completion

Insert the correct word from the vocabulary list into the following sentences.

1. My dad told us a(n) _____ about his childhood that was so funny, none of us could stop laughing.

2. I love to learn the origin of words, so my teacher suggested I might like to read a book on the _____ of language.

3. I _____(d) his smile as accepting my offer.

4. I decided to start my novel with a(n) _____ to get readers thinking about what was to come.

5. The little girl's favorite cartoon is one that uses _____ to tell the story; the silverware, refrigerator, and everything else in the kitchen come to life.

6. When something or someone typifies or embodies a given idea, it is a(n) _____ of that concept.

7. An ideal example of a given type is known as a standard or a(n) _____.

8. A(n) _____ is a play on words.

9. _____ is the art of effective language use.

10. When a character or performer reveals her thoughts without addressing a listener, she is issuing a _____.

11. A brief statement of truth or opinion is known as a(n) _____ or a saying.

12. One is often able to _____, or to reach a conclusion by reasoning or inference.

13. The complex device, _____, is when words are used to express something different from, and opposite to, their literal meaning.

14. _____ is often used in children's books to help kids learn the sounds that animals make, like "moo" for a cow and "meow" for a cat.

15. To _____ is to understand from a hint or implication, rather than from something directly stated.

16. Putting a situation in the proper _____ often requires a certain mental outlook or point of view.

17. A novel's main character, or _____, is central to the action of the text.

18. When a saying, idea, or word is so overused that it fails to evoke interest or convey meaning, we may call it _____.

19. The finest novelists have a real signature to their writing or the _____ they produce.

20. Irony and wit contribute to the makings of an effective _____ that attacks human folly.

Synonyms

The following exercise lists vocabulary words from this chapter. Each word is followed by five answer choices. Four of them are synonyms of the vocabulary word in bold. Your task is to choose the one that is NOT a synonym.

21. archetype
   a. standard
   b. statement
   c. example
   d. ideal
   e. model

22. protagonist
   a. main character
   b. principal figure
   c. fastest player
   d. first actor
   e. leader of a cause

23. perspective
   a. point of view
   b. prescription
   c. evaluation of significance
   d. outlook
   e. perceived interrelations

24. prose
   a. depressing language
   b. ordinary writing
   c. nonmetrical writing
   d. commonplace expression
   e. ordinary speech

25. pun
   a. ambiguous expression
   b. play on words
   c. similar sound
   d. rhetorical joke
   e. powerful understanding

26. satire
   a. classical text
   b. ironic ridicule
   c. witty literature
   d. caricature
   e. lampoon

27. trite
   a. commonplace
   b. habitual
   c. powerful
   d. overused
   e. banal

28. aphorism
   a. saying
   b. adage
   c. statement of truth
   d. euphemism
   e. maxim

29. deduce
   a. conclude
   b. compare
   c. infer
   d. reason
   e. suppose

30. construe
   a. to go against
   b. interpret
   c. render
   d. explain the meaning of
   e. analyze the structure of

True/False

In the space provided, write a *T* if the sentence is true, and an *F* if the sentence is false. If the sentence is false, cross out the false word and write the correct word from the vocabulary list above it.

31. _____ In journalism class, we used the news article as an *archetype* of what quality journalism looks like.

32. _____ In Shakespeare's play, *Hamlet* is not only the title but also the *satire* of the story.

33. _____ Based on the given evidence and circumstances, I was able to *construe* my own hypothesis.

34. _____ *Irony* is when words imitate the sounds associated with the actions to which they refer.

35. _____ My *perspective* on the subject shifted when the author's prose helped me step into another point of view.

36. _____ Cinderella, a well-known *pun*, captivates many readers who dream of transformation.

37. _____ The film was a parody or *soliloquy* of the futuristic genre, as it poked fun at depictions of space travel and alien encounters.

38. _____ Her *prose* was seamless and descriptive as she narrated her travels abroad for a captive audience.

39. _____ Throughout the story, the lion was a *personification* of all things regal and really stood as a symbol of royalty.

40. _____ A word's *epigram* can reveal a great deal about the history of its usages.

Choosing the Right Word

Circle the word in bold that best completes the sentence.

41. I thought she was such a good storyteller as she shared a number of humorous (**anecdotes, archetypes**) about her beloved grandmother.

42. The valentine card included a short, witty (**etymology, epigram**) that I found quite clever.

43. The character was a (**personification, satire**) of fear as she truly embodied the emotion.

44. There was such (**irony, onomatopoeia**) in the way she unexpectedly ended up rejecting the job she had worked for all her career.

45. Sometimes, two words that mean different things yet sound the same provide the opportunity for a (**prose, pun**).

46. The (**rhetoric, protagonist**) in the persuasive essay was so strong it convinced me to change my position.

47. As a reader, I tend to relate to a (**soliloquy, protagonist**) whose experiences reflect mine.

48. Although the poet did have some unique talent, he employed many phrases that were overused and that I found (**trite, ironic**).

49. What was so compelling about the actor's (**soliloquy, satire**) was how the audience came to understand the inner workings of his mind, even though he never addressed them directly.

50. There's an old (**soliloquy, aphorism**) that says, "A watched pot never boils."

Practice Activities

Rent a movie with a friend and try talking about the way the story unfolds: how the actors, screenplay writers, and directors give you, the viewer, your information. In your film (also a literary text) discussion, try to use, in context, a number of words from the vocabulary list

Recommend a book to a friend and in explaining why it is a worthwhile read, try using some of the literary terms you learned in the vocabulary list. Also, read the *New York Times* book review section. You'll see that those literary critics may talk about the quality of *prose*, an author's *rhetorical* gift or style, or the *ironic* plot twist the reader encounters.

TIP

The next time you read a piece of literature, see if you can spot some of the concepts explained in this chapter.

Answers

Words in Context

After reading this paragraph, we understand one literary critic's opinion of new novelist Jane Jackson's *prose*. We understand that *prose* refers to the novelist's writing: written text as opposed to metrical poetry (Jackson is a novelist, not a poet). We are also privy to a direct experience the critic had with the novelist herself. The critic shares this *anecdote*, or story-like episode, in order to convey the *irony*, or unlikelihood, of Jackson being more critical of her own work than any other reader. We are able to recognize *archetype* as meaning ideal or standard both because of the way the critic refers to it as a model of what "good prose" should have, and also because the word is used in conjunction with the word *standard*, a synonym for *archetype*. The three literary terms—*anthropomorphism*, *protagonist*, and *satire*—may be understood in context as the critic explains how they specifically relate to the novelist's *prose*. Jackson evidently writes about a storm that possesses human qualities (*anthropomorphism*) and, in fact, this animated storm operates as the main character (*protagonist*). The critic also describes Jackson's latest novel as a *satire*: a text that exposes and mocks dating in the big city.

Sentence Completion

1. *anecdote.* If you got this question wrong, refer back to the word's definition.
2. *etymology.* If you got this question wrong, refer back to the word's definition.
3. *construe.* If you got this question wrong, refer back to the word's definition.
4. *epigram.* If you got this question wrong, refer back to the word's definition.
5. *anthropomorphism.* If you got this question wrong, refer back to the word's definition.
6. *personification.* If you got this question wrong, refer back to the word's definition.
7. *archetype.* If you got this question wrong, refer back to the word's definition.
8. *pun.* If you got this question wrong, refer back to the word's definition.
9. *rhetoric.* If you got this question wrong, refer back to the word's definition.
10. *soliloquy.* If you got this question wrong, refer back to the word's definition.
11. *aphorism.* If you got this question wrong, refer back to the word's definition.
12. *deduce.* If you got this question wrong, refer back to the word's definition.
13. *irony.* If you got this question wrong, refer back to the word's definition.
14. *onomatopoeia.* If you got this question wrong, refer back to the word's definition.
15. *infer.* If you got this question wrong, refer back to the word's definition.
16. *perspective.* If you got this question wrong, refer back to the word's definition.
17. *protagonist.* If you got this question wrong, refer back to the word's definition.
18. *trite.* If you got this question wrong, refer back to the word's definition.
19. *prose.* If you got this question wrong, refer back to the word's definition.
20. *satire.* If you got this question wrong, refer back to the word's definition.

Synonyms

21. b. *statement.* An archetype is an original model after which other things are patterned, so *statement,* simply something that is said or put forth, would not be a synonym.

22. c. *fastest player.* A protagonist is the main character in a drama or other literary work. In ancient Greek drama, a protagonist is the first actor to engage in dialogue. A protagonist is also a champion or leader of a cause. Speed has little to do with a protagonist's centrality; therefore, fastest player would not be a synonym.

23. b. *prescription.* Perspective is a mental outlook, point of view, or the ability to perceive things as they actually relate to one another. Prescription is the establishment of a claim up front: literally, written beforehand, and would not be a synonym.

24. a. *depressing language.* Prose is ordinary speech or writing, without metrical structure. It is also a term used to denote commonplace expression. That language may be depressing does not define it as prose. Thus, depressing language would not be a synonym.

25. e. *powerful understanding.* A pun is wordplay, sometimes on different senses of the same word and sometimes on the similar sense or sound of different words. Powerful understanding would not be a synonym.

26. a. *classical text.* A satire is a literary work in which human folly or vice is attacked through wit or irony. A text's being considered a classic does not make it a satire. Therefore, classical text would not be a synonym.

27. c. *powerful.* When language is trite, it lacks power to evoke interest because of its overuse or repetition. *Powerful* is in fact the opposite of trite and thus would not be a synonym.

28. d. *euphemism.* An aphorism is a brief statement of truth or opinion: Adage and maxim are essentially synonymous with aphorism while a *euphemism* is a nice way of saying something that may be offensive. Euphemism is not a synonym for aphorism.

29. b. *compare.* To deduce is to reach a conclusion by reasoning or to infer from a general principle. Comparison—considering two things in terms of each other—is not a matter of deductive reasoning. Therefore, compare would not be a synonym.

30. a. *to go against.* To construe is to explain the meaning of, to interpret, or to analyze the structure of a sentence, for example. This does not mean to go against. It is not a synonym for construe.

True/False

31. True
32. False, correct word is protagonist
33. False, correct word is infer
34. False, the correct word is onomatopoeia
35. True
36. False, the correct word is protagonist
37. False, the correct word is satire
38. True
39. True
40. False, the correct word is etymology

Choosing the Right Word

41. *anecdotes.* Context clue is that she is telling stories that are humorous.

42. *epigram.* Context clue is that an epigram or short saying may be described as witty or clever.

43. *personification.* Context clue is that personification refers to a person's typifying or embodying a certain quality: in this case, fear.

44. *irony.* Context clue is that irony conveys the incongruity between what might be expected and what actually occurs.

45. *pun.* Context clue is that a pun is a play on words, such as those that may sound alike.

46. *rhetoric.* Context clue is that rhetoric is the art of using language effectively and persuasively.

47. *protagonist.* Context clue is that a protagonist is the main character of a text whose experiences provide the central action.

48. *trite.* Context clue is that trite phrases are described as overused and here, in contrast to the poet's talent.

49. *soliloquy.* Context clue is that a soliloquy is a dramatic form in which a character talks to himself, revealing his thoughts without addressing a listener.

50. *aphorism.* Context clue is the saying in quotes. An aphorism is a saying or adage.

Across

3 rhetoric
4 trite
7 pun
8 aphorism
9 prose
13 anthropomorphism
15 irony
16 deduce
17 satire
18 construe

Down

1 infer
2 epigram
5 etymology
6 archetype
9 personification
10 onomatopoeia
11 perspective
12 soliloquy
13 anecdote
14 protagonist

13 ▶ SHORT WORDS THAT MEAN A LOT

It is better to learn late than never.
—Publilius Syrus, Roman writer (85 b.c.e.–43 b.c.e.)

CHAPTER SUMMARY

Sometimes, we may falsely assume that vocabulary building means learning a host of long, multisyllabic words. We may hope to throw around these ten-dollar words in our speech and writing in order to sound smart and articulate. Don't forget the little words! Just because a word is short doesn't mean it can't pack a punch.

While a large vocabulary may in fact increase our confidence as well as our comprehension and self-expression skills, these goals do not rest on the length of the words we come to know. After all, how often does *antidisestablishmentarianism* come up in conversation?

This chapter seeks to familiarize you with a number of short but important words that frequently appear in a variety of contexts.

Choose the word from the vocabulary list that best fits into the crossword puzzle. You can check your answers at the end of the chapter following the answers to the questions.

Vocabulary List 10: Short Words That Mean a Lot

acme
awry
bane
cite
crux
dire
dupe
eke
elite
gibe
maim
mete
moot
oust
purge
roil
sham
staid
veer
vie

Across

1 force out
4 to allot
6 fool, chump
8 to cripple
11 askew, twisted
13 cream of the crop, upper crust
15 awful, appalling
17 to contest
18 to jeer or scoff
19 core, kernel

Down

2 a hoax, an impostor
3 serious, somber
5 source of persistent annoyance
7 to cleanse, to rid
9 pinnacle, high point
10 a case no longer of actual significance
12 to quote as an authority
14 to supplement, to make something last
16 to provoke, contaminate
17 to turn, or digress

acme (′ak·mē)

(*noun*)

the highest point, as of achievement or development

When the singer was awarded the Lifetime
    Achievement Award, she knew she had reached
    the _____ of her career.

awry (ə·′rī)

(*adv.*)

in a position that is turned or twisted toward one
    side or away from the correct course; askew

When a number of difficult variables entered into the
    situation, his carefully mapped plans went
    terribly _____.

bane (′bān)

(*noun*)

fatal injury or ruin; a cause of harm, ruin, or death; a
    source of persistent annoyance or exasperation

The persistent beetles that continued to eat away at
    the crop of string beans in spite of all efforts at
    extermination became the _____ of the
    farmer's existence.

cite (′sīt)

(*verb*)

to quote as an authority or example

The historian was careful to _____ a number of
    examples in order to back her claim that
    revolutions happen slowly.

crux (′krəks)

(*noun*)

the basic or central point or feature; a puzzling or
    apparently insoluble problem

After hours of debate, the opponents finally arrived
    at the _____ of the matter and at last the
    central question became clear.

dire (′dīr)

(*adj.*)

warning of, or having dreadful or terrible
    consequences; urgent; desperate

The poorly funded hospital was in _____ need
    of medical supplies given the number of
    neglected patients in desperate need.

dupe (′düp)

(*noun*)

an easily deceived person

The unsuspecting young man felt like a _____
    when he saw his girlfriend walk by in the arms
    of another man.

eke (′ēk)

(*verb*)

to supplement or get with great effort; to make last
    by practicing strict economy

With careful management, the townspeople were
    able to _____ out three more days' use of
    water, although the well had virtually run dry.

elite (ā·′let (i·′lēt, ē·′lēt))

(*noun*)

a group or class of persons or a member of such a
    group or class, enjoying superior intellectual,
    social, or economic status; the best or most
    skilled members of a group

The college's _____ students enjoyed high
    grades and membership in the exclusive and
    esteemed honors program.

gibe (′jīb)

(*verb*)

to make taunting, heckling, or jeering remarks

Mom made it clear that it was not acceptable to
    _____ our younger brother at the dinner
    table even though we insisted our taunting was
    in good fun.

maim   (ˈmām)

(*verb*)

to disable or disfigure; to make imperfect or
    defective; impair

Is it possible that such a seemingly mild car accident
    would _____ the driver to such
    proportions, causing him to lose his eyesight in
    one eye?

mete   (ˈmēt)

(*verb*)

to distribute by or as if by measure; allot

It was the captain's responsibility to carefully
    _____ out the limited rations so that each
    man received an equal amount.

moot   (ˈmüt)

(*noun*)

a hypothetical case argued as an exercise; a case no
    longer of actual significance

Since the position was no longer available, discussing
    who might better fill the spot became a
    _____ point.

oust   (ˈau̯st)

(*verb*)

To eject from a position or place; force out

The community hoped to _____ the
    superintendent from the school district since
    his policies had proved not only ineffective, but
    damaging.

purge   (ˈpərj)

(*verb*)

to free from impurities; purify; to rid of sin, guilt, or
    defilement; to clear a person of a charge; to get
    rid of people considered undesirable

After her candid testimony that evidenced her
    innocence, the woman on the stand was able to
    _____ herself of all criminal charges.

roil   (ˈrŏ i̯əl)

(*verb*)

to make a liquid muddy or cloudy by stirring up
    sediment; to displease or disturb; vex

My husband's disturbing refusal to help with the
    housework began to _____ me.

sham   (ˈsham)

(*noun*)

something false or empty that is said to be genuine;
    one who assumes a false character; an impostor

After a year of marriage, he recognized his wife as a
    _____ and sadly saw that his relationship
    was based on deception and lies.

staid   (ˈstād)

(*adj.*)

characterized by sedate dignity and propriety; sober;
    fixed; permanent

At her mother's funeral, Sue remained _____
    and sober, demonstrating her unwavering
    determination to not show her grief.

veer   (ˈvir)

(*verb*)

to turn aside from a course, direction, or purpose;
    swerve

The car's driver was able to _____ in the other
    direction in order to avoid a dangerous crash
    with an oncoming biker.

vie   (ˈvī)

(*verb*)

to strive for superiority; compete; rival

The two elite players would _____ for the
    championship.

TIP

Play Scrabble! Not only is it a fun way to practice
your vocabulary, but your knowledge of the short
words in this list will give you an advantage.

Words in Context

The following exercise will help you figure out the meaning of some words from the vocabulary list by reading context clues. After you have read and understood the paragraph, explain the context clues that helped you with the meaning of the vocabulary word. Refer to the answer section at the end of this chapter for an explanation of the clues.

There is one big example that I can *cite* to prove that I am one of the biggest *dupes* that ever lived. It involves a situation with one of my friends from work. By the time I realized what a *sham* my so-called friend was, I wondered how I didn't see his scheming ways all along. I tried to straighten things out between us, but everything started to go *awry* anyway when I realized that the money I had given him to put toward opening our own business had mysteriously disappeared. When I confronted him about it, with a lot of prying I was able to barely *eke* out the truth, but by then the situation had already become too *dire*—there was no getting my money back. Unfortunately, I have to see him—the miserable *bane* of my existence—every day!

Sentence Completion

Insert the correct word from the vocabulary list into the following sentences.

1. When a situation goes off course, it is said to have gone _____.

2. To quote as an authority or an example is to _____.

3. The _____ of one's freedom, for example, is the cause of freedom's decay or disappearance.

4. When you reach the _____ of your career, you know you achieved the highest point possible.

5. A(n) _____ is an easily deceived person.

6. One who enjoys superior status in a given arena is considered _____.

7. To _____ out supplies is to distribute them carefully in equal amounts.

8. The _____ of an argument is its basic or central feature.

9. You may be able to _____ out an income by working multiple jobs.

10. A hypothetical case may be considered _____.

11. If your situation is urgent or desperate, you are perhaps in _____ need of assistance.

12. To _____ is to make heckling, taunting remarks.

13. Our teacher instructed us to be careful not to _____ off topic during our oral presentations.

14. To disable or disfigure a person is to _____ his or her body.

15. His _____ composure belied the inner turmoil on his mind.

16. When you disturb or vex another person, you _____ her.

17. You pretended to be genuine, but you are completely false and a total _____!

18. We wondered whether to _____, or force out, the coach after he became unprofessional with his players.

19. It became necessary to _____ his body of toxins in order to purify the system and restore health.

20. The competitive siblings felt they needed to _____ for the approval of their parents.

Synonyms

The following exercise lists vocabulary words from this chapter. Each word is followed by five answer choices. Four of them are synonyms of the vocabulary word in bold. Your task is to choose the one that is NOT a synonym.

21. acme
　　a. summit
　　b. apex
　　c. highest point
　　d. culmination
　　e. average

22. gibe
　　a. jeer
　　b. heckle
　　c. taunt
　　d. applaud
　　e. bother

23. elite
　　a. chosen
　　b. lightweight
　　c. nobility
　　d. superiors
　　e. the best

24. purge
　　a. soil
　　b. cleanse
　　c. clear of charge
　　d. eliminate
　　e. evacuate

25. sham
　　a. imitation
　　b. false pretense
　　c. impostor
　　d. hero
　　e. fake

26. veer
　　a. steer
　　b. swerve
　　c. shift direction
　　d. turn off course
　　e. deviate

27. staid
　　a. serious
　　b. tired
　　c. sedate
　　d. permanent
　　e. proper

28. roil
　　a. displease
　　b. disturb
　　c. cheat
　　d. vex
　　e. stir up

29. bane
   a. curse
   b. killing
   c. ruin
   d. twist
   e. evil

30. awry
   a. turned
   b. elevated
   c. twisted
   d. amiss
   e. askew

Antonyms

Choose the word from the vocabulary list that means the opposite, or most nearly the opposite, of the following groups of words.

31. nadir, bottom, lowest point, underachievement _____

32. soil, condemn, retain, keep _____

33. actual, significant, relevant, important _____

34. protect, retain, house, host _____

35. please, calm, clarify, comfort _____

36. fix, repair, heal, enable _____

37. genuine, trustworthy, sincere, authentic _____

38. inferior, subpar, subordinate, second-rate _____

39. savior, relief, preserver, gift _____

40. straight, direct, right, good _____

TIP

Short words are sometimes hard to remember because they don't have all those helpful prefixes, suffixes, and roots. Try flash cards for this list in particular.

Matching Questions

Match the word in the first column with the corresponding word in the second column.

41. dire   **a.** easily deceived

42. sham   **b.** to get with great effort

43. gibe   **c.** to distribute by measure

44. eke   **d.** to turn aside from a course

45. crux   **e.** to disable or disfigure

46. dupe   **f.** having dreadful consequences

47. mete   **g.** to make taunting remarks

48. veer   **h.** basic or central feature

49. maim   **i.** impostor

50. awry   **j.** askew

Practice Activities

Now that you know these short but important words, they'll turn up everywhere! You may also find, especially if you make a deliberate effort, that ample opportunities arise for you to try these words out for yourself.

These words are very common, so give yourself the challenge of both listening for them when you watch the news, for example, and inserting them into your own common speech. Confide in your friend that things have really gone *awry* in your household (we hope not) or that your mother-in-law has become the *bane* of your existence.

Answers

Words in Context

The narrator begins to explain his situation by saying that he can *cite*, by way of an example, that he is one of the biggest *dupes* that ever lived. We may infer that *cite* means to quote (a situation or example). We can conclude that *dupe(s)* refers to someone who was deceived, based on the statement, "I wondered how I didn't see his scheming ways all along." This same statement, along with the term "so-called friend," can help the reader to infer that *sham* means someone who is scheming, or not loyal. When the narrator says that he tried to straighten things out but that they went *awry* anyway, it is clear that *awry* must mean when things go off course, or askew. When the narrator *ekes* out the truth, he says that it involved a lot of prying, so we can assume that *eke* means to get something like the truth with a lot of difficulty. By the time the narrator gets the truth, he says the situation has already become too *dire*. We can infer that *dire* means extreme or unsalvageable because the narrator says that there was no way to get his money back at that point. The last sentence describes the narrator's "so-called friend" as a miserable *bane* of his existence, or a source of constant misery and annoyance.

Sentence Completion

1. *awry*. If you got this question wrong, refer back to the word's definition.
2. *cite*. If you got this question wrong, refer back to the word's definition.
3. *bane*. If you got this question wrong, refer back to the word's definition.
4. *acme*. If you got this question wrong, refer back to the word's definition.
5. *dupe*. If you got this question wrong, refer back to the word's definition.
6. *elite*. If you got this question wrong, refer back to the word's definition.
7. *mete*. If you got this question wrong, refer back to the word's definition.
8. *crux*. If you got this question wrong, refer back to the word's definition.
9. *eke*. If you got this question wrong, refer back to the word's definition.
10. *moot*. If you got this question wrong, refer back to the word's definition.
11. *dire*. If you got this question wrong, refer back to the word's definition.
12. *gibe*. If you got this question wrong, refer back to the word's definition.
13. *veer*. If you got this question wrong, refer back to the word's definition.
14. *maim*. If you got this question wrong, refer back to the word's definition.
15. *staid*. If you got this question wrong, refer back to the word's definition.
16. *roil*. If you got this question wrong, refer back to the word's definition.
17. *sham*. If you got this question wrong, refer back to the word's definition.
18. *oust*. If you got this question wrong, refer back to the word's definition.
19. *purge*. If you got this question wrong, refer back to the word's definition.
20. *vie*. If you got this question wrong, refer back to the word's definition.

Synonyms

21. **e.** *average.* Acme is the highest point of achievement or development. It is not at all average but, rather, the best one can do. Average would not be a synonym.

22. **d.** *applaud.* Gibe means to make taunting or jeering remarks, so applaud would not be a synonym.

23. **b.** *lightweight.* To be (an) elite is to belong to a group or class of people who enjoy superior status. The elite are chosen, superior, or the best in a given arena. Lightweight would not be a synonym of elite.

24. **a.** *soil.* To purge is to free from impurities, to remove or to eliminate. In law, it means to clear someone of a charge. Soil means to dirty or taint and would not be a synonym of purge.

25. **d.** *hero.* A sham is something or someone false that is purported to be genuine. A hero generally possesses sincere, noble, and admirable qualities. Hero would not be a synonym for sham.

26. **b.** *steer.* To veer is to turn aside from a course, direction or purpose. Swerve and deviate also describe such derailing action. Steer implies guided control and would not be a synonym.

27. **b.** *tired.* Staid characterizes sedate dignity, and serious, sober propriety. It also means fixed or permanent. Fatigue is not necessarily associated with being staid and so, tired would not be a synonym.

28. **c.** *cheat.* To roil is to disturb or displease. It also refers to making a liquid muddy by stirring up sediment. Though one may become vexed or roiled if cheated by another, cheat is not a synonym of roil.

29. **d.** *twist.* Bane describes fatal injury or ruin. Twist would not be a synonym, as it is not necessarily the cause of harm, ruin, or death.

30. **b.** *elevated.* Awry describes a position that is turned or twisted toward one side. Askew and amiss also convey this sense. To elevate means to lift up or raise, not twist or turn, and so would not be a synonym.

Antonyms

31. *acme.* Acme means the highest point of achievement or development, the opposite of the meaning of the words in the group.

32. *purge.* Purge means to free from impurities or guilt, the opposite of soil or condemn. It also means to get rid of, the opposite of retain or keep.

33. *moot.* Moot means a hypothetical case, opposite of actual. It also means no longer of actual significance, opposite of the rest of the words listed.

34. *oust.* Oust means to eject or force out, opposite of the words listed, which mean to keep and comfort in a protected space.

35. *roil.* Roil means to make cloudy or stir up, the opposite of calm or clarify. It also means to disturb or vex, the opposite of please, or comfort.

36. *maim.* To maim is to disable or disfigure, the opposite of the words listed.

37. *sham.* A sham is something or someone false or an impostor, the opposite of the words in the group.

38. *elite.* To be elite is to enjoy superior status, the opposite of the words in the group.

39. *bane.* Bane is fatal injury or the cause of ruin or death, the opposite of the positive, redemptive words in the group.

40. *awry.* Awry means turned or twisted, or off the expected or correct course, the opposite meaning of the words in the group.

Matching Questions

41. f

42. i

43. g

44. b

45. h

46. a

47. c

48. d

49. e

50. j

Across

1 oust
4 mete
6 dupe
8 maim
11 awry
13 elite
15 dire
17 vie
18 gibe
19 crux

Down

2 sham
3 staid
5 bane
7 purge
9 acme
10 moot
12 cite
14 eke
16 roil
17 veer

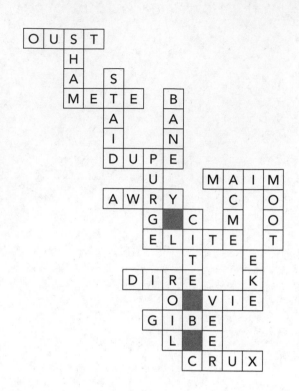

CHAPTER

14 ▶ ADJECTIVES

The adjective is the banana peel of the parts of speech.
—Clifton Paul Fadiman, American author (1904–1999)

CHAPTER SUMMARY

Adjectives are typically understood as words used to describe nouns, that is, people, places, things, and ideas. But, beyond this textbook definition, we may begin to think about the role of adjectives in our experiences as readers, writers, speakers, and listeners.

What does careful description add to a given conversation, story, or explanation? Adjectives add color, definition, and detail to any piece of writing. They serve to qualify and clarify the subject at hand. Consider a mental image coming into focus as additional information is put forth: "There was a man. There was an old man. There was an old, dolorous man." In this way, adjectives help us account for specificity when trying to conjure up a figure, picture, mood, or situation in our minds.

Choose the word from the vocabulary list that best fits into the crossword puzzle. You can check your answers at the end of the chapter following the answers to the questions.

Vocabulary List 11: Adjectives

audacious
churlish
demure
dolorous
epicurean
extenuating
facetious
feisty
flippant
imperious
jaunty
myriad
oblique
ornate
palpable
prodigious
prone
relevant
sardonic
vehement

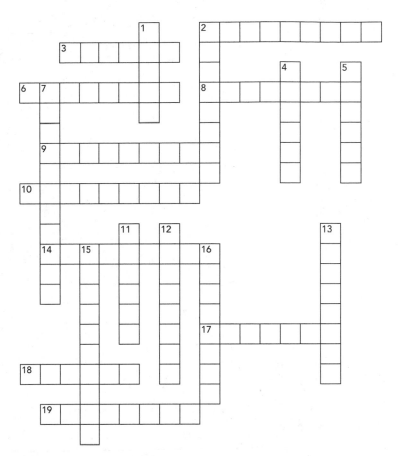

Across

2 something that's meant to be funny
3 shy, modest, reserved
6 relating to
8 touchable, perceptible
9 devoted to the pursuit of sensual pleasure, gourmet
10 bold, adventuresome, insolent
14 commanding
17 indirect, circuitous
18 innumerable
19 surly

Down

1 apt, disposed to
2 glib, lacking appropriate respectfulness
4 stylish, lively
5 spunky, showing aggressiveness, liveliness
7 tempering, moderating
11 elaborate, sumptuous
12 woeful, melancholy
13 intense, desperate
15 amazing, massive
16 cynical, scornful

audacious (ŏ·ʹdā·shəs)

(*adj.*)

fearlessly, often recklessly daring, adventurous, and
    brave; unrestrained by convention or propriety;
    insolent

The student's _____ behavior—swearing at the
    teacher in class—resulted in detention for a
    week.

churlish (ʹchər·lish)

(*adj.*)

boorish or vulgar; having a bad disposition; surly;
    difficult to work with; intractable

The child was immediately punished for his bad
    attitude and _____ behavior.

demure (di·ʹmyŭ r)

(*adj.*)

modest and reserved in manner or behavior; shy

Having always been attracted to the shy and quiet
    type, James predictably fell for the _____
    woman to whom he was introduced.

dolorous (ʹdō·lə·rəs)

(*adj.*)

exhibiting sorrow, grief, or pain

My friend's _____ expression could be explained
    by the painful divorce process in which she
    found herself.

epicurean (e·pi·kyŭ ·ʹrē·ən)

(*adj.*)

devoted to the pursuit of sensual pleasure, especially
    to good food and comfort

The _____ feast lasted for hours as those in
    attendance enjoyed fine wine, delicacies, and
    the host's beautiful home.

extenuating (ik·sten·yə·wāt·ing)

(*adj.*)

lessened the magnitude or seriousness of, especially
    by making partial excuses

After hearing the entire story surrounding the
    supposed crime, the judge realized there existed
    _____ circumstances that put the situation
    in perspective.

facetious (fə·sē·shəs)

(*adj.*)

playfully jocular

"Don't be _____," requested the girl's mother,
    who was tired of her daughter's refusal to take
    the situation seriously.

feisty (ʹfī·stē)

(*adj.*)

touchy; quarrelsome; full of spirit; frisky or spunky

Our new young puppy was extremely _____,
    jumping playfully all over the apartment and
    licking our faces.

flippant (ʹfli·pənt)

(*adj.*)

marked by disrespectful levity or casualness; pert

Her _____ remarks during the interview cost
    her the job as she failed to demonstrate the
    necessary respect for her potential coworkers.

imperious (im·ʹpir·ē·əs)

(*adj.*)

arrogantly domineering or overbearing; dictatorial

"It is my _____, ruthless political strategy that
    will conquer all contesting factions in this city,"
    exclaimed the egocentric, overconfident mayor.

jaunty (ʹjŏ n·tē)

(*adj.*)

having a buoyant or self-confident air; brisk; crisp
    and dapper in appearance

The _____ groom looked dapper in his stylish
    suit and hat as he confidently entered the
    church on his wedding day.

myriad (ˈmir·ē·əd)
(***adj.***)
constituting a very large, indefinite number; innumerable; composed of numerous diverse elements or facets
(***noun***)
a great number, countless
The _____ species of fish, plants, and micro-organisms populate the ocean.

oblique (ō·ˈblēk)
(***adj.***)
having a slanting or sloping direction, course, or position; indirect or evasive; devious, misleading, or dishonest
While the president's _____ political maneuvers were expedient, they did not earn him the trust of the general public.

ornate (ŏr·ˈnāt)
(***adj.***)
elaborately and often excessively ornamented; showy or flowery
The actress's _____ style of dress was tastelessly overdone.

palpable (ˈpal·pə·bəl)
(***adj.***)
capable of being handled, touched, or felt; tangible
The tension in the room was so _____ one felt it could be cut with a knife.

prodigious (prə·ˈdi·jəs)
(***adj.***)
impressively great in size, force, or extent; extraordinary; marvelous
A _____ talent like the great golfer Tiger Woods doesn't come along very often.

prone (ˈprōn)
(***adj.***)
lying with the front or face downward; having a tendency; inclined
Chloe is quite clumsy and _____ to accidents.

relevant (ˈre·lə·vənt)
(***adj.***)
having a bearing on or connection with the matter at hand
Gabriel brought up a point that at first didn't seem _____, but later, we all realized that it had a direct bearing on the situation.

sardonic (sär·ˈdä·nik)
(***adj.***)
scornfully or cynically mocking
I tend to gravitate toward people with a _____ sense of humor because I, too, have a cynical outlook.

vehement (ˈvē·ə·mənt)
(***adj.***)
characterized by forcefulness of expression or intensity of emotion or conviction; fervid; intense
His reaction was _____, so it was clear there was no convincing him to change his mind.

Words in Context

The following exercise will help you figure out the meaning of some words from the vocabulary list by reading context clues. After you have read and understood the paragraph, explain the context clues that helped you with the meaning of the vocabulary word. Refer to the answer section at the end of this chapter for an explanation of the clues.

When my young daughter Tanya came home one day claiming she had adopted a lost puppy, I thought this an *audacious* move. After all, we live in a small two-bedroom apartment, and further, Tanya knows her sister is *prone* to allergies, especially around long-haired dogs like this pup she found. Under normal circumstances, I probably would have demanded we let the dog go. Yet, there were *extenuating* circumstances that seemed *relevant* to the decision I had to make. The playful and *feisty* puppy reminded us so very much of Jelly, the playful dog next door who, three months ago, was tragically killed by a speeding car. The loss had stayed with my daughters and me; our sadness was *palpable,* filling our home with gloom. And so I agreed that the sweet stray would become a member of our family.

TIP

Sometimes when you're writing, it can be hard to decide which adjective to use. If you get stuck, brainstorm a short list of possibilities, and then insert one word at a time to see which adjective best fits your sentence.

Sentence Completion

Insert the correct word from the vocabulary list into the following sentences.

1. Because James is quite shy, he tends to get along with girls who have a(n) _____ nature.

2. Her _____ behavior was shocking, as she was normally shy and reserved.

3. The _____ circumstances helped to justify why the normally conscientious student didn't turn in his term paper.

4. I enjoyed my job until I had to work closely with the _____ Louise—she is impossible to get along with!

5. I tend to like people with a(n) _____ disposition, as I like a personality with spirit and spunk.

6. It was no surprise that the day Kathryn lost her job, she had a(n) _____ expression on her face.

7. Jason is so playful that it is hard to tell when he is being _____ or serious.

8. It was clear by Paul's _____ behavior that he didn't care about the project.

9. Andrew's _____ tastes inspired him to go to cooking school and open his own restaurant.

10. After Sandy let it slip about the surprise party for Johnny, there was a _____ feeling of awkwardness in the room.

11. There are _____ cultural activities to choose from in New York City.

12. Because of my pale skin, I am _____ to getting freckles in the sun.

13. I had to leave my last job because of my _____ boss; he thought that the best way to manage a department was by being dictatorial.

14. Bob's _____ strategies may work in the short term, but eventually, his sneaky dealings will get him in trouble.

15. Her coworkers respond well to Lauren's _____ demeanor, as everyone likes to be around someone who is self-confident.

16. Your _____ denial is so insistent that I no longer believe that you are responsible.

17. The room was too _____ for my taste with its gaudy, elaborate decor.

18. The _____ storm was so huge, I thought it the most intense weather we had experienced all year.

19. He never seemed open to new experiences; he and his _____ attitude mocked everything even remotely unfamiliar.

20. My past experiences proved _____ to the situation once I was able to make the connection.

Synonyms

The following exercise lists vocabulary words from this chapter. Each word is followed by five answer choices. Four of them are synonyms of the vocabulary word in bold. Your task is to choose the one that is NOT a synonym.

21. feisty
a. energetic
b. rambunctious
c. frisky
d. touchy
e. laid-back

22. demure
a. prudish
b. graceful
c. shy
d. solemn
e. modest

23. dolorous
a. demure
b. sorrowful
c. unpleasant
d. painful
e. distressful

24. flippant
a. careless
b. flexible
c. disrespectful levity
d. rudely casual
e. pert

25. ornate
a. showy
b. flowery
c. epicurean
d. highly decorated
e. excessively ornamented

26. jaunty
a. dapper
b. buoyant
c. self-confident
d. athletic
e. stylish

27. palpable
a. substantial
b. touchable
c. weighable
d. tangible
e. sensitive

28. sardonic
a. sarcastic
b. prodigious
c. cynical
d. caustic
e. scornfully mocking

29. vehement
   a. fervid
   b. passionate
   c. relevant
   d. zealous
   e. forceful

30. myriad
   a. plenty
   b. numerous
   c. indefinite
   d. countless
   e. oblique

Antonyms

31. conservative, restrained, reserved, timid   _____

32. polite, poised, tractable, malleable   _____

33. respectful, mindful, serious, courteous   _____

34. joyful, blissful, happy, mirthful   _____

35. finite, numerical, limited, homogenous   _____

36. clear, straight, honest, direct   _____

37. plain, unadorned, modest, simple   _____

38. irrelevant, disconnected, moot, unrelated   _____

39. intangible, imperceptible, subtle, untouchable   _____

40. boastful, uplifting, positive   _____

TIP

When using adjectives, it's important to keep in mind a word's connotation, as different adjectives have different feelings associated with them.

Choosing the Right Word

Circle the word in bold that best completes the sentence.

41. I found your casual, (**flippant, feisty**) attitude during the formal ceremony very disrespectful.

42. "Might makes right!" declared the (**facetious, imperious**) dictator.

43. It's difficult to know whether you are serious when you are so (**facetious, jaunty**) with me.

44. It was very (**audacious, churlish**) to stand up before the crowd and recklessly begin speaking without having prepared at all.

45. I can't work with you in this professional environment when you are so (**extenuating, churlish**).

46. How can you afford your (**epicurean, extenuating**) tastes; they are so lavish and luxurious!

47. Can't you forgive me considering the (**extenuating, feisty**) circumstances?

48. Did you notice how (**dolorous, feisty**) she became when the touchy subject came up?

49. His (**oblique, jaunty**) answers to my simple questions left me at a loss for understanding.

50. She became (**prodigious, prone**) to illness when her immune system began to fail her.

Practice Activities

Go to your favorite magazine and, while reading an article, story, or any considerably lengthy feature, circle all the adjectives (words that describe or qualify nouns) you come across. Take note of the nouns (people, places, things) they describe or qualify, and then ask yourself how the presence of adjectives contributes to the piece in specific cases, and also as a whole.

The next time you write an e-mail or an old-fashioned letter to a friend, see what happens to the quality and character of your prose when you make a point of including carefully selected adjectives, including those you learned in the vocabulary list.

Answers

Words in Context

Tanya's move of bringing home the puppy was seen as *audacious,* or bold and even reckless, considering both the size of her family's apartment and the fact that her sister is *prone,* or susceptible, to allergies. Yet Tanya's reasonable mother is willing to consider the *relevant* (having bearing on the matter at hand) *extenuating* circumstances, which allow her to make an exception. All things considered (namely her family's *palpable,* or tangible gloom when the neighbor's dog died), it wouldn't be a bad idea for this *feisty* puppy—so obviously playful and full of spirit—to stay.

Completing the Sentence

1. *demure.* If you got this question wrong, refer back to the word's definition.
2. *audacious.* If you got this question wrong, refer back to the word's definition.
3. *extenuate.* If you got this question wrong, refer back to the word's definition.
4. *churlish.* If you got this question wrong, refer back to the word's definition.
5. *feisty.* If you got this question wrong, refer back to the word's definition.
6. *dolorous.* If you got this question wrong, refer back to the word's definition.
7. *facetious.* If you got this question wrong, refer back to the word's definition.
8. *flippant.* If you got this question wrong, refer back to the word's definition.
9. *epicurean.* If you got this question wrong, refer back to the word's definition.
10. *palpable.* If you got this question wrong, refer back to the word's definition.
11. *myriad.* If you got this question wrong, refer back to the word's definition.
12. *prone.* If you got this question wrong, refer back to the word's definition.
13. *imperious.* If you got this question wrong, refer back to the word's definition.
14. *oblique.* If you got this question wrong, refer back to the word's definition.
15. *jaunty.* If you got this question wrong, refer back to the word's definition.
16. *vehement.* If you got this question wrong, refer back to the word's definition.
17. *ornate.* If you got this question wrong, refer back to the word's definition.
18. *prodigious.* If you got this question wrong, refer back to the word's definition.
19. *sardonic.* If you got this question wrong, refer back to the word's definition.
20. *relevant.* If you got this question wrong, refer back to the word's definition.

Synonyms

21. e. *laid-back.* Feisty means frisky or spunky, so laid-back is not a synonym of the word.
22. b. *graceful.* Demure describes modest and reserved behavior. Graceful describes pleasing, attractive movement, and though one may find modesty graceful, it would not be a synonym for demure.
23. a. *demure.* Dolorous means exhibiting pain, grief, or sorrow. Demure means mild-mannered or shy and would not be a synonym.
24. b. *flexible.* Flippant means marked by disrespectful levity. Being overly casual in a disrespectful manner or being pert or careless would also describe this attitude. Flexible means able to bend, change, or move, and would not be a synonym.
25. c. *epicurean.* Ornate means elaborately and excessively ornamented. Something ornate may also be considered showy or flowery.

Epicurean means devoted to the pursuit of sensual pleasures and thus would not be a synonym.

26. d. *athletic.* Jaunty means having a buoyant or self-confident air. It also means having a crisp, dapper, stylish appearance. Athletic, meaning good at sports, would not be considered a synonym.

27. e. *sensitive.* Palpable means capable of being handled, touched, or felt. All the words in the group except sensitive denote this characteristic. Sensitive means highly receptive to senses (including, but not exclusively to, touch) and is not a synonym.

28. b. *prodigious.* Sardonic means scornfully or cynically mocking. All the words and groups of words suggest this disposition except for prodigious. Prodigious means extraordinary or impressively great in size or force and would not be a synonym.

29. c. *relevant.* Vehement means characterized by forcefulness or intensity. The word choices are all useful vocabulary terms that have similar meanings to vehement except for relevant, which means having a connection with the matter at hand. Relevant would not be a synonym.

30. e. *oblique.* Myriad means constituting a very large or indefinite number. Oblique would not be considered a synonym, as it means indirect or evasive.

Antonyms

31. *audacious.* Audacious means bold, the opposite of the meaning of the words in the group.

32. *churlish.* Churlish means vulgar or difficult to work with, the opposite of the meaning of the words in the group.

33. *flippant.* Flippant means marked by disrespectful levity or casualness, the opposite of the meaning of the words in the group.

34. *dolorous.* Dolorous means marked by sorrow, the opposite of the meaning of the words in the group.

35. *myriad.* Myriad means indefinite, the opposite of the meaning of the words in the group.

36. *oblique.* Oblique means slanting or misleading, the opposite of the meaning of the words in the group.

37. *ornate.* Ornate means elaborately ornamented, the opposite of the meaning of the words in the group.

38. *relevant.* Relevant means having a bearing on, or a connection with, the matter at hand, the opposite of the meaning of the words in the group.

39. *palpable.* Palpable means capable of being touched or felt, the opposite of the meaning of the words in the group.

40. *sardonic.* Sardonic means scornfully or cynically mocking, the opposite of the words in the group.

Choosing the Right Word

41. *flippant.* Context clue is that flippant means marked by disrespectful casualness. Though being overly feisty may also be considered disrespectful, considering the context clues, flippant is the stronger choice.

42. *imperious.* Context clue is that imperious means dictatorial and domineering.

43. *facetious.* Context clue is that facetious means playfully jocular; when one is facetious, it may sometimes be difficult to determine whether one is joking or not.

44. *audacious.* Context clue is that audacious means recklessly daring.

45. *churlish.* Context clue is that churlish means difficult to work with, specifically on the grounds of vulgarity (that would be problematic in the mentioned "professional" environment).

46. *epicurean.* Context clue is that epicurean means devoted to the pursuit of sensual pleasure, especially fine food.

47. *extenuating.* Context clue is that extenuating means lessening the magnitude or seriousness of (in this case, whatever the speaker did for which she asks forgiveness).

48. *feisty.* Context clue is that feisty means touchy or quarrelsome (argumentative being a synonym thereof).

49. *oblique.* Context clue is that oblique means indirect or evasive; such responses would not yield clarity or understanding.

50. *prone.* Context clue is that prone means susceptible or inclined toward.

Across

2 facetious
3 demure
6 relevant
8 palpable
9 epicurean
10 audacious
14 imperious
17 oblique
18 myriad
19 churlish

Down

1 prone
2 flippant
4 jaunty
5 feisty
7 extenuating
11 ornate
12 dolorous
13 vehement
15 prodigious
16 sardonic

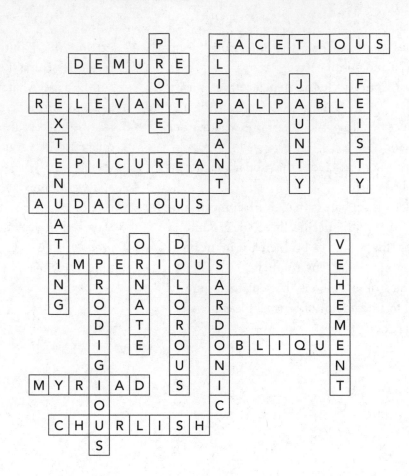

CHAPTER 15 ▶ **ACRONYMS**

The only place success comes before work is in the dictionary.
—Vince Lombardi, American football coach (1913–1970)

CHAPTER SUMMARY

What is an acronym? While this term may in itself be a new vocabulary word for you, you are probably familiar with more acronyms than you think. Have you ever written RSVP at the bottom of an invitation? Have you wondered about the amount of RAM on your latest computer? Both are commonly used acronyms.

An acronym is a word formed from the initial letter or letters of each of the successive parts (or major parts) of a compound term. The roots *acr* or *acro* mean *beginning,* thus, the *first* letters of each word in a term work together to make a single new word: an acronym.

In a way, understanding acronyms is like breaking a code. Each of the letters, or initials in the acronym, represent an entire other word. For example, the letters in *scuba* stand for Self Contained Underwater Breathing Apparatus. And it makes sense: That's really what scuba diving is all about, right?

Choose the word from the vocabulary list that best fits into the crossword puzzle. You will use 19 words from the vocabulary list to solve this puzzle. You can check your answers at the end of the chapter following the answers to the questions.

Vocabulary List 12: Acronyms

ASAP
CAT scan
CD-ROM
dinks
DOS
ESL
FAQ
HTML
ISP
LAN
laser
modem
moped
radar
RAM
REM
scuba
snafu
URL
yuppie

Across

2 a type of computer access memory that can be accessed randomly
3 the coding on many Web page documents
6 local area network
8 a compact disc that contains data a computer can read
9 self-contained underwater breathing device
10 English as a second language
13 a company that provides access to the Internet
14 a device that generates electromagnetic radiation
16 as soon as possible
17 frequently asked questions
18 rapid eye movement

Down

1 the address of documents and resources on the Web
4 a motor-powered bike that can also be pedaled
5 a mix-up
7 a device that converts signals from digital to analog to transmit over phone lines
8 a 3D image of a body structure
11 disk operating system
12 a young, professional adult who works and lives in or near a city
15 radio detecting and ranging

ASAP   (ā·s·ā·p)

(*adv.*)

an abbreviation for **A**s **S**oon **A**s **P**ossible

Please don't waste any time; I need you to complete this assignment _____.

CAT scan   (ˈkat·ˈskan)

(*noun*)

Computerized **A**xial **T**omography scan—a three-dimensional image of a body structure made from a series of cross-sectional images and put together by a computer

John had to check into the hospital after his car accident for a routine _____ to make sure he did not have a concussion.

CD-ROM   (sē·dē·ˈräm)

(*noun*)

Compact **D**isk-**R**ead **O**nly **M**emory—a compact disk that contains data a computer can read

That SAT study guide comes with a _____ you can put in your computer to practice test questions.

dink (a subset of yuppies)   (ˈdĩk)

(*noun*)

double **i**ncome couple, **n**o **k**ids

I confess, we are sometimes a bit envious of the thirty-something _____ next door, though we would never trade in our children for their wealth.

DOS   (ˈdäs)

(*noun*)

the **D**isk **O**perating **S**ystem used on personal computers (PCs)

When you are having a technical problem with your personal computer, it is often a good idea to return to _____, the opening screen, to see what may be wrong.

ESL   (ē·es·el)

(*noun*)

English as a **S**econd **L**anguage

It is critical that we have _____ programs in our schools so that the immigrant youth population may improve its English and not be at a disadvantage in the classroom.

FAQ   (ef·ā·kyü)

(*noun*)

an abbreviation for **F**requently **A**sked **Q**uestions

Before you raise your hand, please note that in the back of the driver's ed manual you will find the _____ section, and perhaps your question will be included there.

HTML   (āch·tē·em·ˈel)

(*noun*)

Hypertext **M**arkup **L**anguage—a system of tagging documents to define a document's structure and appearance on a Web page

Each Web page on our website must be coded in _____ before it gets posted on the Internet.

ISP   (ī·es·pē)

(*noun*)

Internet **S**ervice **P**rovider—a company that provides Internet access to consumers

It may be difficult to select an _____ when there are so many—Compuserve, AOL, Earthlink—from which to choose.

LAN   (l·ā·n)

(*noun*)

Local **A**rea **N**etwork—a network of directly con-nected machines that are close together and provide high-speed communication over, for example, fiber optics or coaxial cable (like for phone service or cable TV)

I've been satisfied with my _____ as I never have any trouble making local calls, and the customer service is excellent.

laser ('lā·zər)

(*noun*)

light **a**mplification by **s**timulated **e**mission of **r**adiation—a device that generates electro-magnetic radiation

It is now possible to remove your tattoos with _____ surgery where no needles are involved: only light and radiation.

modem ('mō·dəm)

(*noun*)

modulator/**dem**odulator—a device used to convert digital signals into analog signals—and vice versa—for transmissions over phone lines

This old _____ on my computer is so slow; it connects to the Internet at only 14,400k. The newer models connect at up to 56,000k.

moped ('mō·ped)

(*noun*)

motor **ped**al—a small, light, motor-powered bike that can also be pedaled

While I have never ridden a _____, I imagine it is just like riding a bike, only motorized!

radar ('rā·där)

(*noun*)

radio **d**etecting **a**nd **r**anging—a device that sends out radio waves and processes them for display; usually used for locating objects or surface features of an object (such as a planet)

What's amazing is how I was able to pick up your signal on my _____ even though you were out of sight.

RAM ('ram)

(*noun*)

Random-**A**ccess **M**emory (on a computer)—a type of computer memory that can be accessed randomly

With so many programs installed on your home computer, it's no wonder you no longer have enough _____ available for new files.

REM ('rem)

(*noun*)

Rapid **E**ye **M**ovement (in sleep)—a rapid movement of the eyes associated with REM sleep and dreaming

I guessed you were dreaming in your deep sleep when I saw your eyes twitching under their lids in _____.

scuba ('skü·bə)

(*noun*)

self-**c**ontained **u**nderwater **b**reathing **a**pparatus—equipment used for breathing underwater

Jim packed up all his _____ gear, including his flippers, goggles, and tank, before he left for his trip to the Caribbean.

snafu (sna·'fü)

(*noun*)

situation **n**ormal **a**ll **f**ouled **u**p

As it turns out, we ran into a major _____ and we need your help!

URL (ü·ar·el)

(*noun*)

Uniform **R**esource **L**ocator—the address of documents and resources on the Internet

Our auto company's _____ is not too original, but it is sure easy to remember: www.cars.com.

yuppie ('yə·pē)

(*noun*)

young **u**rban **p**rofessional—a young, college-educated adult who works and lives in or near a large city

Since when have you become such a _____, with your upscale clothes and cars, and at such a young age!

TIP

Acronyms have their own built-in mnemonic devices. Remember what the letters stand for and you'll remember the meaning!

Words in Context

The following exercise will help you figure out the meaning of some words from the vocabulary list by reading context clues. After you have read and understood the paragraph, explain the context clues that helped you with the meaning of the vocabulary word. Check the answer section at the end of this chapter for an explanation of the clues.

> I finally took it upon myself to become more knowledgeable when it comes to using my home computer. My resolution set in when I was trying to attach a simple text file to an e-mail document and ran into a frustrating *snafu*. Everything froze and I thought my PC had crashed. Quickly turning to the *FAQ* section in my user's manual, I realized that the problem was really with my *modem*. That's why my e-mail wasn't going through. I called my *ISP* to verify my diagnosis of the problem. The customer service agent on the phone said he had to check on it, but that he would call me back *ASAP*. Though he said that it would only take a second, I found myself waiting for hours. Born of my own impatience, my goal to become more independently computer-savvy was born!

Sentence Completion

Insert the correct word from the vocabulary list into the following sentences.

1. I love my _____ because it's as small as a bike but much faster.

2. An unexpected _____ caused us to be late.

3. I know it's short notice, but can you have the report to me _____?

4. In my state, it's illegal to use a(n) _____ that tells you when a police car is nearby.

5. When I came to the United States, I took _____ classes to learn English.

6. I had to have a(n) _____ to see if I had suffered a concussion while sparring with my boxing partner.

7. This neighborhood used to be full of artists until all of the _____ from Wall Street moved in.

8. Many websites have a convenient _____ page, so be sure to look there before you call customer service.

9. The first time I went _____ diving, I was amazed at all the underwater life I saw.

10. If you look up a nonprofit organization on the Internet, the _____ most likely ends in "org."

11. I bought a(n) _____ that had the entire world atlas on a single disk!

12. I took a class in _____ coding so that I would know how to build a Web page.

13. There was no incision involved when I had _____ surgery on my eyes, only light amplification from radiation.

14. We know a couple of _____ who have a lot of money to spend; they have no children to support, and both his and her jobs are quite lucrative.

15. Your _____ made me know you were in deep sleep.

16. My _____ is offering a good deal now so you may want to switch and have them be your service provider.

17. I think your disk may not be working due to a malfunction in _____.

18. The _____ was busy putting in new phone lines in our area after the storm did so much damage.

19. Out Internet connection wasn't working very well, but it turned out that all we needed to do was dust off our _____.

20. When I bought my new computer, I increased the amount of _____ so that it would have enough memory to handle all these programs.

Matching Questions

Match the acronym in the first column with the corresponding definition in the second column.

21. dinks   **a.** self-contained underwater breathing apparatus

22. ISP   **b.** rapid eye movement

23. FAQ   **c.** young urban professional

24. laser   **d.** as soon as possible

25. CD-ROM   **e.** double income couple, no kids

26. ASAP   **f.** compact disk read-only memory

27. RAM   **g.** light amplification by stimulated emission of radiation

28. moped   **h.** Internet service provider

29. HTML   **i.** English as a second language

30. radar   **j.** hypertext markup language

31. scuba   **k.** modulator/demodulator

32. LAN   **l.** random-access memory

33. REM   **m.** situation normal all fouled up

34. yuppie   **n.** radio detecting and ranging

35. URL   **o.** motor pedal

36. CAT scan   **p.** local area network

37. DOS   **q.** computerized axial tomography scan

38. ESL   **r.** disk operating system

39. modem   **s.** frequently asked questions

40. snafu   **t.** uniform resource locator (World Wide Web address)

True/False

In the space provided, write a *T* if the sentence is true and an *F* if the sentence is false. If the sentence is false, cross out the misused word and write the correct word from the vocabulary list above it.

41. _____ The operating system used in IBM compatible computers is called *DOS*.

42. _____ The computerized axial tomography scan one might receive to check for internal injury is a *CD-ROM*.

43. _____ Double income couples without any children are sometimes referred to as *dinks*.

44. _____ Before I left for my diving adventure in Indonesia, I purchased some state of the art _radar_ gear.

45. _____ If you want something done quickly, you may ask for it _ASAP_.

46. _____ At the new planetarium, I saw an amazing _laser_ light show amplified on the ceiling!

47. _____ A _yuppie_ is a person who lives in a city.

48. _____ The _LAN_ section of a user's manual may be of tremendous use if you have questions and are struggling to put something together—a bicycle, for example.

49. _____ My computer is overloaded with so many programs that I probably have to upgrade my _HTML_.

50. _____ Having the correct _URL_ enabled me to get to the website with ease.

Practice Activities

It is _relatively_ easy (though no piece of cake) to remember what an acronym stands for because the letters that make it up serve as clues. For example, when completing the matching section, you may have quickly associ-

ated the acronym ISP with its definition—Internet Service Provider—since the corresponding letters I-S-P probably jumped out at you. The next step in committing these acronyms to your vocabulary repertoire is _really_ understanding what they mean. Try to go beyond simply relying on remembering what each letter stands for.

A suggestion is to check out a website or a trade magazine relating to the subject of the acronym. And just because you may _never_ scuba dive doesn't mean your vocabulary and literacy won't benefit from visiting a scuba website to learn how all the gear is a self-contained underwater breathing apparatus. Flipping through _Wired_ magazine or the Science section of the _New York Times_ might allow you to more deeply, in context, read explications and applications of some of the acronyms relating to science and technology.

TIP

Since acronyms shorten a phrase down to one word, use them to be more concise in your writing.

Answers

Words in Context

When this computer novice's computer freezes, it may be understood as a *snafu*: A normal situation of trying to attach a file becomes fouled up! For guidance, he turns to the *FAQ* section of the user's manual, thinking that perhaps others have had similar problems and asked similar questions. The fact that his e-mail was not going through indicates that perhaps the *modem* was the source of the problem, as a modem allows for the necessary connection to the Internet. The logical company to contact at that point would be one's *ISP*: the Internet Service Provider. The customer service representative explains that he will get back to the customer momentarily: as soon as he is able, or *ASAP*. As the customer impatiently waits, he resolves to learn to rectify such *snafus* on his own.

Sentence Completion

1. *moped.* If you got this question wrong, refer back to the word's definition.
2. *snafu.* If you got this question wrong, refer back to the word's definition.
3. *ASAP.* If you got this question wrong, refer back to the word's definition.
4. *radar.* If you got this question wrong, refer back to the word's definition.
5. *ESL.* If you got this question wrong, refer back to the word's definition.
6. *CAT scan.* If you got this question wrong, refer back to the word's definition.
7. *yuppie.* If you got this question wrong, refer back to the word's definition.
8. *FAQ.* If you got this question wrong, refer back to the word's definition.
9. *scuba.* If you got this question wrong, refer back to the word's definition.
10. *URL.* If you got this question wrong, refer back to the word's definition.
11. *CD-ROM.* If you got this question wrong, refer back to the word's definition.
12. *HTML.* If you got this question wrong, refer back to the word's definition.
13. *laser.* If you got this question wrong, refer back to the word's definition.
14. *dinks.* If you got this question wrong, refer back to the word's definition.
15. *REM.* If you got this question wrong, refer back to the word's definition.
16. *ISP.* If you got this question wrong, refer back to the word's definition.
17. *DOS.* If you got this question wrong, refer back to the word's definition.
18. *LAN.* If you got this question wrong, refer back to the word's definition.
19. *modem.* If you got this question wrong, refer back to the word's definition.
20. *RAM.* If you got this question wrong, refer back to the word's definition.

Matching

21. e
22. h
23. s
24. g
25. f
26. d
27. l
28. o
29. j
30. n
31. a
32. p
33. b
34. c
35. t
36. q
37. r
38. i
39. k
40. m

True/False

41. True

42. False, correct word is CAT scan

43. True

44. False, correct word is scuba

45. True

46. True

47. True

48. False, correct word is FAQ

49. False, correct word is RAM

50. True

Across

2 RAM
3 HTML
6 LAN
8 CD-ROM
9 scuba
10 ESL
13 ISP
14 laser
16 ASAP
17 FAQ
18 REM

Down

1 URL
4 moped
5 snafu
7 modem
8 CAT scan
11 DOS
12 yuppie
15 radar

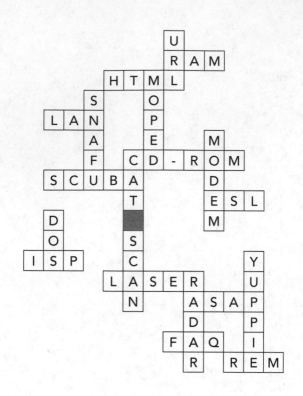

16 ▶ COMMONLY TESTED WORDS

The difference between the right word and the almost right word is the difference between lightning and a lightning bug.

—MARK TWAIN, American writer (1835–1910)

CHAPTER SUMMARY

In this chapter, you will learn words that don't fit neatly into any particular category but are used occasionally in adult-level writing and very often found on standardized tests. It can sometimes seem as if test makers have some magical list of words that they think will trip up the average test taker. Of course, that is not the case, but if you had never encountered these words before seeing them on a test, they could certainly be intimidating. Perhaps many of these words are somewhat familiar from your reading or studies, but they are the type of words that you skip over and hope you don't need to know to understand the reading passage. By learning and mastering the words in this chapter, you can give yourself the extra advantage you need on tests and in your reading.

Choose the word from the vocabulary list that best fits into the crossword puzzle. You can check your answers at the end of the chapter following the answers to the questions.

Vocabulary List 13: Commonly Tested Words

anomaly
badinage
brusque
cower
diffident
dross
extricate
fodder
garrulous
hyperbole
malapropism
pertinacity
plausible
prehensile
rancor
resolute
ruminate
simian
stolid
succor

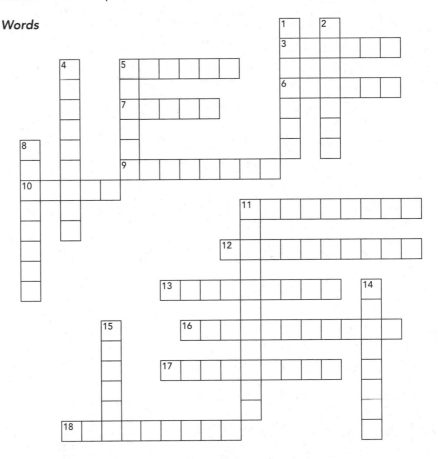

Across

3 animosity
5 apathetic, impassive
6 related to, or resembling an ape
7 to cringe
9 ponder, muse
10 waste
11 possible
12 adapted for wrapping around, grabbing
13 bashful
16 misuse
17 to set free, disentangle
18 wordy

Down

1 blunt, brief
2 deviation from the norm
4 exaggeration
5 aid, assistance
8 banter
11 obstinance
14 determined
15 coarse food for cows and horses

anomaly   (ə·ˈnä·mə·lē)

(*noun*)

abnormality; irregularity; deviation from the norm
    or usual

The one year the company did not break even was
    just an _____.

badinage   (ba·dən·ˈäzh)

(*noun*)

playful and joking conversation or banter

The two men never met without beginning a little
    _____ that entertained us all.

brusque   (ˈbrəsk)

(*adj.*)

abrupt, blunt, or short in manner or speech

His _____ manner was often mistaken for
    rudeness by people who did not know him
    better.

cower   (ˈkaŭ·ə̯r)

(*verb*)

to shrink and tremble, as from someone's anger or
    threats; to cringe

It was unnerving to watch the dog _____ in the
    corner when he misbehaved.

diffident   (ˈdi·fə·dənt)

(*adj.*)

modest, shy, reserved, bashful, humble

Her _____ smile seemed to indicate that she
    would dance if only someone would encourage
    her.

dross   (ˈdräs)

(*noun*)

the worthless part of something that is separated
    from the better part; waste; garbage

The cook trimmed the fillet and swept the
    _____ away.

extricate   (ˈek·strə·kāt)

(*verb*)

to set free or release; to disentangle, as from a
    difficulty or embarrassment

She hung up the phone and wondered how she
    would ever _____ herself from really
    having to attend the luncheon.

fodder   (ˈfä·dər)

(*noun*)

dry, coarse food for cattle, horses, or sheep, like hay
    or straw; often also used in expressions
    unrelated to animals

We were waiting by the barn for the new _____
    to be delivered.

garrulous   (ˈgar·ə·ləs)

(*adj.*)

overly talkative about unimportant things; chattering

I regretted striking up a conversation with him when
    I remembered how _____ he can be.

hyperbole   (hī·ˈpər·bə·lē)

(*noun*)

exaggeration for effect, not to be taken literally

He often spoke with _____, as when he said he
    was so hungry he could eat a horse.

malapropism   (ˈma·lə·prä·pi·zəm)

(*noun*)

a ridiculous or humorous misuse of words, usually
    due to a resemblance in sound

She was quite amusing with her frequent
    _____(s), like when she excused herself
    from the table to go to the laboratory.

pertinacity   (per·tən·′a·sə·tē)

(**noun**)

firm or unyielding adherence to some purpose; stubbornness; persistence

No matter what anyone said, there was no way to reason with his _____.

plausible   (′plŏ·zə·bəl)

(**adj.**)

seemingly true and acceptable, but usually used with implied disbelief; possible

The excuse seemed _____, so we had to accept their apology for not attending our dinner party.

prehensile   (prē·′hen͜t͵·səl)

(**adj.**)

adapted to grasp, seize, or hold

Chimpanzees and humans both have a _____ hand.

rancor   (′rã·kər)

(**noun**)

a continuing and bitter hatred or ill will

The negotiators worked for peace among the opposing factions, despite their obvious _____.

resolute   (′re·zə·lüt)

(**adj.**)

determined; firm of purpose; resolved

I would try to stop you, but I can see you are _____ in your decision.

ruminate   (rü·mə·nāt)

(**verb**)

to meditate on or ponder something; to think over

One could see him _____ over the question for a few moments before he answered.

simian   (′si·mē·ən)

(**adj.**)

dealing with apes or monkeys; apelike

The researcher was investigating several aspects of _____ behavior.

stolid   (′stä·ləd)

(**adj.**)

showing little or no emotion or awareness; unexcitable; expressionless

We wondered how he could remain so _____ upon hearing such awful news.

succor   (′sə·kər)

(**noun**)

aid; help; assistance, especially that which relieves and ends stress, need, or a difficulty

She gladly offered _____ when he had nowhere else to turn.

Words in Context

The following exercise will help you figure out the meaning of some words from the vocabulary list by reading context clues. After you have read and understood the paragraph, explain the context clues that helped you with the meaning of the vocabulary word. Refer to the answer section at the end of this chapter for an explanation of the clues.

I will never forget the day I accompanied Professor Mackey into the apes' facility for the first time. He delighted in introducing me to all their unique *simian* behaviors. There were several apes who remained quite *diffident* during our visit, but most went about their normal behavior, and a few even came forward to greet us. One charmer even offered us a piece of food with his *prehensile* hand. The professor pointed out the leader, who remained a *stolid* observer of all the proceedings in the cage. Mackey explained that when the leader did move about, all the apes would become scared and excited and even *cower* in the corner. Two of the apes fought violently during our visit, but fortunately their *rancor* seemed focused solely on each other. Undoubtedly, the most fascinating resident was one of the males named Yankee. When the professor closed the cage door after he had brought the apes their lunch, Yankee came to the door and looked for the keyhole. I watched him *ruminate* there for a few minutes, staring intently at the door and the keys on the bench beside us. He then tried every imaginable way to *extricate* himself from the cage, and regardless of how impossible it would be without the keys, he seemed *resolute* enough to continue for hours. Indeed, the professor said he was still trying when he returned later that evening.

TEST-TAKING TIP

Make sure you get enough sleep the night before the test.

Sentence Completion

Insert the correct word from the vocabulary list into the following sentences.

1. Maleek was _____ when he was younger, but now he is confident and outgoing.

2. I didn't believe the solution to the mystery because it just didn't seem _____.

3. Because dogs do not have a(n) _____ hand, they have to grab things with their jaws.

4. New Yorkers are stereotyped as being _____, but this is not usually the case.

5. "He is the very pineapple of politeness," is a famous _____ said by a character in the play *The Rivals*.

6. I was unable to _____ myself from an uncomfortable situation when I realized I was seated next to the woman I had beat out for a promotion.

7. Because there were so many stray animals, the shelter could not provide _____ to all of them.

8. He was known for using _____ to make his point, but sometimes, it became tedious to hear him exaggerate every situation.

9. Natalie's turning in the report late is really a(n) _____, as she is always on time with her work.

10. I think that sometimes horses get tired of eating the same _____ every day, but experts say that the animals don't get bored of it.

11. When Hannah makes up her mind to do something, she is _____ about it and doesn't stop until she has achieved her goal.

12. I try to avoid getting into a conversation with Judy, as she is so _____ that I can't ever seem to end a conversation with her.

13. During the trial, the defendant remained so _____ that no one could tell what he was thinking.

14. It is his nature to _____ over new ideas; he does not make quick decisions.

15. My dog might surprise you with her _____ ; she will not give up when it comes to getting attention.

16. We kept the few minerals we found in the sample and just brushed the _____ away.

17. His stooped posture, long arms, and wild hair cast an almost _____ aspect to his appearance.

18. Nothing pleases me more than a little _____ with someone who has a quick wit.

19. The _____ between them had existed for years, and it was rumored to have begun from some long-forgotten argument.

20. The booming thunder made the two children _____ under the covers and reach to hold on to one another.

Synonyms

The following exercise lists vocabulary words from this chapter. Each word is followed by four answer choices. Three of them are synonyms of the vocabulary word in bold. Your task is to choose the one that is NOT a synonym.

21. pertinacity
   a. persistence
   b. stubbornness
   c. loudness
   d. determination

22. garrulous
   a. quiet
   b. talkative
   c. chatty
   d. loquacious

23. brusque
   a. courteous
   b. brief
   c. abrupt
   d. blunt

24. rancor
   a. hatred
   b. fondness
   c. dislike
   d. contempt

25. cower
   a. cringe
   b. tremble
   c. rip
   d. shrink away

26. succor
   a. aid
   b. assistance
   c. help
   d. stress

27. plausible
   a. deceitful
   b. true
   c. believable
   d. possible

28. diffident
   a. shy
   b. reserved
   c. furious
   d. bashful

29. anomaly
    a. irregularity
    b. abnormality
    c. deviation
    d. average

30. simian
    a. apelike
    b. concerning apes
    c. having to do with animals
    d. having to do with monkeys

Antonyms

Choose the word from the vocabulary list that means the opposite, or most nearly the opposite, of the following groups of words.

31. treasure, valuables, prize   _____

32. fact, literal truth, exactness   _____

33. approach, stand up to, hold firm   _____

34. excited, enthusiastic, upset   _____

35. love, friendship, affection   _____

36. quiet, solemn, serious   _____

37. cuisine, delicacy, feast   _____

38. careless, indecisive, uncertain   _____

39. catch, imprison, confine   _____

40. impossible, unlikely, false   _____

TIP

You won't be able to predict what words will be on a test, so give yourself an advantage by knowing your prefixes, suffixes, and roots. If you don't know a word, you'll be able to make an educated guess at its meaning.

Choosing the Right Word

Circle the word in bold that best completes the sentence.

41. It is a very interesting offer, but I will need to (**extricate, ruminate**) on it a bit before I give you my answer.

42. The lecturer explained the tremendous advantages that our earliest ancestors had over other species—the evolution of a (**stolid, prehensile**) hand.

43. She showed amazing (**pertinacity, hyperbole**) at the meeting and eventually succeeded in persuading the entire room.

44. He acted very (**simian, diffident**) when we approached, and we wondered if our forwardness made him uncomfortable.

45. The employee was warned about being so (**dross, garrulous**) on the phone, and he was advised to be more professional and direct.

46. The pitcher who made the all-star team was not just a(n) (**anomaly, malapropism**); he was the cream of the crop.

47. The press was delighted when he came out of the building, but he was (**brusque, badinage**) with them and rushed out a moment later.

48. I believe your theory is (**prehensile, plausible**), but I still think we should do a little more research.

49. The neighbor was shocked at the boy's strange (**diffident, simian**) behavior and decided to notify his parents later that day.

50. All they could do was (**cower, succor**) in fear as the bears approached them; they were so afraid that they couldn't even run away.

Practice Activities

Write a letter to a friend, teacher, or coworker using at least 5–7 of the words from this chapter's vocabulary list. Perhaps your letter could be a description of an unusual visit (like this chapter's visit to the apes), or a problem you have noticed that needs addressing. Look back over the list and try to see a few connections between the words. When an idea comes to you, go with it. The most important thing is to try to use as many new words as possible in the correct manner.

Try to discover as many alternate forms of the words from the word list as you can. For example, *diffident* is an adjective used to describe someone who is shy or reserved, and *diffidence* is the noun form that identifies that shyness or modesty. Jot down as many alternate forms of the words as you can guess, and then check the words in a dictionary. Can you use each of the forms of the words in a sentence?

Answers

Words in Context

The paragraph is a recollection of a visit to see the apes and the behaviors noticed by the narrator; thus we should certainly conclude that *simian* means apelike or concerning apes. When we read that some apes remained *diffident* but others came forward to greet the visitors, we can understand that *diffident* could mean shy or reserved. The friendly ape that offers food in his *prehensile* hand must surely have a hand that is capable of holding something. Since the leader of the apes remains a *stolid* observer of all the activities, we can guess that he is showing no emotion or expression, because he is juxtaposed with his fellow apes who get excited. The apes that become scared when the leader moves about *cower* in the corner, so we can understand that they are cringing and trembling in fear of him. The two apes that fight during the visit apparently have *rancor* only for each other, so we should know that *rancor* means hatred or ill will. The ape Yankee seems to be staring at the door and trying to figure out a means of escape, so we can conclude that *ruminate* means to think over or ponder. Yankee's attempts to *extricate* himself from the cage, despite it being impossible without the keys, indicate that *extricate* must mean free or release. Finally, since we are told Yankee is *resolute* enough to continue his attempt for hours, we can understand that *resolute* must mean determined and firm of purpose.

Sentence Completion

1. *diffident.* If you got this question wrong, refer back to the word's definition.
2. *plausible.* If you got this question wrong, refer back to the word's definition.
3. *prehensile.* If you got this question wrong, refer back to the word's definition.
4. *brusque.* If you got this question wrong, refer back to the word's definition.
5. *malapropism.* If you got this question wrong, refer back to the word's definition.
6. *extricate.* If you got this question wrong, refer back to the word's definition.
7. *succor.* If you got this question wrong, refer back to the word's definition.
8. *hyperbole.* If you got this question wrong, refer back to the word's definition.
9. *anomaly.* If you got this question wrong, refer back to the word's definition.
10. *fodder.* If you got this question wrong, refer back to the word's definition.
11. *resolute.* If you got this question wrong, refer back to the word's definition.
12. *garrulous.* If you got this question wrong, refer back to the word's definition.
13. *stolid.* If you got this question wrong, refer back to the word's definition.
14. *ruminate.* If you got this question wrong, refer back to the word's definition.
15. *pertinacity.* If you got this question wrong, refer back to the word's definition.
16. *dross.* If you got this question wrong, refer back to the word's definition.
17. *simian.* If you got this question wrong, refer back to the word's definition.
18. *badinage.* If you got this question wrong, refer back to the word's definition.
19. *rancor.* If you got this question wrong, refer back to the word's definition.
20. *cower.* If you got this question wrong, refer back to the word's definition.

Synonyms

21. **c.** *loudness.* Pertinacity means firm or unyielding adherence to some purpose. Since loudness means the audible volume of something, it is not a synonym.

22. **a.** *quiet.* Garrulous means overly talkative and chatty, so quiet is not a synonym.

23. **a.** *courteous.* Brusque means being short or abrupt in manner or speech. Since courteous means polite and gracious, it is not a synonym.

24. **b.** *fondness.* Rancor means continuing hatred or ill will. Since fondness means warm affection, it is not a synonym.

25. **c.** *rip.* Cower means to cringe or tremble in fear. Since rip means to tear or shred something, it is not a synonym.

26. **d.** *stress.* Succor means aid or assistance in a time of need. Since stress means tension or pressure, it is not a synonym.

27. **a.** *deceitful.* Plausible means seemingly true and acceptable. Since deceitful means dishonest and fraudulent, it is not a synonym.

28. **c.** *furious.* Diffident means shy and reserved. Since furious means violently angry and raging, it is not a synonym.

29. **d.** *average.* Anomaly means an irregularity or abnormality. Since average means usual or commonplace, it is not a synonym.

30. **c.** *having to do with animals.* Simian means apelike or having to do with apes or monkeys. Since having to do with animals is too broad a definition, it is not a synonym.

Antonyms

31. *Dross* means the waste or worthless part of something, the opposite of the words listed.

32. *Hyperbole* means an exaggeration for effect, not to be taken literally, the opposite of the words listed.

33. *Cower* means to shrink and tremble, the opposite of the words listed.

34. *Stolid* means showing little emotion or awareness, the opposite of the words listed.

35. *Rancor* means continuing hatred or ill will, the opposite of the words listed.

36. *Garrulous* means overly talkative about unimportant things or chattering, the opposite of the words listed.

37. *Fodder* means dry, coarse food for cattle, horses, or sheep, the opposite of the words listed.

38. *Resolute* means determined and firm of purpose, the opposite of the words listed.

39. *Extricate* means to set free or release, the opposite of the words listed.

40. *Plausible* means seemingly true and possible, the opposite of the words listed.

Choosing the Right Word

41. *ruminate.* Extricate means free or release, so surely the person will have to think over or ruminate on the offer.

42. *prehensile.* Context clues indicate that the hand evolved to be an advantage, so it is logical that it is capable of holding something, or prehensile.

43. *pertinacity.* Pertinacity means persistence or stubbornness, so undoubtedly, this quality is what helped her persist and eventually persuade the entire room.

44. *diffident.* Diffident means shy and reserved, so it is logical that he would act that way if the others made him feel uncomfortable when they met. But he would not act simian or apelike.

45. *garrulous.* Garrulous means overly talkative and chattering, which would be something an employee might be warned against. Dross means the unusable part of something, or waste.

46. *anomaly.* Since the one good player stands out on the team, he or she must be an anomaly, or an abnormality or deviation from the norm. A malapropism is a humorous misuse of words that sound alike.

47. *brusque.* Brusque means abrupt, blunt, or short in manner or speech. Badinage is playful or joking banter.

48. *plausible.* Plausible means seemingly true and possible, so it would apply to a theory that the speaker believes but still wants to research further. Prehensile means adapted to seize or hold something.

49. *simian.* Simian means apelike, so if the boy was acting that way, it may be an exaggeration, but the neighbor might easily be shocked and want to notify the parents. Diffident means shy and reserved, so that would not be shocking.

50. *cower.* Cower means tremble or cringe in fear, which could be an appropriate response to approaching bears. Succor is aid or assistance in a time of need.

Across

3 rancor
5 stolid
6 simian
7 cower
9 ruminate
10 dross
11 plausible
12 prehensile
13 diffident
16 malapropism
17 extricate
18 garrulous

Down

1 brusque
2 anomaly
4 hyperbole
5 succor
8 badinage
11 pertinacity
14 resolute
15 fodder

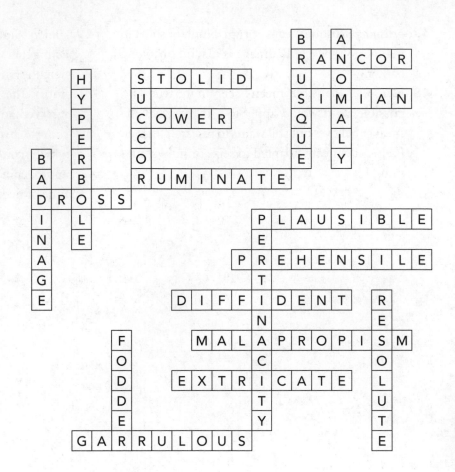

17 ▶ MORE COMMONLY TESTED WORDS

Always desire to learn something useful.

> —Sophocles, Greek poet (496 B.C.E.–406 B.C.E.)

CHAPTER SUMMARY

This chapter introduces you to another group of words that are commonly found on standardized tests. No doubt you have encountered some of them before in your reading, but you may also be seeing many of the words for the first time. Be sure to say the words aloud to yourself as you read over the list, as this helps commit them to memory.

Choose the word from the vocabulary list that best fits into the crossword puzzle. You can check your answers at the end of the chapter following the answers to the questions.

Vocabulary List 14: More Commonly Tested Words

addle
ambivalent
bevy
disconsolate
genteel
guffaw
guttural
inert
insouciance
mutable
obtuse
omniscient
pallor
partisan
purloin
resonant
rubric
smidgen
sycophant
wallow

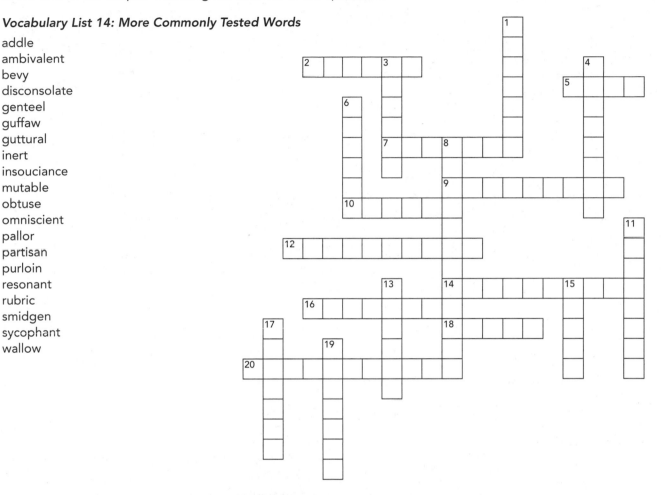

Across

2 indulge
5 a large group or collection
7 small amount
9 a person who tries to get ahead by flattering people of wealth or power
10 a category
12 having conflicting or divided feelings
14 all-knowing
16 throaty
18 confuse or fluster
20 carefree, easy-going

Down

1 steal
3 dull or dense
4 vibrant, full, resounding
6 paleness, wanness, pastiness
8 melancholy
11 strongly in favor of one side or one political party
13 hearty chuckle
15 stationary, inactive
17 refined, polite
19 changeable

addle ('a·dəl)
(*verb*)
to confuse, fluster, or muddle
He likes to _____ his opponent by being overly
confident.

ambivalent (am·'bi·və·lənt)
(*adj.*)
having at the same time two conflicting feelings or
emotions toward another person or thing, such
as love and hate; having divided feelings about
something or someone; equivocal; uncertain
I am _____ about inviting her to the wedding.

bevy ('be·vē)
(*noun*)
a large group or collection; or a flock of birds
Because Ivan was trying to find a date for the prom,
he was delighted to see that there was a
_____ of girls at my birthday party.

disconsolate (dis·'kän(t)'sə'lət)
(*adj.*)
hopeless, sad, melancholy, dejected
The grieving child was _____ when her mother
passed away.

genteel (jen·'tē(ə)l)
(*adj.*)
refined, polite, elegant, gentlemanly, or ladylike
Though Deborah was raised in a carefree way—her
parents let her do whatever she wanted—her
manners are quite _____.

guffaw (gə·'fŏ)
(*noun*)
a loud, rough burst of laughter
Martin tends to _____ rather than laugh quietly.

guttural ('gə·tə·rəl)
(*adj.*)
throaty; used to describe sounds that originate in the
throat, like the *k* in *kite*
When my dog wants to play, she tries to get your
attention by making _____ noises, like the
beginnings of a growl.

inert (i·'nərt)
(*adj.*)
inactive, sluggish, without power to move
It was so hot last Sunday that I remained _____;
I lay on the couch all day and enjoyed the air-
conditioning.

insouciance (in·'sü·sē·ən(t)s)
(*noun*)
carefree, unconcerned
Her _____ at losing her job made us all think
that she was independently wealthy.

mutable ('myü·tə·bəl)
(*adj.*)
changeable, unstable, variable
Unfortunately, my schedule this week is not
_____, as I have clients coming in from out
of town that I must meet.

obtuse (äb·'tüs)
(*adj.*)
dull, not sharp or acute; when used to describe a
person, it means slow to understand or notice,
or insensitive
Even though Robert is a brilliant man, he can be
_____ about the simplest of concepts.

omniscient (äm·'ni·shənt)
(*adj.*)
all-knowing; having universal knowledge of all things
The Judeo-Christian God is believed to be _____.

pallor (ˈpa·lər)

(*noun*)

lack of color; unnatural paleness, often used to
    describe a face

She was struck by the eerie _____ of the strange
    man who always peered out from the windows
    of his dark house.

partisan (ˈpär·tə·zən)

(*adj.*)

strongly in favor of one side or political party; blindly
    or unreasonably devoted to a party

The senator knew he would not be able to persuade
    his _____ peers.

purloin (pər·ˈlȯin)

(*verb*)

to steal

Did you _____ that new coat you're wearing?
    You can't afford one like that!

resonant (ˈre·zən·ənt)

(*adj.*)

used to describe sounds, it usually means vibrant,
    full, ringing, intensified, resounding, rich

Everyone loved to hear his _____ bass voice fill
    the concert hall.

rubric (ˈrü·brik)

(*noun*)

a formal way to say *name* or *title,* or a category of
    something; an established rule or tradition

We found what we were looking for under the gen-
    eral _____ of *respiratory diseases.*

smidgen (ˈsmi·jən)

(*noun*)

a very small particle; an insignificant piece or amount

I am not sure what it does, but my aunt always adds a
    _____ of dill to the dish.

sycophant (ˈsi·kə·fənt)

(*noun*)

a person who tries to get ahead by flattering people
    of wealth or power

Only a shameless _____ could tell the boss that
    his horribly ugly orange tie is nice.

wallow (ˈwä·lō)

(*verb*)

to roll about pleasantly in water or mud; can also be
    used to mean to overindulge in something

We watched the pigs _____ in the mud and lis-
    tened to their squeals of delight.

Words in Context

The following exercise will help you figure out the
meaning of some words from the vocabulary list by
reading context clues. After you have read and understood the paragraph, explain the context clues that
helped you with the meaning of the vocabulary word.
Refer to the answer section at the end of this chapter
for an explanation of the clues.

After we rang the doorbell, someone let us
in, and we immediately turned on our
most *genteel* manners. We mingled a little
with the adults and some of the other kids
there, and no one seemed to realize that we
were crashing the party. Our plan was
working smoothly when Pete suddenly
erupted with a loud *guffaw* after Joe
whispered a wisecrack in his ear. Pete's
insouciance is one of the things we love
about him, but sometimes such a happy-
go-lucky attitude can be a problem. He can
be absolutely *obtuse* about when and where
he ought to restrain himself. When those
around us quieted and cast disapproving
stares in our direction, we wandered off in
search of a *bevy* of young ladies to enter-
tain. We found a few in the large dining
room. Pete approached one with an oddly

attractive *pallor* to her face, which was accentuated by her beautiful dark eyes and gorgeous black hair. He made them all laugh within a few moments, and then Pete introduced us to the pale girl's two friends. We asked the three of them to dance. Two said yes, but the third remained *inert*, so I stayed to talk to her. She was *disconsolate*. I soon learned she had recently broken up with the boy she had been dating and had come to the party only at her friends' insistence. She had been making a few attempts to enjoy herself, but she was *ambivalent* about meeting anyone or trying to have a good time. Knowing that a good remedy for an aching heart can be two moving feet, I pulled her out onto the dance floor. By the end of the party, she was laughing and singing, and on the way out all three girls thanked the hostess for inviting such charming young gentlemen to dance with. She laughed and said it was her pleasure, but as we exited past the woman's puzzled, smiling face, I could see her confusion. Of course, when Pete said this party had been better than her last and gave the woman a good-bye kiss, it did nothing but *addle* her further.

Sentence Completion

Insert the correct word from the vocabulary list into the following sentences.

1. I hate to be such a(n) _____, but it seems the only way to get the boss to notice the hard work I am doing is to make her feel like she is the genius who came up with the idea in the first place.

2. We suspected that the suspicious-looking man in the dark sunglasses was attempting to _____ the valuable sculpture.

3. His _____ manners were a pleasant, new side to him we had not seen before.

4. The cord was unplugged and I knew the blades were _____, so I thought it was safe to try and repair the fan.

5. I don't like my tea very sweet, so I'll just have a _____ of sugar.

6. If a story is written from a(n) _____ point of view, the reader can learn what all of the characters are thinking.

7. Joe felt _____ about hearing his best friend had been accepted at the university because it was so far from home.

8. Because the clay was still _____, she was able to alter the nose of the statue to make it a better likeness.

9. The mother warned her children to avoid the mud, but she knew if they passed the big puddle in the back yard they would _____ in it until they were filthy.

10. Even in the brightly lit laboratory, the unnatural _____ of the corpse unnerved us.

11. Once it was clear that no rescue party would be coming, several of the survivors grew completely _____, and it seemed nothing could ease their minds.

12. When the models posed for the picture, everyone could see what a(n) _____ of beauties they were.

13. If she can put aside her _____ beliefs for the sake of the public good, I think she will make an excellent governor.

14. I am working hard on the project, but if I answer the phone it will just _____ me and make me lose my train of thought.

15. I wish I had my brother's _____ so I would not worry so much about finding a job this summer.

16. I think that goes under the general _____ of "things that will get you fired in under an hour."

17. Jill's new guitar has such a beautiful, _____ tone.

18. I heard a(n) _____ from across the room, and I knew my comical uncle must have been telling some of his jokes again.

19. The pain in my side was not _____; I felt sharp stabs of pain every time my torso twisted even just a bit.

20. Some strange _____ sound rose from the sleeping patient's mouth.

Synonyms

The following exercise lists vocabulary words from this chapter. Each word is followed by four answer choices. Three of them are synonyms of the vocabulary word in bold. Your task is to choose the one that is NOT a synonym.

21. inert
- **a.** inactive
- **b.** sluggish
- **c.** boisterous
- **d.** incapable of moving

22. genteel
- **a.** polite
- **b.** soft
- **c.** refined
- **d.** well mannered

23. sycophant
- **a.** one who is rude to the boss
- **b.** one who flatters the boss
- **c.** one who always showers compliments on the boss
- **d.** one who offers to pick up the dry cleaning for the boss

24. wallow
- **a.** roll around in
- **b.** bask
- **c.** indulge
- **d.** avoid

25. insouciance
- **a.** a carefree attitude
- **b.** anxiety
- **c.** lightheartedness
- **d.** unconcern

26. resonant
- **a.** vibrant
- **b.** ringing
- **c.** resounding
- **d.** weak

27. smidgen
a. crumb
b. particle
c. plenty
d. drop

28. guffaw
a. frown
b. laugh
c. giggle
d. chuckle

29. bevy
a. group
b. crowd
c. bunch
d. example

30. disconsolate
a. melancholy
b. ecstatic
c. hopeless
d. dejected

TEST-TAKING TIP

Read the question carefully and look for tricky words like *not* and *opposite*.

Antonyms

Choose the word from the vocabulary list that means the opposite, or most nearly the opposite, of the following groups of words.

31. sharp, acute, sensitive _____

32. explain, teach, illustrate _____

33. fixed, permanent, stable _____

34. impartial, unbiased, unprejudiced _____

35. certain, decided, sure _____

36. ignorant, naïve, limited in knowledge _____

37. avoid, reject, eschew _____

38. rude, impolite, discourteous _____

39. color, brightness, tint _____

40. give, present, donate _____

Matching Questions

Match the word in the first column with the corresponding word in the second column.

41. inert   **a.** changeable

42. smidgen   **b.** throaty

43. addle   **c.** group

44. guttural   **d.** inactive

45. obtuse   **e.** resounding

46. purloin   **f.** dull

47. mutable   **g.** small particle

48. resonant   **h.** sad

49. bevy   **i.** confuse

50. disconsolate **j.** steal

TIP

Sometimes it's easier to eliminate than it is to choose. Always see if you can eliminate any wrong answers on a test question.

Practice Activities

Many of the words in this chapter's vocabulary list have several synonyms. Find a good thesaurus and look up the synonyms for each word. Try to list five synonyms for each word. If you have difficulty finding the word in the thesaurus, use an alternate form of the word (like resonate for resonant). Your synonyms may be one word long or you may choose to write a few words in a phrase that makes the meaning clear.

To practice your spelling skills, as well as your understanding of the meanings of the words from this chapter's vocabulary list, construct another crossword puzzle. Choose one of the longer words to start with, and write it down in the middle of a page. Then find a word that you can connect to this word because they both share a letter, and write the second word going down through this word. Then try to connect a word to that word, and continue doing this until you have connected every word on the list. Draw boxes around all the letters (or just use graph paper), and place a number in the box with the first letter in each word. Finally, make a list of clues for your crossword puzzle for both the across and the down words. Can any of your friends solve your puzzle?

Answers

Words in Context

Because the boys in this passage are trying their best to blend in at a fancy party they were not invited to, we can guess that when they put on their best *genteel* manners upon arriving, they are trying to be polite, refined, and gentlemanly. Pete's loud *guffaw* that disrupts the room after Joe whispers a joke in his ear helps us understand that *guffaw* means a loud, rough burst of laughter. The next sentence helps us identify Pete's lovable *insouciance* as his troublesome, happy-go-lucky attitude. Since the narrator feels Pete can be *obtuse* about noticing when to restrain himself, we can conclude that *obtuse* can mean insensitive, or slow to understand or notice. Since the boys search for and find a *bevy* of young ladies, we must assume that *bevy* is a group of some kind. The pale girl's dark eyes and hair accentuate her *pallor,* making it possible for us to guess that *pallor* means lack of color or unnatural paleness. The third girl chooses not to dance and remains *inert,* so we can read *inert* as inactive or incapable of moving. The reason she won't dance is because she is heartbroken, which helps us understand that the word *disconsolate* means sad, hopeless, or dejected. Since she seems to have mixed feelings about being at the party, trying to meet new people, and enjoying herself, we should assume that *ambivalent* means divided and uncertain feelings, or feeling two opposite feelings at the same time. Finally, Pete's humorous attempts to add to the hostess's confusion at not recognizing the party crashers helps us conclude that *addle* must mean confuse, fluster, or muddle.

Sentence Completion

1. *sycophant.* If you got this question wrong, refer back to the word's definition.
2. *purloin.* If you got this question wrong, refer back to the word's definition.
3. *genteel.* If you got this question wrong, refer back to the word's definition.
4. *inert.* If you got this question wrong, refer back to the word's definition.
5. *smidgen.* If you got this question wrong, refer back to the word's definition.
6. *omniscient.* If you got this question wrong, refer back to the word's definition.
7. *ambivalent.* If you got this question wrong, refer back to the word's definition.
8. *mutable.* If you got this question wrong, refer back to the word's definition.
9. *wallow.* If you got this question wrong, refer back to the word's definition.
10. *pallor.* If you got this question wrong, refer back to the word's definition.
11. *disconsolate.* If you got this question wrong, refer back to the word's definition.
12. *bevy.* If you got this question wrong, refer back to the word's definition.
13. *partisan.* If you got this question wrong, refer back to the word's definition.
14. *addle.* If you got this question wrong, refer back to the word's definition.
15. *insouciance.* If you got this question wrong, refer back to the word's definition.
16. *rubric.* If you got this question wrong, refer back to the word's definition.
17. *resonant.* If you got this question wrong, refer back to the word's definition.
18. *guffaw.* If you got this question wrong, refer back to the word's definition.
19. *obtuse.* If you got this question wrong, refer back to the word's definition.
20. *guttural.* If you got this question wrong, refer back to the word's definition.

Synonyms

21. **c.** *boisterous.* Inert means not moving or not able to move, and boisterous means noisy and exuberant, which is not a synonym.

22. **b.** *soft.* Genteel means polite, refined, and gentlemanly or ladylike. You may have confused soft and its synonym gentle with genteel.

23. **a.** *one who is rude to the boss.* A sycophant is one who tries to get ahead by flattery. Choice **a** is the only choice that is not appropriate.

24. **d.** *avoid.* Wallow means to overindulge in something, making a spectacle of oneself, like the way a pig will roll about in the mud. Avoid means to steer clear of, so it is not a synonym.

25. **b.** *anxiety.* Insouciance is an easygoing and happy-go-lucky attitude. Since anxiety means painful uneasiness of the mind, or worry, it is not a synonym.

26. **d.** *weak.* Resonant is used to describe sounds and means vibrant, full, and resounding. Weak would not be a synonym because resonant sounds are strong, loud sounds.

27. **c.** *plenty.* A smidgen is a very small particle or amount. Since plenty means an abundance or full supply of something, it is not a synonym.

28. **a.** *frown.* A guffaw is a loud burst of laughter. Since a frown is a look of displeasure or disapproval, it is not a synonym.

29. **d.** *example.* A bevy is a group or flock. Since an example is a model or specimen of something, it is not a synonym.

30. **b.** *ecstatic.* Disconsolate means sad, dejected, and hopeless, so ecstatic is not a synonym.

Antonyms

31. *Obtuse* means dull and not sharp, or slow to notice, the opposite of the words listed.

32. *Addle* means to confuse, fluster, or muddle, the opposite of the words listed.

33. *Mutable* means changeable or variable, the opposite of the words listed.

34. *Partisan* means strongly devoted to one side in a conflict or a political party, the opposite of the words listed.

35. *Ambivalent* means having conflicting feelings about something, the opposite of the words listed.

36. *Omniscient* means all knowing, the opposite of the words listed.

37. *Wallow* means to overindulge, the opposite of the words listed.

38. *Genteel* means refined, polite, and elegant, the opposite of the words listed.

39. *Pallor* means a lack of color, or an unnatural paleness, the opposite of the words listed.

40. *Purloin* means to steal, the opposite of the words listed.

Matching Questions

41. d

42. g

43. i

44. b

45. f

46. j

47. a

48. e

49. c

50. h

Across

2 wallow
5 bevy
7 smidgen
9 sycophant
10 rubric
12 ambivalent
14 omniscient
16 guttural
18 addle
20 insouciance

Down

1 purloin
3 obtuse
4 resonant
6 pallor
8 disconsolate
11 partisan
13 guffaw
15 inert
17 genteel
19 mutable

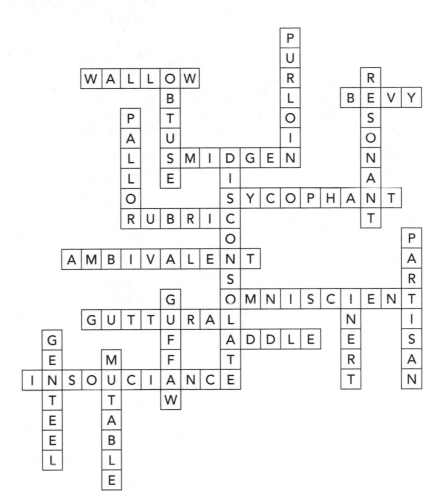

CHAPTER

18 ▶ PHILOSOPHICAL TERMS

There is nothing so strange and so unbelievable that it has not been said by one philosopher or another.

—René Descartes, French philosopher
and mathematician (1596–1650)

CHAPTER SUMMARY

Some of the most influential work done over the last few thousand years has been done not by anyone who built a famous building, won a great battle, or discovered a new land, but by people who pondered the world around them. They have investigated the nature of the world, explored the meanings of concepts like truth, honor, and love, and tried to determine the ultimate purpose of life. These people were philosophers, and their work and study is called philosophy. Everyone is a bit of a philosopher in his or her own right, because each of us must decide what values we will live by and what our life's purpose is. Some people may think about these matters occasionally or very briefly, while others will spend their lives searching for answers.

In this chapter, you will study some new words that are commonly used to discuss concepts and ideas in various fields such as philosophy, politics, and religion. Many of the words are also used every day in the newspaper or on television. Perhaps once you have mastered the words in this chapter, you too will begin to use them in your writing and speech, and someone will wonder if you yourself are a philosopher.

Choose the word from the vocabulary list that best fits into the crossword puzzle. You can check your answers at the end of the chapter following the answers to the questions.

Vocabulary List 15: Philosophical Terms

abstraction
altruism
antithesis
banal
dichotomy
dogma
empiric
erudite
hedonism
ideology
logic
paradigm
paradox
pragmatism
semantic
syllogism
tautology
teleology
tenet
utopia

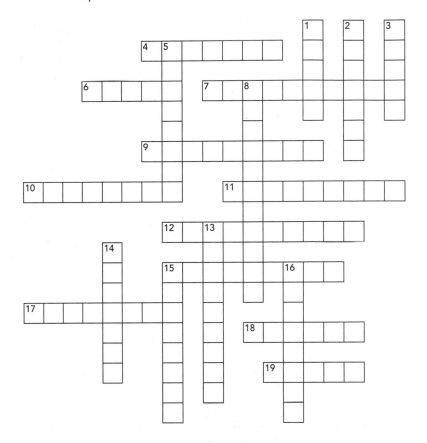

Across

4 a statement that seems to contradict itself
6 a belief that is asserted to be true
7 a practical or realistic attitude
9 division of a subject into two opposite classes or aspects
10 the belief in a pleasure-seeking lifestyle
11 redundancy
12 the exact opposite
15 logical reasoning that leads to a conclusion
17 an example or model
18 paradise
19 the science of reasoning

Down

1 worn out by overuse, trite
2 a quack
3 official beliefs or teachings of particular politics, philosophy, or religion
5 unselfish concern for others
8 theoretical idea or concept
13 "all natural processes occur for a reason"
14 scholarly, learned
15 subtle differences between word meanings
16 doctrines

abstraction (ab·′strak·shən)

(*noun*)

something that is not concrete or tangible, but is more of a theoretical idea or concept, like truth or beauty

We were discussing our relationships when Franklin reminded us that love itself could be looked at as just an _____.

altruism (′al·trŭ·i·zəm)

(*noun*)

unselfish concern for the welfare of others

The couple's _____ had an immeasurable effect on the entire community.

antithesis (an·′ti·thə·səs)

(*noun*)

the exact opposite of something, or an extreme contrast

I was really hoping for a promotion, but I received its _____, a demotion to another office.

banal (bə·′nal)

(*adj.*)

trivial, worn out by overuse, or used so commonly as to have lost all interest and novelty

Long after people had stopped saying "far out," Tim continued to use the _____ expression.

dichotomy (dī·′kä·tə·mē)

(*noun*)

the division of a subject into two opposite classes or aspects, such as internal and external

We were intrigued by all the interesting possibilities that the _____ of the experience presented: are ghosts real or illusions?

dogma (′dog·mə)

(*noun*)

the official beliefs, principles, or teachings, such as those of a religion, political party, or philosophy, used most often with the added implication that these beliefs or teachings should be strictly adhered to

He lived faithfully by the _____ of his religion.

empiric (im·′pir·ik)

(*noun*)

someone who begins a practice such as law or medicine without the proper professional education and experience; a popular slang term for this is a *quack*; or one who is ignorant of the scientific principles and relies completely on practical experience

Bethany recommended I see her friend for the pain in my back, but I had met him and was sure he was just an _____.

erudite (′er·ə·dīt)

(*adj.*)

scholarly, learned, well read, having extensive knowledge

Her _____ opinion easily impressed the instructor and persuaded us all to agree with her.

hedonism (hē·dən·i·zəm)

(*noun*)

the belief that everything in life should be done to bring pleasure; a pleasure-seeking lifestyle

The _____ we practiced in our youth brought us as many problems as it did pleasures.

ideology (ī·dē·′ä·lə·′jē)

(*noun*)

the doctrines, beliefs, or opinions of a person, group, or school of thought

He explained his _____ to us, and then we better understood the way he chose to live.

logic (′lä·jik)

(*noun*)

the science of correct reasoning used to discover truths, or any method of reasoning, whether it reveals true and valid statements or not

If we use some _____, I am sure we can figure out this riddle.

paradigm   ('par·ə·dīm)
(*noun*)
a pattern, example, or model
After hours of fruitless discussion about the project, the director presented us with a _____ that made our goal much clearer.

paradox   ('par·ə·däks)
(*noun*)
a statement that seems contradictory, unbelievable, or absurd but may actually be true; or something that is not fully understood because of contradictory appearances, statements, or actions
That is an interesting _____; I guess you really were lucky to be so unlucky.

pragmatism   ('prag·mə·'ti·'zəm)
(*noun*)
a way of thinking or an attitude that stresses the value of being practical, realistic, and useful
We were all glad he showed such _____ at the meeting and that he was not too idealistic about achieving our goal in just a few weeks.

semantic   (si·'man·tik)
(*adj.*)
concerning the meaning of something; usually used in discussing words and language and the subtle differences between the meanings of similar words
The lawyers disputed the wording of part of the contract, but I did not have the patience to deal with _____ issues just then.

syllogism   ('si·lə·ji·zəm)
(*noun*)
a form of logical reasoning that begins with two true statements and ends with a logical conclusion drawn from them, using deductive reasoning, which proceeds from general statements to the specific

Objects that can float in water are less dense than water, and I can float in water, so therefore I must be less dense than water. Is that a valid _____?

tautology   (tŏ·'tä·lə·'jē)
(*noun*)
needless repetition of an idea in a different word or phrase; redundancy
Can we eliminate any of this _____? We certainly know that the "requirements" are "necessary," so can we just call them "requirements?"

teleology   (te·lē·'ä·lə·jē)
(*noun*)
the study of final causes; or the belief that all natural processes and events occur for a reason, and nature is directed by some kind of purpose
Looking at the forest fire with _____, one can see how the fire renews and rejuvenates the forest in an essential way.

tenet   ('te·nət)
(*noun*)
an opinion, principle, or belief that a person, religion, or school of thought believes and asserts to be true and important; a doctrine
He did not question the _____ itself, but only asked that his teacher clarify the different implications this new doctrine had for daily life.

utopia   (yŭ·'tō·pē·ə)
(*noun*)
a place or state of ideal perfection, usually imaginary; a paradise
When we arrived at their camp by the river, it seemed to be an unbelievable _____.

TIP

Philosophy can be intimidating, so just take it one word at a time. You don't have to be a philosopher to understand and use these concepts.

Words in Context

The following exercise will help you figure out the meaning of some words from the vocabulary list by reading context clues. After you have read and understood the paragraph, explain the context clues that helped you with the meaning of the vocabulary word. Refer to the answer section at the end of this chapter for an explanation of the clues.

It always inspires me to remember my old teacher. He was one of the few people who really believed we could make the world a better place, and he had this wonderful vision of a future *utopia* that he was absolutely convinced was inevitable. For him, *altruism* was not just some *abstraction*, some big word that you could discuss in a philosophy class and then forget about; it was a way of life. It was a basic *tenet* of his that each person should do all that they can to help others, and he certainly taught us well enough by his own example. But his *pragmatism* also kept him well grounded and focused on real solutions to local concerns, and perhaps that is why none of his critics could dismiss him. Many did not understand that the fabulous entertaining he did was all part of his mission and not just some selfish *hedonism*. Rather, he was motivating and rewarding his team, and you could not leave one of his parties without understanding his unique *ideology* a little better, resolved to commit even more fully to a life of public service.

Sentence Completion

Insert the correct word from the vocabulary list into the following sentences.

1. The _____ that we based this on is outdated, so we will need a new model for the upcoming project.

2. I know that she is certified as a "healer," but I don't trust her methods—I think she is just a(n) _____.

3. Studying about Chinese culture did not prepare me for the _____ between the two cultures that I experienced when I lived in Shanghai for a year.

4. As an inexperienced writer, her work was replete with _____, but in time, she learned how to spot and eliminate redundancies.

5. This may sound like a _____, but I think that standing in one place is more tiring than walking.

6. I tried to fill him with hope, the _____ of despair, which is what he has been feeling ever since he lost his job.

7. My favorite science fiction book describes a(n) _____, a place that is perfect in its social, political, and moral characteristics.

8. Sandra's _____ has rubbed off on me, and now I am much more practical in my approach to life.

9. My _____, or ideas about life and work, has been largely influenced by my parents.

10. Sophie is known for her _____, as she donates a lot of time to help those in need.

11. One would think that most young people don't adhere to the popular _____, "All humans are mortal, and I am human; therefore, I must be mortal," because they act as if they think they're invincible.

12. One of the _____(s) of physical science says that no two objects can occupy the same space at the same time.

13. I wish I could abandon all my responsibilities, follow them down there on their vacation, and join them in their carefree _____.

14. It was a(n) _____ opinion, and I had to respect his thorough research, but nonetheless, I still disagreed and thought the procedure should be banned.

15. If we just use a little bit of _____, we should be able to figure out a solution to our problem.

16. It is not just a small _____ mistake; you just introduced me as someone you work *with*, when we both know that I hired you to work *for me*.

17. In all the years I have known him, I have never known him to question the _____ of his church.

18. He mocked us and told us we were foolish to spend our time discussing such a(n) _____, but we knew that few things were more important than trying to better understand just what *honor* really meant.

19. I subscribe to a similar _____, and I also believe that birds have an important purpose that would be well worth understanding.

20. It is amusing to hear some people use so many _____ expressions that they probably have just learned from television.

Synonyms

The following exercise lists vocabulary words from this chapter. Each word is followed by four answer choices. Three of them are synonyms of the vocabulary word in bold. Your task is to choose the one that is NOT a synonym.

21. paradox
   a. mystery
   b. contradiction
   c. puzzle
   d. clue

22. antithesis
   a. an opposite
   b. a statement
   c. the reverse
   d. a contrast

23. semantic
   a. concerning the meaning of
   b. related to the different definitions of
   c. using too many words
   d. distinguishing different contexts

24. tenet
   a. prejudice
   b. belief
   c. opinion
   d. principle

25. hedonism
    a. pleasure-seeking
    b. debauchery
    c. solitude
    d. indulgence

26. teleology
    a. belief that nature is purposeful
    b. belief that natural processes occur for a reason
    c. belief that nature is haphazard
    d. belief that everything that occurs in the natural world is part of some higher plan

27. paradigm
    a. model
    b. pattern
    c. example
    d. drawing

28. abstraction
    a. theoretical
    b. conceptual
    c. tangible
    d. intangible

29. logic
    a. confusion
    b. reasoning
    c. figuring out
    d. analyzing the truth of something

30. erudite
    a. scholarly
    b. knowledgeable
    c. discourteous
    d. well read

Antonyms

Choose the word from the vocabulary list that means the opposite, or most nearly the opposite, of the following groups of words.

31. unity, universality, oneness   _____

32. idealism, dreaminess, impracticality   _____

33. a professional, one who is properly trained, a qualified authority   _____

34. new, exciting, fresh   _____

35. selfishness, greediness, hostility   _____

36. concise writing, succinctness, speech that is not redundant   _____

37. a world of horrors, a "hell on Earth," future world of suffering and misery   _____

38. ignorant, uneducated, illiterate   _____

39. hard fact, physical evidence, tangible object   _____

40. answer, evidence, clue   _____

Choosing the Right Word

Circle the word in bold that best completes the sentence.

41. The two men were known for their wild (**utopia, hedonism**); they had a reputation for always eating at the best restaurants and cafes, and taking spontaneous vacations to exotic locales.

42. His speech was very (**erudite, tautology**), and he received good reviews for his display of such fine research.

43. Her volunteer work at the nursing home was just another example of her admirable (**pragmatism, altruism**).

44. It is a(n) (**antithesis, tenet**) that followers of the faith often have difficulty with.

45. I don't know what to make of it; it sure seems like a (**paradox, paradigm**) to me.

46. Have you ever heard such a (**banal, semantic**) expression? I am just so tired of hearing that over and over again.

47. If you really analyze the first premise of that (**abstraction, syllogism**), you will see that the conclusion cannot possibly be valid.

48. She always closely followed the (**dichotomy, dogma**) of her religion, and often helped instruct others who had questions about it themselves.

49. Don't panic. Let's try to use a little (**logic, paradox**) and see if we can figure out what must have happened to the keys.

50. This place is like a little hidden (**utopia, empiric**) that we have been fortunate to find before anyone else ruined it.

Practice Activities

Go to the library and look up a book on philosophy. Not only will you read some interesting ideas by some of humankind's best thinkers, but you will no doubt see the words from this chapter in the text, as well as many others that you may not recognize. Find ten new words that you do not know the definition of, and look up those words in the dictionary. Then practice using each word in a sentence.

Use an Internet search engine and look up some of the words from this chapter. Does the search engine have links for the word? Go to a few of those websites and see why they used that word. Is the word part of the name of the website, or is it used in the text of the site? See how many words you can find from this list.

TIP

It might help to talk to someone about the ideas in this list. You'd be surprised at how many of these words relate to ideas in your own life, and the more you use or think about a word on a daily basis, the easier it is to remember.

Answers

Words in Context

The reader can understand that the narrator's former teacher's optimistic belief in a *utopia* is a belief in a better world that lies somewhere in the future. One gets the sense that this place must be almost like a paradise where, finally, no one would need the kind of help the teacher always gives. Thus, we can understand from the context of the passage that *altruism* must be an admirable quality that means an unselfish concern for others, which would explain the teacher's commitment to doing all he can for others and living a life of public service. We can conclude that an *abstraction* is a theoretical idea, but that the professor does not consider altruism to be just a word one only discusses in a philosophy class and does not practice. The narrator explains the teacher's *tenet* is that one must always strive to do more for others, so we can conclude that *tenet* means an opinion or belief of a person, religion, or school of thought. Since the teacher's *pragmatism* keeps him grounded and focused on practical efforts to help others, we should know that *pragmatism* is a way of thinking that emphasizes being realistic and useful. The teacher's choice to celebrate and throw parties is defended as not being selfish *hedonism,* so we can assume that *hedonism* means a pleasure-seeking lifestyle or philosophy. Finally, since the narrator states that he understands his teacher's unique *ideology* better after the celebrations, we can guess that *ideology* means those beliefs, opinions, or doctrines that he adheres to.

Sentence Completion

1. *paradigm.* If you got this question wrong, refer back to the word's definition.
2. *empiric.* If you got this question wrong, refer back to the word's definition.
3. *dichotomy.* If you got this question wrong, refer back to the word's definition.
4. *tautology.* If you got this question wrong, refer back to the word's definition.
5. *paradox.* If you got this question wrong, refer back to the word's definition.
6. *antithesis.* If you got this question wrong, refer back to the word's definition.
7. *utopia.* If you got this question wrong, refer back to the word's definition.
8. *pragmatism.* If you got this question wrong, refer back to the word's definition.
9. *ideology.* If you got this question wrong, you may have mistakenly chosen dogma, a close synonym of ideology. However, dogma implies a belief system that is more strictly adhered to, and the context of this sentence indicates that the belief system was only loosely adhered to.
10. *altruism.* If you got this question wrong, refer back to the word's definition.
11. *syllogism.* If you got this question wrong, you may have mistakenly chosen logic. It is true that logic is being used in the reasoning of the example but in the unique form of a syllogism. It also would be inappropriate to use logic in the blank because the next phrase asks if the piece of reasoning presented is logical, and thus, it would be somewhat repetitive to use logic.
12. *tenet.* If you got this question wrong, you may have mistakenly chosen dogma or ideology. Since tenet refers to a specific belief, and dogma and ideology refer to an entire set of beliefs, tenet would be the best answer because this example presents only one specific belief.
13. *hedonism.* If you got this question wrong, refer back to the word's definition.
14. *erudite.* If you got this question wrong, refer back to the word's definition.
15. *logic.* If you got this question wrong, refer back to the word's definition.
16. *semantic.* If you got this question wrong, refer back to the word's definition.

17. *dogma.* Here, again, you may have chosen the closely related terms ideology or tenet. Tenet refers to one specific doctrine or teaching. The context of this sentence tells us that, for several years, the man has not questioned his church's teachings, implying that the entire set of beliefs is being discussed. Dogma would be a better choice than ideology, because the man seems to strictly adhere to his church's teachings. The connotation of ideology emphasizes the beliefs themselves, whereas the connotation of dogma stresses required obedience and adherence to the teachings of the religion or group.

18. *abstraction.* If you got this question wrong, refer back to the word's definition.

19. *teleology.* If you got this question wrong, refer back to the word's definition.

20. *banal.* If you got this question wrong, refer back to the word's definition.

Synonyms

21. **d.** *clue.* Paradox means something that is hard to understand because it contains a contradiction. Since clue means a hint or slight indication toward solving some mystery, it is not a synonym.

22. **b.** *statement.* Antithesis means the exact opposite of something. Since a statement is a saying or an expression, it is not a synonym.

23. **c.** *using too many words.* Semantic means concerning the different meanings of closely related words. Using too many words is not a correct answer because it deals with the number of words involved and not the meanings of the words.

24. **a.** *prejudice.* A tenet is a belief, opinion, or principle that a person or an organized group holds to be true and important. A prejudice is a bias against something or a preconception prior to meeting or experiencing it, so it is not a synonym.

25. **c.** *solitude.* Hedonism is the belief that pleasure is the most important goal in life. Solitude is the state of being alone and by oneself, so it is not a synonym.

26. **c.** *belief that nature is haphazard.* Teleology is the belief that all natural processes and events happen for a reason, directed by some kind of purpose. Haphazard means accidental or careless, so choice **c** could not be a synonym.

27. **d.** *drawing.* Paradigm means a pattern or model, often used to help organize or conceptualize an idea. A drawing could serve the same purpose, but it always refers to a hand-drawn, visual presentation, so it is too specific and narrow to be a synonym.

28. **c.** *tangible.* An abstraction is something that is not tangible, so tangible is actually an antonym of abstraction.

29. **a.** *confusion.* Logic is the science of using correct reasoning to discover a truth. Confusion is puzzlement or bewilderment, so it is not a synonym.

30. **c.** *discourteous.* Erudite means scholarly, learned, and having an extensive knowledge. Discourteous means rude and impolite, so it is not a synonym.

Antonyms

31. *dichotomy.* Dichotomy means the division of something into two opposite classes or aspects, usually for discussion or analysis, the opposite of the words listed.

32. *pragmatism.* Pragmatism means belief in the value of being practical, realistic, and useful.

33. *empiric.* An empiric is someone who begins a practice such as medicine or law without the proper professional education and experience, the opposite of the words listed.

34. *banal.* Banal means trite, hackneyed, and worn out by overuse, the opposite of the words listed.

35. *altruism.* Altruism is the unselfish concern for the welfare of others, the opposite of the words listed.

36. *tautology.* Tautology is the needless repetition of an idea in slightly different words, the opposite of the words listed.

37. *utopia.* A utopia is an imaginary place of ideal perfection, the opposite of the words listed.

38. *erudite.* Erudite means scholarly, knowledgeable, and well read, the opposite of the words listed.

39. *abstraction.* An abstraction is a concept or idea that is theoretical or hypothetical and is not material or physical, the opposite of the words listed.

40. *paradox.* A paradox is a mystery or something that is unclear, the opposite of the words listed.

Choosing the Right Word

41. *hedonism.* Hedonism can mean a pleasure-seeking lifestyle. Utopia means an imaginary perfect place.

42. *erudite.* Erudite means scholarly and knowledgeable. Tautology is the needless repetition of similar meaning words or phrases.

43. *altruism.* Altruism is the unselfish concern for the welfare of others, and is exemplified by volunteer work in a nursing home. Pragmatism is the attitude or belief that the practical, realistic, and useful are most important.

44. *tenet.* A tenet is a belief or principle of a person, religion, or school of thought. Antithesis is the exact opposite of something.

45. *paradox.* A paradox is a mystery, or something that is unclear or not fully understood because of some contradiction. A paradigm is a pattern, example, or model.

46. *banal.* Banal means worn out by overuse, or trite. Semantic means concerning the slightly different meanings of similar words.

47. *syllogism.* A syllogism is a specific form of logical reasoning that begins with two premises and derives a conclusion from them. An abstraction is something that does not exist in the physical world, but is rather a concept or theoretical idea.

48. *dogma.* Dogma is the official set of beliefs and teachings of a religion, political party, or philosophy. Dichotomy means the division of a subject into two opposite classes or aspects for analysis or discussion.

49. *logic.* Logic is the science of correct reasoning used to discover truths. A paradox is a puzzling statement that is difficult to fully understand because it contains a contradiction.

50. *utopia.* Utopia means a place of ideal perfection. Empiric means someone who lacks the necessary and proper training and experience to practice a profession.

Across

4 paradox
6 tenet
7 pragmatism
9 dichotomy
10 hedonism
11 tautology
12 antithesis
15 syllogism
17 paradigm
18 utopia
19 logic

Down

1 banal
2 empiric
3 dogma
5 altruism
8 abstraction
13 teleology
14 erudite
15 semantic
16 ideology

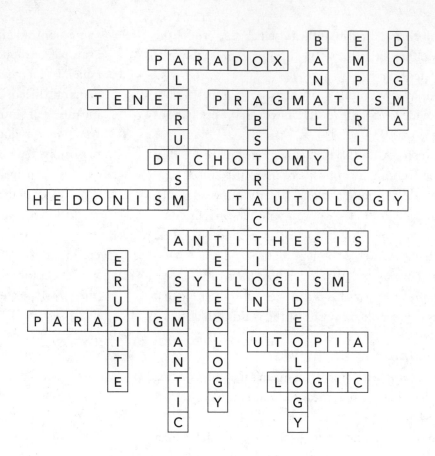

CHAPTER

19 ▶ POSTTEST

Now that you've built your vocabulary and spelling skills, you're ready to test them out. Take this posttest and compare your score with your pretest's to see how far you've come. You should go back and review any words you forgot until you know every word in this book.

1.	ⓐ	ⓑ	ⓒ	ⓓ		31.	ⓐ	ⓑ	ⓒ	ⓓ
2.	ⓐ	ⓑ	ⓒ	ⓓ		32.	ⓐ	ⓑ	ⓒ	ⓓ
3.	ⓐ	ⓑ	ⓒ	ⓓ		33.	ⓐ	ⓑ	ⓒ	ⓓ
4.	ⓐ	ⓑ	ⓒ	ⓓ		34.	ⓐ	ⓑ	ⓒ	ⓓ
5.	ⓐ	ⓑ	ⓒ	ⓓ		35.	ⓐ	ⓑ	ⓒ	ⓓ
6.	ⓐ	ⓑ	ⓒ	ⓓ		36.	ⓐ	ⓑ	ⓒ	ⓓ
7.	ⓐ	ⓑ	ⓒ	ⓓ		37.	ⓐ	ⓑ	ⓒ	ⓓ
8.	ⓐ	ⓑ	ⓒ	ⓓ		38.	ⓐ	ⓑ	ⓒ	ⓓ
9.	ⓐ	ⓑ	ⓒ	ⓓ		39.	ⓐ	ⓑ	ⓒ	ⓓ
10.	ⓐ	ⓑ	ⓒ	ⓓ		40.	ⓐ	ⓑ	ⓒ	ⓓ

Spelling
Choose the word that is spelled correctly.

1. a. disinterrested
   b. dissinterested
   c. disinterested
   d. disintirested

2. a. belligerent
   b. belligarent
   c. belligerrent
   d. beligerent

3. a. diffident
   b. difident
   c. diffidant
   d. difidant

4. a. contraban
   b. contriband
   c. conttraban
   d. contraband

5. a. omnishint
   b. omniscient
   c. onmscient
   d. omniscint

Choose the word that is misspelled.

6. a. mutable
   b. hedonism
   c. dicotomy
   d. simian

7. a. snaffu
   b. laser
   c. jaunty
   d. dolorous

8. a. guffaw
   b. extricate
   c. anomaly
   d. idealogy

9. a. synthisis
   b. deferment
   c. bigotry
   d. larceny

10. a. biodegradable
    b. phillanthropy
    c. protracted
    d. malevolent

Sentence Completion
Write the word from Group 1 that best fits in the blank. You can check your answers at the end of the posttest.

Group 1

imperious	palpable	antipathy	brusque
plausible	exhume	aphorism	purloin
prodigious	succor	guttural	dire
dogma	utopia	malaise	retrospect
parity	venerate	fluctuate	benevolent

11. It is not a simple matter to _____ a body from a grave; a judge has to deem that there is a very good reason for it.

12. I am generally a happy person, but during winter, I always experience a feeling of _____.

13. Her story is not _____ because she would have had to be in two places at once.

14. The author's _____ body of work was impressive to the novice writer, who hadn't even published one book.

15. After the power failed, we realized the situation had grown _____ and that we would need someone to come to our aid.

Write the word from Group 2 that best fits in the blank. You can check your answers at the end of the posttest.

Group 2

capital	affidavit	illegible	simian
attribute	pathos	recapitulate	naïve
fiscal	cower	tenure	database
ambivalent	construe	mete	myriad
prone	verify	addle	paradox

16. Some people like to _____ in their seats as they watch a scary movie, but I'd rather be rapt by a good love story.

17. It's very frustrating when Derek handwrites his memos, as they are completely _____.

18. I always call the airlines to _____ that my flight is leaving on time before I leave for the airport.

19. Selfishness is not a very desirable _____, so I tried to make sure that my children understood the importance of sharing.

20. Ben was _____ to headaches, so he kept some medication with him at all times.

Choosing the Right Word

Circle the bold word that best fits into the context of the sentence.

21. The workers' union and the board of directors finally decided to go to (**arbitration, collusion**) because their negotiations were fruitless.

22. I found the answer in the (**FAQ, ASAP**) section of the brochure.

23. I can't read this memo because it is filled with (**nepotism, jargon**) that I don't understand.

24. She is well known for her (**syllogism, pragmatism**), so I think she will be a very successful manager.

25. Everything was fine until we had a little (**snafu, yuppie**) while on the train.

26. I am sure I know the sound of that (**addle, guffaw**), so Joe must be here, and it sounds like he is having a good time.

27. She can't sell her car because there is still a (**lien, tort**) against it.

28. The hackers tried, but they could not figure out our company's (**cache, encryption**) methods, so the files remain secure.

29. The map was so old that it was no longer (**vehement, relevant**).

30. The poet used (**personification, abstraction**) so well in the poem that the ocean actually seemed alive.

Synonyms

The following exercise lists vocabulary words from this book. Each word is followed by four answer choices. Three of them are synonyms of the vocabulary word in bold. Your task is to choose the one that is NOT a synonym.

31. minimize
- **a.** shrink
- **b.** expand
- **c.** stunt
- **d.** subtract

32. rancor
- **a.** hatred
- **b.** ill will
- **c.** dislike
- **d.** ignorance

33. recapitulate
- **a.** summarize
- **b.** introduce
- **c.** go back over
- **d.** review

34. rendezvous
- **a.** parting
- **b.** meeting
- **c.** engagement
- **d.** appointment

35. flippant
- **a.** too casual
- **b.** rude
- **c.** tired
- **d.** disrespectful

36. puerile
- **a.** childish
- **b.** silly
- **c.** immature
- **d.** cautious

37. archetype
- **a.** model
- **b.** replication
- **c.** example
- **d.** standard

38. relentless
- **a.** occasional
- **b.** unstoppable
- **c.** harsh
- **d.** continuing

39. purge
- **a.** cleanse
- **b.** eliminate
- **c.** ruin
- **d.** empty

40. cryptic
- **a.** hidden
- **b.** secret
- **c.** ambiguous
- **d.** ancient

Antonyms

Write the word in the blank that is most nearly the opposite of the words listed.

41. clear, unmistakable, easily read _____

42. give, restore, buy _____

43. exact words, literal meaning, unexaggerated speech _____

44. hidden, secret, possible to miss or pass by _____

45. sluggish, lethargic, inactive _____

46. fair hiring, promotions given to those most deserving, merit-based personnel decisions _____

47. remain constant, resist change, stay the same always _____

48. worldly, experienced, wise _____

49. selfishness, greediness, lack of concern for others _____

50. excellent, extraordinary, skillful _____

Word Pairs

Write *S* if the words are synonyms, or *A* if the words are antonyms.

51. vehement, blasé _____

52. stolid, staid _____

53. genteel, urbane _____

54. avant-garde, banal _____

55. altruism, hedonism _____

56. relentless, tenacious _____

57. evident, conspicuous _____

58. laudable, churlish _____

59. gregarious, diffident _____

60. obsolescence, irrelevance _____

Denotation and Connotation

The following words are all synonyms with the same denotation, but with different connotations. Write *POS* in the blank if the word carries a positive connotation, *NEG* in the blank if the word carries a negative connotation, and *N* if the word carries a neutral connotation.

Example

1. _____ project _____ enterprise _____ scheme

Answer

1. *Project* carries a neutral connotation—the reader doesn't have any idea who or what might be creating or working on the project. In contrast, enterprise carries a positive connotation—*enterprise* is often associated with a business venture or a new and exciting project, thus giving the word a positive connotation. In contrast, *scheme* carries a negative connotation—criminals and lawlessness are often associated with schemes.

61. _____ exorbitant _____ copious

62. _____ puerile _____ naïve
_____ facetious

63. _____ loquacious _____ garrulous

64. _____ gregarious _____ jaunty

65. _____ collusion _____ consortium

66. _____ resolute _____ tenacious
_____ relentless

67. _____ entrepreneur _____ empiric

68. _____ furtive _____ cryptic
_____ incognito

69. _____ audible _____ resonant

70. _____ aficionado _____ partisan

71. _____ provocative _____ litigious

72. _____ bane _____ antipathy

73. _____ audacious _____ flippant

74. _____ feisty _____ vivacious

75. _____ relevant _____ tangential
_____ non sequitur

Answers

Spelling

1. **c.** disinterested
2. **a.** belligerent
3. **a.** diffident
4. **d.** contraband
5. **b.** omniscient
6. **c.** *Dicotomy* should be spelled *dichotomy*.
7. **a.** *Snaffu* should be spelled *snafu*.
8. **d.** *Idealogy* should be spelled *ideology*.
9. **a.** *Synthisis* should be spelled *synthesis*.
10. **b.** *Phillanthropy* should be spelled *philanthropy*.

Sentence Completion

11. *exhume.* Exhume means remove from a grave.
12. *malaise.* A malaise is a vague feeling of illness.
13. *plausible.* Plausible means seemingly true and acceptable.
14. *prodigious.* Prodigious means very large or numerous.
15. *dire.* Dire means urgent or threatening.
16. *cower.* Cower means tremble in fear.
17. *illegible.* Illegible means not able to be easily read.
18. *verify.* Verify means to establish the truth of something.
19. *attribute.* An attribute is a special quality or characteristic.
20. *prone.* Prone means having a tendency toward something.

Choosing the Right Word

21. *arbitration.* Arbitration is the process by which disputes are settled by a third party, in order to end fruitless negotiations.
22. *FAQ.* FAQ means Frequently Asked Questions, which is where one would find the answer one sought. *ASAP* is As Soon As Possible.
23. *jargon.* Jargon is the specialized vocabulary of an industry or interest group.

24. *pragmatism.* Pragmatism is the belief in, and emphasis on, the practical, possible, and useful.
25. *snafu.* Snafu means situation normal all fouled up.
26. *guffaw.* A guffaw is a loud burst of laughter.
27. *lien.* A lien is a charge against property for the satisfaction of a debt imposed by the courts.
28. *encryption.* Encryption refers to the technology term for translating information into secret code.
29. *relevant.* Relevant means having a bearing on or a connection to the matter at hand.
30. *personification.* Personification is a literary device in which inanimate objects are given human qualities.

Synonyms

31. **b.** *expand.* Minimize means to make smaller or decrease in size.
32. **d.** *ignorance.* Rancor is hatred, ill will, or dislike of something or someone.
33. **b.** *introduce.* Recapitulate means to summarize, go back over, or review.
34. **a.** *parting.* Rendezvous means a meeting, engagement, or appointment.
35. **c.** *tired.* Flippant means too casual, rude, or disrespectful.
36. **d.** *cautious.* Puerile means childish, silly, or immature.
37. **b.** *replication.* Archetype means model, example, or standard.
38. **a.** *occasional.* Relentless means unstoppable, harsh, or continuing.
39. **c.** *ruin.* Purge means to cleanse, eliminate, or empty.
40. **d.** *ancient.* Cryptic means hidden, secret, or ambiguous.

Antonyms

41. *illegible.* Illegible means not easily read, the opposite of the words listed.

42. *purloin.* Purloin means to steal, the opposite of the words listed.

43. *hyperbole.* Hyperbole means exaggerated speech or writing, the opposite of the words listed.

44. *conspicuous.* Conspicuous means highly visible, the opposite of the words listed.

45. *vivacious.* Vivacious means full of spirit and lively, the opposite of the words listed.

46. *nepotism.* Nepotism is the hiring and promoting of friends or family members, the opposite of the words listed.

47. *fluctuate.* Fluctuate means to change or vary, the opposite of the words listed.

48. *naïve.* Naïve means innocent, simple, and lacking knowledge of the world, the opposite of the words listed.

49. *altruism.* Altruism is the unselfish concern for the welfare of others, the opposite of the words listed.

50. *mediocre.* Mediocre means average, the opposite of the words listed.

Word Pairs

51. *A*
52. *S*
53. *S*
54. *A*
55. *A*
56. *S*
57. *S*
58. *A*
59. *A*
60. *S*

Denotation and Connotation

61. *Exorbitant* carries a negative connotation, implying excessive behavior, and is often associated with showy and ostentatious displays of wealth. *Copious* carries a positive connotation, since it means abundant and plentiful and is often associated with generosity.

62. *Puerile* carries a negative connotation and is often used to condemn or criticize. *Naïve* usually carries a neutral connotation; it can be used to objectively describe someone or an idea, or it can be used with a negative connotation to criticize someone who was expected to have known something they did not know. *Facetious* carries a positive connotation, and it is used to describe playful, joking behavior, or to excuse an offensive remark, as in "I was just being *facetious.*"

63. *Loquacious* carries a neutral connotation, as it means talkative, an attribute that could be either positive or negative depending on the speaker's own subjective view. *Garrulous*, however, carries a negative connotation, as it means overly talkative and chattering about unimportant things.

64. Both of these words carry positive connotations. *Gregarious* means sociable, and *jaunty* means confident and presenting a sharp appearance.

65. *Collusion* carries a negative connotation and is used to identify fraudulent or deceitful business conspiracies. *Consortium* carries a neutral connotation, as it simply means a coming together of two or more businesses for a specific purpose, and there is no implication that this purpose is either honest or deceitful.

66. *Resolute* carries a neutral connotation and does not indicate whether the firmness of purpose indicated is directed toward a positive or negative end. *Tenacious* carries a slightly negative connotation and is often used to criticize negative stubbornness. *Relentless* also usually carries a negative connotation and is used to describe persistent efforts or assaults that are unwelcome.

67. *Entrepreneur* carries a positive connotation, and identifies someone who takes on the challenge and risk of starting his or her own business. *Empiric* has a negative connotation because it identifies someone who, though he or she also shows initiative, begins a practice such as law or medicine without the proper training and experience, assuming they will learn on the job.

68. *Furtive* has a negative connotation, as it means done in a sly, stealthy, underhanded manner. *Cryptic* has a neutral connotation and means secret or hidden, but with no implied ill will. *Incognito* has a positive connotation, because although it means disguised, it is rarely used to describe negative characters and often carries a connotation of good-hearted mischief or adventure.

69. *Audible* carries a neutral connotation and simply means able to be heard. *Resonant* carries a positive connotation, as it describes sounds that are rich, full, and vibrant.

70. *Aficionado* carries a positive connotation, as it means a person who likes, knows about, and is devoted to a particular activity or thing. It is rarely used with any negative connotations, but rather is most often used as a compliment. *Partisan* has a negative connotation because it means strongly in favor of one view or political party, usually with the connotation of blindly following the party line and not considering an issue on its own or in terms of the bigger picture.

71. *Provocative* carries a negative connotation, like its root word provoke. *Provocative* means exciting emotion in a negative way and likely to stir up action or cause a riot. *Litigious* carries a negative connotation also, and is used to describe something that is disputed and needs to be settled in court. The negative connotation arises from most people's dislike of going to court, and the hassle and expense involved.

72. Both of these words have strong negative connotations. *Bane* means the source of continued annoyance or exasperation, or the cause of ruin or death. *Antipathy* means a revulsion or strong dislike of something.

73. *Audacious* carries a negative connotation. Though it means fearless, adventurous, and daring, it usually means recklessly so. *Flippant* also carries a negative connotation, as it is used to describe disrespectful levity or casualness.

74. *Feisty* carries a negative connotation, as it means full of spirit, but in a quarrelsome way. *Vivacious* carries a positive connotation because it means lively and full of spirit and is used as a compliment.

75. *Relevant* carries a positive connotation. It means related to, or concerning, the subject at hand, and implies that there is other material that is not relevant and therefore does not matter. *Tangential* carries a neutral or negative connotation, and describes something that is slightly related to the subject at hand. *Non sequitur* carries a negative connotation because a *non sequitur* is a statement that has no relation to the one before it and therefore is not a good conversation piece or argument.

STUDYING FOR SUCCESS

How successful you are at studying has less to do with how much time you put into it than with how you do it. That's because some ways of studying are much more effective than others, and some environments are much more conducive to studying than others. Another reason is that not everyone retains information in the same way. On the following pages, you will discover how to adapt your studying strategies to the ways you learn best. You will probably pick up some new preparation techniques for your test and gain insight on how to prepare for standardized tests.

Learning Styles

Think for a minute about what you know about how you learn. For example, if you need directions to a new restaurant, would you:

- Ask to see a map showing how to get there.
- Ask someone to tell you how to get there.
- Copy someone's written directions.

Most people learn in a variety of ways: seeing, touching, hearing, and experiencing the world around them. Many people find, however, that they are more likely to absorb information better from one learning source than from others. The source that works best for you is called your dominant learning method.

There are three basic learning methods: visual, auditory, and kinesthetic (also known as tactile).

- Visual learners understand and retain information best when they can **see** the map, the picture, the text, the word, or the math example.
- Auditory learners learn best when they can **hear** the directions, the poem, the math theorem, or the spelling of a word.
- Kinesthetic learners need to **do**—they must write the directions, draw the diagram, or copy down the phone number.

Visual Learners

If you are a visual learner, you learn best by seeing. Pay special attention to illustrations and graphic material when you study. If you color code your notes with colorful inks or highlighters, you may find that you absorb information better. Visual learners can learn to map or diagram information later in this chapter.

Auditory Learners

If you are an auditory learner, you learn best by listening. Read material aloud to yourself, or talk about what you are learning with a study partner or a study group. Hearing the information will help you to remember it. Some people like to tape-record notes and play them back on the tape player. If you commute to work or school by car or listen to a personal tape player, you can gain extra preparation time by playing the notes to yourself on tape.

Kinesthetic Learners

If you are a kinesthetic learner, you learn best by doing. Interact a lot with your print material by underlining and making margin notes in your textbooks and handouts. Rewrite your notes onto index cards. Recopying material helps you remember it.

How to Study Most Effectively

If studying efficiently is second nature to you, you're very lucky. Most people have to work at it. Try some of these helpful study methods to make studying easier and more effective for you.

Make an Outline

After collecting all the materials you need to review or prepare for the test, the first step for studying any subject is to reduce a large body of information into smaller, more manageable units. One approach to studying this way is to make an outline of text information, handout materials, and class notes.

The important information in print material is often surrounded by lots of extra words and ideas. If you can highlight just the important information, or at least the information you need to know for your test, you can help yourself narrow your focus so that you can study more effectively. There are several ways to make an outline of print material. They include annotating, outlining, and mapping. The point of all three of these strategies is that they allow you to pull out just the important information that you need to prepare for the test.

Annotating

Annotations help you pull out main ideas from the surrounding text to make them more visible and accessible to you. Annotation means that you underline or highlight important information that appears in print material. It also involves responding to the material by engaging yourself with the writer by making margin notes. Margin notes are phrases or sentences in the margins of print material that summarize the content of those passages. Your margin notes leave footprints for you to follow as you review the text.

Here is an example of a passage that has been annotated and underlined.

Loction, Location, Location

Find a quiet spot, use a good reading light, and turn the radio off.

Find Quiet Places

For many adult test takers, it's difficult to find a quiet spot in their busy lives. Many adults don't even have a bedroom corner that isn't shared with someone else. Your quiet spot may be in a different place at different times of the day.

For example, it could be the kitchen table early in the morning before breakfast, your workplace area when everyone else is at lunch, or a corner of the sofa late at night. If you know you'll have to move around when you study, make sure your study material is portable.

Keep your notes, practice tests, pencils, and other supplies together in a folder or bag. Then you can easily carry your study material with you and study in whatever quiet spot presents itself.

If quiet study areas are nonexistent in your home or work environment, you may need to find a space elsewhere. The public library is the most obvious choice. Some test takers find it helpful to assign themselves study hours at the library in the same way that they schedule dentist appointments, class hours, household tasks, or other necessary uses of daily or weekly time. Studying away from home or work also minimizes the distractions of other people and other demands when you are preparing for a test.

Lights

Libraries also provide good reading lights. For some people, this may seem like a trivial matter, but the eyestrain that can come from working for long periods in poor light can be very tiring—which you can't afford when you're studying hard.

At home, the bedside lamp, the semidarkness of a room dominated by the television, or the bright sunlight of the back porch will be of little help to tired eyes.

Margin notes:
- Different quiet places at different times
- Portable study material
- Library!
- Need good light

Outlining

You are probably familiar with the basic format of the traditional outline:

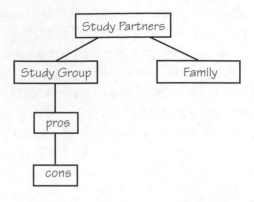

    I.   Main idea 1
        A.   Major detail
        B.   Major detail
            1. Minor detail
            2. Minor detail
   II.   Main idea 2
        A.   Major detail
        B.   Major detail

You may have used an outline in school to help you organize a writing assignment or take notes. When you outline print material, you're looking for the basic ideas that make up the framework of the text. When you are taking out the important information for a test, then you are looking for the basic ideas that the author wants to convey to you.

Mapping

Mapping is a more visual kind of outline. Instead of making a linear outline of the main ideas of a text, when you map, you make a diagram of the main points in the text that you want to remember. The following diagrams show the same information in a map form.

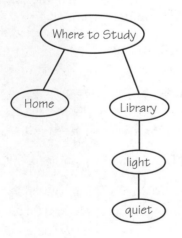

Make Study Notes

The next step after you have pulled out all the key ideas is to make notes from which you will study. You will use these notes for the intensive and ongoing study you'll do over the period of time before the test. They're the specific items that you targeted as important to know for the test. Your notes should help you understand the information you need to know and, in many cases, commit it to memory. You should be sure to include:

- the main ideas you underlined or highlighted in the text
- the main ideas and important details you outlined or mapped from the text
- specific terms, words, dates, formulas, names, facts, or procedures that you need to memorize

How Do You Make Study Notes?

Some people like to write study notes in the back pages of their notebooks or on paper folded lengthwise so that it can be tucked between the pages of a text or review book. This format is good to use for notes that can be written as questions and answers, cause and effect, or definition and examples. You can also make notes on index cards.

Using Index Cards

It can be very helpful to write your study notes—especially those that contain material to be memorized—on index cards. Vocabulary words are significantly easier to learn using index cards.

Advantages of making notes on index cards are:

- The information on each card is visually separated from other information. Therefore, it's easier to concentrate on just that one item, separate from the surrounding text. You remember the look of a vocabulary word or a math equation more clearly when it is set off by itself.
- Cards are small and portable. They can be carried in a purse or a pocket and pulled out at any time during the day for review.
- Study cards can help you with the necessary task of memorizing. If you write the key word or topic you are trying to learn on one side, and the information you must know on the other side, you have an easy way to quiz yourself on the material. This method is especially good for kinesthetic learners, who learn by doing.

Making Memorizing Easier

There are many ways to take the drudgery out of memorizing information.

Take Small Bites of Time

Most people memorize information best when they study in small periods over a long period of time.

Memorizing facts from index cards that can be carried with you and pulled out for a few ten-minute sessions each day will yield better results than sitting down with a textbook for an hour straight. Index card notes can be pulled out in odd moments: while you are sitting in the car waiting to pick up your friend, during the 15 minutes you spend on the bus in the morning, while you wait to be picked up from school or work, and so on.

You'll find that these short but regular practices will greatly aid your recall of lots of information. They're a great way to add more study time to your schedule.

Break It Up

When you have a list to memorize, break the list into groups of seven or any other odd number. People seem to remember best when they divide long lists into shorter ones—and, for some reason, shorter ones that have an odd number of items in them. So instead of trying to memorize ten vocabulary or spelling words, split your list into smaller lists of seven and three, or five and five, to help you remember them.

Create Visual Aids

Give yourself visual assistance in memorizing. If there's a tricky combination of letters in a word you need to spell, for example, circle or underline it in red or highlight it in the text. Your eye will recall what the word looks like. With some information, you can even draw a map or picture to help you remember.

Do It Out Loud

Give yourself auditory assistance in memorizing. Many people learn best if they *hear* the information. Sit by yourself in a quiet room and say aloud what you need to learn. Or give your notes to someone else and let that person ask you or quiz you on the material.

Use Mnemonics

Mnemonics, or memory tricks, are things that help you remember what you need to know.

The most common type of mnemonic is the acronym. One acronym you may already know is **HOMES**, for the names of the Great Lakes (**H**uron, **O**ntario, **M**ichigan, **E**rie, and **S**uperior). **ROY G. BIV** reminds people of the colors in the spectrum (**r**ed, **o**range, **y**ellow, **g**reen, **b**lue, **i**ndigo, and **v**iolet).

You can make a mnemonic out of anything. In a psychology course, for example, you might memorize the stages in death and dying by the nonsense word **DABDA** (**D**enial, **A**nger, **B**argaining, **D**epression, and

Acceptance). Another kind of mnemonic is a silly sentence made out of words that each begin with the letter or letters that start each item in a series. You may remember "**P**lease **E**xcuse **M**y **D**ear **A**unt **S**ally" as a device for remembering the order of operations in math (**P**arentheses, **E**xponents, **M**ultiply, **D**ivide, **A**dd, and **S**ubtract).

Sleep on It

When you study right before sleep and don't allow any interference—such as conversation, radio, television, or music—to come between study and sleep, you remember material better. This is especially true if you review first thing after waking as well. A rested and relaxed brain seems to hang on to information better than a tired and stressed-out brain.

On the following pages, try out some of the learning strategies you discovered in this lesson. Then check your answers.

The following is a passage from this text to underline and annotate. Make margin summaries of the key points in each paragraph. Then make a mnemonic based on your margin notes.

Take Small Bites of Time

Most people memorize information best when they study in small periods over a long period of time.

Memorizing facts from index cards that can be carried with you and pulled out for a few ten-minute sessions each day will yield better results than sitting down with a textbook for an hour straight. You'll find that these short but regular practices will greatly aid your recall of lots of information. They're a great way to add more study time to your schedule.

Break It Up

When you have a list to memorize, break the list into groups of seven or any other odd number. People seem to remember best when they divide long lists into shorter ones—and, for some reason, shorter ones that have an odd number of items in them. So instead of trying to memorize ten vocabulary or spelling words, split your list into smaller lists of seven and three, or five and five, to help you remember them.

Create Visual Aids

Give yourself visual assistance in memorizing. If there's a tricky combination of letters in a word you need to spell, for example, circle or underline it in red or highlight it in the text. Your eye will recall what the word looks like.

Do It Out Loud

Give yourself auditory assistance in memorizing. Many people learn best if they hear the information. Sit by yourself in a quiet room and say aloud what you need to learn. Or give your notes to someone else and let that person quiz you on the material.

Use Mnemonics

Mnemonics, or memory tricks, are things that help you remember what you need to know.

The most common type of mnemonic is the acronym. One acronym you may already know is **HOMES**, for the names of the Great Lakes (**H**uron, **O**ntario, **M**ichigan, **E**rie, and **S**uperior). **ROY G. BIV** reminds people of the colors in the spectrum (**r**ed, **o**range, **y**ellow, **g**reen, **b**lue, **i**ndigo, and **v**iolet).

Note Cards

Make note cards with definitions for each kind of learning modality:

- visual
- auditory
- kinesthetic

Mapping

Here is an outline of the learning strategies covered in this chapter. Using the same information, make a map or diagram of the same material.

    I.   How to study most effectively
        A.   Annotating
        B.   Outlining
        C.   Mapping
   II.   How to make study notes
        A.   Notebook pages
        B.   Index cards
             1. Reasons for using index cards
 III.   Memory methods

Completed Sample Annotation

Take Small Bites of Time

[Distributed practice]

Most people memorize information best when they study in <u>small periods over a long period of time</u>.

Memorizing facts from portable index cards that can be carried with you and pulled out for a few ten-minute sessions each day will yield better results than sitting down with a textbook for an hour straight. You'll find that these short but regular practices will greatly aid your recall of lots of information. They're a great way to add more study time to your schedule.

Break It Up

[Divide lists]

When you have a list to memorize, <u>break the list into groups of seven or any other odd number</u>. People seem to remember best when they divide long lists into shorter ones—and, for some reason, shorter ones that have an odd number of items in them. So instead of trying to memorize ten vocabulary or spelling words, split your list into smaller lists of seven and three, or five and five, to help you remember them.

Create Visual Aids

[Visual Aids]

<u>Give yourself visual assistance in memorizing</u>. If there's a tricky combination of letters in a word you need to spell, for example, circle or underline it in red or highlight it in the text. Your eye will recall what the word looks like.

Do It Out Loud

[Auditory]

<u>Give yourself auditory assistance in memorizing</u>. Many people learn best if they hear the information. Sit by yourself in a quiet room and say aloud what you need to learn. Or give your notes to someone else and let that person ask you questions and quiz you on the material.

Use Mnemonics

<u>Mnemonics</u>, or memory tricks, are things that help you remember what you need to know.

[Acronym]

The most common type of mnemonic is the <u>acronym</u>. One acronym you may already know is **HOMES**, for the names of the Great Lakes (**H**uron, **O**ntario, **M**ichigan, **E**rie, and **S**uperior). **ROY G. BIV** reminds people of the colors in the spectrum (**R**ed, **O**range, **Y**ellow, **G**reen, **B**lue, **I**ndigo, and **V**iolet).

Sample Mnemonics
DDVAA

Note Cards
Here are samples of how your note cards might look:

FRONT OF CARD

Visual Modality	Auditory Modality	Kinesthetic Modality

BACK OF CARD

learning by seeing	learning by listening	learning by doing

Mapping
Here is an example of how your map or diagram might look:

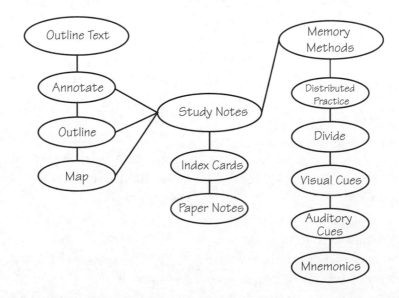

Preparing for Standardized Tests

Most of us get nervous about tests, especially standardized tests, where our scores can have a significant impact on our future. Nervousness is natural—and it can even be an advantage if you know how to channel it into positive energy.

The following pages provide suggestions for overcoming test anxiety both in the days and weeks before the test and during the test itself.

Two to Three Months before the Test

The number one best way to combat test anxiety is to **be prepared**. That means two things: Know what to expect on the test and review the material and skills on which you will be tested.

Review the Material and Skills You'll Be Tested On

The fact that you are reading this book means that you've already taken this step. Now, are there other steps you can take? Are there other subject areas you need to review? Can you make more improvement in this or other areas? If you are really nervous or if it has been a long time since you reviewed these subjects and skills, you may want to buy another study guide, sign up for a class in your neighborhood, or work with a tutor.

The more you know about what to expect on test day and the more comfortable you are with the material and skills to be tested, the less anxious you will be and the better you will do on the test itself.

The Days before the Test
Review, Don't Cram

If you have been preparing and reviewing in the weeks before the exam, there's no need to cram a few days beforehand. Cramming is likely to confuse you and make you nervous. Instead, schedule a relaxed review of all you have learned.

Physical Activity

Get some exercise in the days preceding the test. You'll send some extra oxygen to your brain and allow your thinking performance to peak on the day you take the test. Moderation is the key here. Don't exercise so much that you feel exhausted, but a little physical activity will invigorate your body and brain. Walking is a terrific, low-impact, energy-building form of exercise.

Balanced Diet

Like your body, your brain needs proper nutrients to function well. Eat plenty of fruits and vegetables in the days before the test. Foods high in lecithin, such as fish and beans, are especially good choices. Lecithin is a protein your brain needs for peak performance. You may even consider a visit to your local pharmacy to buy a bottle of lecithin tablets several weeks before your test.

Rest

Get plenty of sleep the nights before the test. Don't overdo it, though, or you'll make yourself as groggy as if you were overtired. Go to bed at a reasonable time, early enough to get the hours of rest you need to function **effectively**. You'll feel relaxed and rested if you've gotten plenty of sleep in the days before you take the test.

Trial Run

At some point before the test, make a trial run to the testing center to see how long it takes to get there. Rushing raises your emotional energy and lowers your intellectual capacity, so you want to allow plenty of time on test day to get to the testing center. Arriving ten or fifteen minutes early gives you time to relax and get situated.

Motivation

Plan some sort of celebration—with family or friends, or just by yourself—for after the test. Make sure it's something you'll really look forward to and enjoy. If you have something planned for after the test, you may find it easier to prepare and keep moving during the test.

Test Day

It's finally here, the day of the big test. Set your alarm early enough to allow plenty of time to get to the testing center. Eat a good breakfast. Avoid anything that's really high in sugar, such as donuts. A sugar high turns into a sugar low after an hour or so. Cereal and toast, or anything with complex carbohydrates is a good choice. Eat only moderate amounts. You don't want to take a test feeling stuffed! Your body will channel its energy to your digestive system instead of your brain.

Pack a high-energy snack to take with you. You may have a break sometime during the test when you can grab a quick snack. Bananas are great. They have a moderate amount of sugar and plenty of brain nutrients, such as potassium. Most proctors won't allow you to eat a snack while you're testing, but a peppermint shouldn't pose a problem. Peppermints are like smelling salts for your brain. If you lose your concentration or suffer from a momentary mental block, a peppermint can get you back on track. Don't forget the earlier advice about relaxing and taking a few deep breaths.

Leave early enough so you have plenty of time to get to the test center. Allow a few minutes for unexpected traffic. When you arrive, locate the restroom and use it. Few things interfere with concentration as much as a full bladder. Then, find your seat and make sure it's comfortable. If it isn't, tell the proctor and ask to move to something more suitable.

Now relax and think positively! Before you know it, the test will be over, and you'll walk away knowing you've done as well as you can.

Combating Test Anxiety

Okay—you know what the test will be on. You've reviewed the subjects and practiced the skills on which you will be tested. So why do you still have that sinking feeling in your stomach? Why are your palms sweaty and your hands shaking?

Even the brightest, most well-prepared test takers sometimes suffer bouts of test anxiety. But don't worry; you can overcome it. Here are some specific strategies to help you.

Take the Test One Question at a Time

Focus all your attention on the one question you're answering. Avoid thoughts about questions you've already read or concerns about what's coming next. Concentrate your thinking where it will do the most good—on the question you're answering now.

Develop a Positive Attitude

Keep reminding yourself that you're prepared. In fact, if you've read this book or any other in the LearningExpress Skill Builders series, you're probably better prepared than most other test takers. Remember, it's only a test, and you will do your **best**. That's all anyone can ask of you. If that nagging drill sergeant voice inside your head starts sending negative messages, combat them with positive ones of your own. Tell yourself:

- "I'm doing just fine."
- "I've prepared for this test."
- "I know exactly what to do."
- "I know I can get the score I'm shooting for."

You get the idea. Remember to drown out negative messages with positive ones of your own.

If You Lose Your Concentration

Don't worry about it! It's normal. During a long test, it happens to everyone. When your mind is stressed or overexerted, it takes a break whether you want it to or not. It's easy to get your concentration back if you simply acknowledge the fact that you've lost it and take a quick break. You brain needs very little time (seconds, really) to rest.

Put your pencil down and close your eyes. Take a deep breath, hold it for a moment, and let it out slowly. Listen to the sound of your breathing as you repeat this two more times. The few seconds this takes is really all the time your brain needs to relax and refocus. This exercise also helps you control your heart rate, so you can keep anxiety at bay.

Try this technique several times before the test when you feel stressed. The more you practice, the better it will work for you on test day.

If You Freeze

Don't worry about a question that stumps you even though you're sure you know the answer. Mark it and go on to the next question. You can come back to the "stumper" later. Try to put it out of your mind completely until you come back to it. Just let your subconscious mind chew on the question while your conscious mind focuses on the other items (one at a time—of course). Chances are, the memory block will be gone by the time you return to the question.

If you freeze before you even begin the test, here's what to do:

1. Do some deep breathing to help yourself relax and focus.
2. Remind yourself that you're prepared.
3. Take some time to look over the test.
4. Read a few of the questions.
5. Decide which ones are the easiest and start there.

Before long, you'll be in the groove.

Time Strategies

One of the most important—and nerve-wracking—elements of a standardized test is time. You'll only be allowed a certain number of minutes for each section, so it is very important that you use your time wisely.

Pace Yourself

The most important time strategy is **pacing yourself**. Before you begin, take just a few seconds to survey the test, noting the number of questions and the sections that look easier than the rest. Then make a rough time schedule based on the amount of time available to you.

Mark the halfway point on your test and make a note beside that mark of the time when the testing period is half over.

Keep Moving

Once you begin the test, **keep moving**. If you work slowly in an attempt to make fewer mistakes, your mind will become bored and begin to wander. You'll end up making far more mistakes if you're not concentrating. Worse, if you take too long to answer questions that stump you, you may end up running out of time before you finish.

So don't stop for difficult questions. Skip them and move on. You can come back to them later if you have time. A question that takes you five seconds to answer counts as much as one that takes you several minutes, so pick up the easy points first. Besides, answering the easier questions first helps build your confidence and gets you in the testing groove. Who knows? As you go through the test, you may even stumble across some relevant information to help you answer those tough questions.

Don't Rush

Keep moving, but **don't rush**. Think of your mind as a seesaw. On one side is your emotional energy; on the other side, your intellectual energy. When your emotional energy is high, your intellectual capacity is low. Remember how difficult it is to reason with someone when you're angry? On the other hand, when your intellectual energy is high, your emotional energy is low. Rushing raises your emotional energy and reduces your intellectual capacity. Remember the last time you were late for work? All that rushing around probably caused you to forget important things—like your lunch. Move quickly to keep your mind from wandering, but don't rush and get yourself flustered.

Check Yourself

Check yourself at the halfway mark. If you're a little ahead, you know you're on track and may even have a little time left to check your work. If you're a little behind, you have a couple choices. You can pick up the pace a little, but do this *only* if you can do it comfortably. Remember—**don't rush!** You can also skip around in the remaining portion of the test to pick up as many easy points as possible. This strategy has one drawback, however. If you are marking a bubble-style answer sheet, and you put the right answers in the wrong bubbles—they're wrong. So pay close attention to the question numbers if you decide to do this.

Avoiding Errors

When you take the test, you want to make as few errors as possible in the questions you answer. Here are a few tactics to keep in mind.

Control Yourself

Remember that comparison between your mind and a seesaw? Keeping your emotional energy low and your intellectual energy high is the best way to avoid mistakes. If you feel stressed or worried, stop for a few seconds. Acknowledge the feeling (Hmmm! I'm feeling a little pressure here!), take a few deep breaths, and send yourself a few positive messages. This relieves your emotional anxiety and boosts your intellectual capacity.

Directions

In many standardized testing situations, a proctor reads the instructions aloud. Make certain you understand what is expected. If you don't, **ask**. Listen carefully for instructions about how to answer the questions and make certain you know how much time you have to complete the task. Write the time on your test if you don't already know how long you have to take the test. If you miss this vital information, **ask for it**. You need it to do well on your test.

Answers

This may seem like a silly warning, but it is important. Place your answers in the right blanks or the corresponding ovals on the answer sheet. Right answers in the wrong place earn no points—you may even lose

points. It's a good idea to check every five to ten questions to make sure you're in the right spot. That way, you won't need much time to correct your answer sheet if you have made an error.

Choosing the Right Answers by Process of Elimination

Make sure you understand what the question is asking. If you're not sure of what's being asked, you'll never know whether you've chosen the right answer. So determine what the question is asking. If the answer isn't readily apparent, look for clues in the answer choices. Notice the similarities and differences in the answer choices. Sometimes, this helps to put the question in a new perspective, making it easier to answer. If you're still not sure of the answer, use the process of elimination. First, eliminate any answer choices that are obviously wrong. Then reason your way through the remaining choices. You may be able to use relevant information from other parts of the test. If you can't eliminate any of the answer choices, you might be better off to skip the question and come back to it later. If you can't eliminate any answer choices to improve your odds when you return, make a guess and move on.

If You're Penalized for Wrong Answers

You **must know** whether there's a penalty for wrong answers before you begin the test. If you don't, ask the proctor before the test begins. Whether you make a guess depends on the penalty. Some standardized tests are scored in such a way that every wrong answer reduces your score by one-fourth or one-half of a point. Whatever the penalty, if you can eliminate enough choices to make the odds of answering the question better than the penalty for getting it wrong, make a guess.

Let's imagine you are taking a test in which each answer has four choices and you are penalized one-fourth of a point for each wrong answer. If you have no clue and cannot eliminate any of the answer choices, you're better off leaving the question blank because the odds of answering correctly are one in four. This makes the penalty and the odds equal. However, if you can eliminate one of the choices, the odds are now in your favor. You have a one in three chance of answering the question correctly. Fortunately, few tests are scored using such elaborate means, but if your test is one of them, know the penalties and calculate your odds before you take a guess on a question.

If You Finish Early

Use any time you have left at the end of the test or test section to check your work. First, make certain you've put the answers in the right places. As you're doing this, make sure you've answered each question only once. Most standardized tests are scored in such a way that questions with more than one answer are marked wrong. If you've erased an answer, make sure you've done a good job. Check for stray marks on your answer sheet that could distort your score.

After you've checked for these obvious errors, take a second look at the more difficult questions. You've probably heard the folk wisdom about never changing an answer. It's not always good advice. If you have a good reason for thinking a response is wrong, change it.

After the Test

Once you've finished, *congratulate yourself*. You've worked hard to prepare; now it's time to enjoy yourself and relax. Remember that celebration you planned before the test? Go to it!

B ▶ ADDITIONAL RESOURCES

The following resources will help you build your vocabulary beyond the words in this book. In this list, you will find print material to help you on your way to further word study. Before you look at any of the books listed, you should get a good dictionary. For general reference at home, a collegiate or college dictionary will suffice. Try Merriam-Webster's Collegiate Dictionary, 11th Edition (Merriam-Webster, Inc., 2003). You can also refer to an online dictionary, such as Merriam-Webster's online dictionary, found at www.m-w.com.

Recommended Books

1001 Vocabulary & Spelling Questions, 2nd Edition (NY: LearningExpress, 2003).

Bromberg, Murray, and Julius Liebb. *601 Words You Need to Know to Pass Your Exam, Fourth Edition* (NY: Barron's Educational Series, 2005).

Bromberg, Murray, and Melvin Gordon. *1100 Words You Need to Know, 5th Edition* (NY: Barron's Educational Series, 2008).

Contemporary Vocabulary (NY: St. Martin's Press, 1995).

Cornog, Mary Wood. *Merriam Webster's Vocabulary Builder* (Springfield, MA: Merriam-Webster Publishing, Inc., 1994).

Elster, Charles Harrinton. *Verbal Advantage: 10 Steps to Powerful Vocabulary* (NY: Random House Reference, 2000).

Funk, Wilfred John, and Norman Lewis. *30 Days to a More Powerful Vocabulary* (NY: Pocket Books, 1991).

Keen, Dennis. *Developing Vocabulary Skills* (Boston, MA: Heinle & Heinle ITP Publishers, 1994).

Kolby, Jeff. *Vocabulary 4000: The 4000 Words Essential for an Educated Vocabulary* (Los Angeles, CA: Nova Press, 2000).

Lewis, Norman. *Word Power Made Easy* (NJ: BBS Publishing Corporation, 1995).

Randol, Susan. (editor). *Random House Webster's Power Vocabulary Builder* (NY: Ballantine Books, 1996).

Robinson, Adam. *Word Smart: Building an Educated Vocabulary* (Princeton, NJ: Princeton Review Series, 2001).

Schur, Norman W. *1000 Most Important Words* (NY: Ballantine Books, 1982).

Glossary

abrogate   to abolish by authoritative action

abstraction   something that is not concrete or tangible, but is more of a theoretical idea or concept, like truth or beauty

acme   the highest point, as of achievement or development

addle   to confuse, fluster, or muddle

adjudicate   to act as a judge, to settle judicially

affidavit   a sworn statement in writing made under oath

aficionado   a person who likes, knows about, and is devoted to a particular activity or thing

agrarian   having to do with agriculture or farming

altruism   unselfish concern for the welfare of others

ambivalent   having at the same time two conflicting feelings or emotions toward another person or thing, such as love and hate; having divided feelings about something or someone; equivocal; uncertain

anecdote   a short account of an interesting or humorous incident

anomaly   abnormality; irregularity; deviation from the norm or usual

antagonist   one that contends with or opposes another

antecedent   going before in time

anthropomorphism   attribution of human motivation, characteristics, or behavior to inanimate objects, animals, or natural phenomenon

antipathy   revulsion, any object of strong dislike

antithesis   the exact opposite of something, or an extreme contrast

antonym   a word that means the opposite of the word to which it is being compared. For example, "shiny" and "dull" are antonyms.

aphorism   a brief statement of a truth or opinion; a saying or an adage

appellate   having the power to review the judgment of another court

application   a software program that lets you complete a task on your computer, such as word processing

arbitrage   the buying of "paper"—stocks, bonds, and securities—to resell for a quick profit

arbitration   the process by which disputes are settled by a third party

archetype   an original model or type after which other similar things are patterned

ASAP   an abbreviation for As Soon As Possible

audacious   fearlessly, often recklessly daring, adventurous, and brave; unrestrained by convention or propriety; insolent

avant-garde   a group of people who develop innovative and experimental concepts, especially in the arts

awry   in a position that is turned or twisted toward one side or away from the correct course; askew

badinage   playful and joking conversation or banter

banal   trivial, worn out by overuse, or used so commonly as to have lost all interest and novelty

bandwidth   the amount of information that one can send through a connection, usually measured in bits per second

bane   fatal injury or ruin; a cause of harm, ruin, or death; a source of persistent annoyance or exasperation

beneficiary   one who will benefit from something

bequest   the act of bequeathing; the act of leaving someone something in a will, something that is bequeathed

bevy   a group; a flock of birds

bigotry   unreasonable zeal in favor of a party, sect, or opinion; excessive prejudice

bitmap   the representation in rows and columns of dots of an image in computer memory

blasé   apathetic to pleasure or excitement as a result of excessive indulgence in something

bourgeois   having the attributes and beliefs of the middle class, marked by materialistic concerns

brusque   abrupt, blunt, or short in manner or speech

cache   a high-speed storage mechanism that allows a computer to store frequently accessed information locally

capital   accumulated wealth, used to gain more wealth

CAT scan   Computerized Axial Tomography scan—a three-dimensional image of a body structure made from a series of cross-sectional images and put together by a computer

CD-ROM   Compact Disk-Read Only Memory—a compact disk that contains data a computer can read

churlish   boorish or vulgar; having a bad disposition; surly; difficult to work with; intractable

circumvent   to go around; to catch in a trap; to gain superiority over; to prevent from happening

cite   to quote as an authority or example

cliché   a phrase or saying that has been overused and, as a result, has little significance or meaning

collusion   a secret agreement for a deceitful or fraudulent purpose; conspiracy

connotation   the tone or implied meaning of a word; the emotion a word evokes within its reader

consensus   agreement, especially in opinion

consortium   a joining of two or more businesses for a specific purpose

construe   to explain the meaning of; interpret; to analyze the grammatical structure of (a sentence)

consummate   to complete, to carry to the utmost degree

context   the surrounding text in which a word is used

contraband   illegal or prohibited exporting or importing of goods

contraction   formed by putting two words together and omitting one or more letters. In a contraction, an apostrophe is added to the word to show that letters have been left out, and that two words have merged.

controversy   a discussion of question in which opposing views clash

cookie   a message given to a Web browser by a Web server that is stored in the browser and sent back to the server every time the browser contacts the server for a Web page

copious   abundant; plentiful; in great quantities

cower   to shrink and tremble, as from someone's anger or threats; to cringe

crux   the basic or central point or feature; a puzzling or apparently insoluble problem

cryptic   hidden; secret; having a hidden or ambiguous meaning

cursor   a symbol, usually a blinking line that shows where the next letter will be typed on a computer screen

database   information stored and organized so that a computer can quickly retrieve selected pieces of information

debut   a first appearance

decimate   to destroy or kill a large portion of something, to take or destroy a tenth part of something

deduce   to reach a conclusion by reasoning; to infer from a general principle; to trace the origin of

deduction   the subtraction of a cost from income

deferment   the act of putting off or delaying; postponement

demote   to lower in grade or position

demure   modest and reserved in manner or behavior; shy

denotation   the dictionary definition of a word

deposition   testimony under oath, taken down in writing

dichotomy   the division of a subject into two opposite classes or aspects, such as internal and external

diffident   modest, shy, reserved, bashful, humble

dink   double income couple, no kids—a subset of yuppies

dire   warning of, or having dreadful or terrible consequences; urgent; desperate

disconsolate   hopeless, sad, melancholy, dejected

discrimination   the act of making distinctions, the act of distinguishing between one group of people and another and treating people differently as a result, prejudiced actions or treatment

disinterested   not motivated by personal interest or selfish motives

dogma   the official beliefs, principles, or teachings, such as those of a religion, political party, or philosophy, used most often with the added implication that these beliefs or teachings should be strictly adhered to

dolorous   exhibiting sorrow, grief, or pain

DOS   the Disk Operating System used on personal computers (PCs)

download   the process of copying a document or file from an online source to your own computer

dross   the worthless part of something that is separated from the better part; waste; garbage

dupe   an easily deceived person

eke   to supplement or get with great effort; to make last by practicing strict economy

élan   spirit, enthusiasm, or excitement

elite   a group or class of persons or a member of such a group or class, enjoying superior intellectual, social, or economic status; the best or most skilled members of a group

empiric   someone who begins a practice such as law or medicine without the proper professional education and experience; a popular slang term for a quack; one who is ignorant of the scientific principles and relies completely on practical experience

encryption   the translation of information into a secret code

entitlement   special privilege or benefit allowed to a group of people

entrepreneur   a person who takes on the challenge and risk or starting his or her own business

epicurean   devoted to the pursuit of sensual pleasure, especially to good food and comfort

epigram   a short, witty poem expressing a single thought or observation; a concise, clever, often paradoxical statement or saying

epitome   an exact example of something; someone or something that embodies the essence of a concept or type

equity   fairness or evenness of treatment, or the value of property after all claims have been made against it

erudite   scholarly, learned, well read, having extensive knowledge

ESL   English as a Second Language

Ethernet   a common method of enabling computers in the same Local Area Network (LAN)

etymology   the origin and historical development of a word's forms, meanings, and usages

euphemism   the use of a word or phrase that is considered less distasteful or offensive than another

exacerbate   to make more violent, bitter, or severe

exempt   excused from some rule or job

exhume   to remove from a grave; to bring back from neglect or obscurity

exorbitant   going beyond what is reasonable and proper

extenuating   lessened the magnitude or seriousness of, especially by making partial excuses

extradite   to surrender an alleged criminal to the stat or country in which he or she can be tried

extricate   to set free or release; to disentangle, as from a difficulty or embarrassment

facetious   playful; jocular

fait-accompli   something that is complete and seemingly irreversible

FAQ   Frequently Asked Questions

feisty   touchy; quarrelsome; full of spirit; frisky or spunky

firewall   a system (using either hardware or software) that prevents unauthorized access to and from a private network

fiscal   pertaining to money or finance

flippant   marked by disrespectful levity or casualness; pert

fodder   dry, coarse food for cattle, horses, or sheep, like hay or straw; also often used in expressions unrelated to animals

franchise   a business that is owned by a parent company but run by independent operators under rules set by the parent company

furtive   done in a stealthy manner; sly and underhanded

garrulous   overly talkative about unimportant things; chattering

gauche   lacking social graces or sophistication

genteel   refined, polite, elegant, gentlemanly or ladylike

geology   the study of the history of the earth and its life, especially as recorded in rocks

gibe   to make taunting, heckling, or jeering remarks

guffaw   a loud rough burst of laughter

guttural   throaty; used to describe sounds that originate in the throat, like the "k" in kite

harassment   the act of irritating or annoying persistently; sexual harassment

hedonism   the belief that everything in life should be done to bring pleasure; a pleasure-seeking lifestyle

homonyms   words that sound the same but have different meanings or definitions. Homonyms are pronounced the same way, but are not spelled the same way and do not mean the same thing.

hyperbole   exaggeration for effect, not to be taken literally

ideology   the doctrines, beliefs, or opinions of a person, group, or school of thought

illegible   not able to be read

imbroglio   a complicated or embarrassing situation due to a misunderstanding

imperious   arrogantly domineering or overbearing; dictatorial

inert   inactive, sluggish, without power to move

infer   to conclude or reason from evidence, premises, or circumstances; to hint or imply

information technology (IT)   the broad subject of anything concerning processing or managing information, especially in a large company

ingénue   a young girl or woman, an actress playing such a role

insouciance   carefree, unconcerned

intermittent   stopping and starting again at intervals

intestate   one who dies without a will

ipso facto   by the very fact or act, an inevitable act

irony   the use of words to express something different from, and often opposite to, their literal meaning; a literary style employing such contrasts for witty effect; incongruity between what might be expected and what actually occurs

ISP   Internet Service Provider

jargon   the specialized vocabulary of an industry or interest group

jaunty   having a buoyant or self-confident air; brisk; crisp and dapper in appearance

jurisprudence   a system of laws, the science or philosophy of the law

keyword   a word that specifies a particular record or file in programming a specific command

laissez-faire   a doctrine opposing government control of economic matters except in the case of maintaining peace and the concept of property

larceny   the unlawful taking of someone else's property with the intention of not giving it back

laser   light amplification by stimulated emission of radiation—a device that generates electromagnetic radiation

laudable   praiseworthy

lien   a charge against real or personal property for the satisfaction of a debt or duty originally arising from the law

litigious   contentious situation, prone to litigation

logic   the science of correct reasoning used to discover truths, or any method of reasoning, whether it reveals true and valid statements or not

loquacious   talkative

maim   to disable or disfigure; to make imperfect or defective; impair

malaise   the vague feeling of illness

malapropism   a ridiculous or humorous misuse of words, usually due to a resemblance in sound

malevolent   having an evil disposition toward others

malfeasance   wrongdoing or misconduct, especially by a public official

mete   to distribute by or as if by measure; allot

minimize   to play down; to keep to a minimum

moot   a hypothetical case argued as an exercise; a case no longer of actual significance

motherboard   the main circuit board of a computer

mutable   changeable, unstable, variable

mutation   the act or process of changing

myriad   constituting a very large, indefinite number; innumerable; composed of numerous diverse elements or facets

naïve   innocent, simple, lacking knowledge of the world

nepotism   the employment or promotion of friends and family members

network   a group of two or more computers linked together

nominal   in name only, small amount

non sequitur   a statement that has no connection to the previous statement or idea

oblique   having a slanting or sloping direction, course, or position; indirect or evasive; devious, misleading, or dishonest

obtuse   dull, not sharp or acute; when used to describe a person, it means slow to understand or notice, or insensitive

omniscient   all-knowing; having universal knowledge of all things

onomatopoeia   the formation or use of words that imitate the sounds associated with the objects or actions to which they refer

ornate   elaborately and often excessively ornamented; showy or flowery

oust   to eject from a position or place; force out

pallor   lack of color; unnatural paleness, often used to describe a face

palpable   capable of being handled, touched, or felt; tangible

paradigm   a pattern, example, or model

paradox   a statement that seems contradictory, unbelievable, or absurd but may actually be true; or something that is not fully understood because of contradictory appearances, statements, or actions

partisan   strongly in favor of one side or political party; blindly or unreasonably devoted to a party

pathos   suffering; feeling of sympathy or pity

perjury   lying or intentionally omitting information under oath

perquisite   a privilege or bonus given in addition to regular salary

personification   a person or thing typifying a certain quality or idea; an embodiment or exemplification; a figure of speech in which inanimate objects or abstractions are endowed with human qualities or are represented as possessing human form

perspective   a mental view or outlook; a point of view; the ability to perceive things in their actual interrelations or comparative importance

pertinacity   firm or unyielding adherence to some purpose; stubbornness; persistence

plagiarism   the act of passing off someone else's work as your own

plausible   seemingly true and acceptable, but usually used with implied disbelief; possible

plug-in   a piece of hardware or software that adds a specific feature to a larger, already existing system

pragmatism   a way of thinking or an attitude that stresses the value of being practical, realistic, and useful

precursor   a forerunner, a harbinger, one who or that which goes before

prefix   word part placed at the beginning of a word. The prefix is usually one syllable, and its job is to add to the meaning of a word.

prehensile   adapted to grasp, seize, or hold

prodigious   impressively great in size, force, or extent; extraordinary; marvelous

prognosis   a forecast; especially in medicine

prone   lying with the front or face downward; having a tendency; inclined

prose   ordinary speech or writing, without metrical structure (as in poetry)

prospectus   a published report of a business and its plan for a program or offering

protagonist   the main character in a drama or other literary work

protracted   drawn out in time, prolonged

pun   play on words

purge   to free from impurities; purify; to rid of sin, guilt, or defilement; to clear a person of a charge; to get rid of people considered undesirable

purloin   to steal

rancor   a continuing and bitter hatred or ill will

rejected   sent back, refused, discarded

relevant   having a bearing on or connection with the matter at hand

rendezvous   to meet at a meeting place

resolute   determined; firm of purpose; resolved

resonant   used to describe sounds, it usually means vibrant, full, ringing, intensified, resounding, rich

retrospect   to think about the past

rhetoric   the art or study of using language effectively and persuasively

roil   to make a liquid muddy or cloudy by stirring up sediment; to displease or disturb; vex

root   the original, direct meaning of a word. Most root words are Greek or Latin in origin.

rubric   a formal way to say name or title, or a category of something; an established rule or tradition

ruminate   to meditate on or ponder something; to think over

sanction   authoritative permission or approval that makes a course of action valid, a law or decree

sardonic   scornfully or cynically mocking

satire   a literary work in which human vice or folly is attacked through irony or wit

search engine   a program that searches documents, websites, and databases for a keyword and then provides a list of those documents

semantic   concerning the meaning of something; usually used in discussing words and language and the subtle differences between the meanings of similar words

server   a computer on a network that manages network resources

sham   something false or empty that is said to be genuine; one who assumes a false character; an imposter

simian   dealing with apes or monkeys; apelike

smidgen   a very small particle; an insignificant piece or amount

soliloquy   a dramatic or literary form of disclosure in which a character talks to himself or herself or reveals his or her thoughts without addressing a listener

sophisticated   knowledgeable; refined, experienced, and aware

staid   characterized by sedate dignity and propriety; sober; fixed; permanent

stolid   showing little or no emotion or awareness; unexcitable; expressionless

subordinate   inferior to or placed below another in rank, power, or importance

subsidy   a grant of money for a particular purpose

succor   aid; help; assistance, especially that which relieves and ends stress, need, or a difficulty

suffix   word part placed at the end of a word. The suffix signals how a word is being used in a sentence and identifies the word's part of speech. Different suffixes categorize the word within different parts of speech.

sycophant   a person who tries to get ahead by flattering people of wealth and power

syllogism   a form of logical reasoning that begins with two true statements and ends with a logical conclusion drawn from them, using deductive reasoning, which proceeds from general statements to the specific

synonym   a word that has the same, or nearly the same, meaning as another word to which it is being compared. For example, "happy" and "joyful" are synonyms.

synthesis   putting of two or more things together to form a whole

tautology   needless repetition of an idea in a different word or phrase; redundancy

teleology   the study of final causes; or the belief that all natural processes and events occur for a reason, and nature is directed by some kind of purpose

tenacious   unwilling to let go, stubborn

tenet   an opinion, principle, or belief that a person, religion, or school of thought believes and asserts to be true and important; a doctrine

tenure   the state or period of holding a particular position, or a guarantee of employment to teachers who have met particular standards

tort   wrongdoing for which damages can be claimed; an unintentional violation of someone's rights, which can result in civil action but not criminal proceedings

transcend   to go beyond the limits

trite   lacking power to evoke interest through overuse or repetition; hackneyed

trivial   of little worth or importance

upload   the opposite of download; to transmit documents from your computer to an online source

utopia   a place or state of ideal perfection, usually imaginary; a paradise

veer   to turn aside from a course, direction, or purpose; swerve

vehement   characterized by forcefulness of expression or intensity of emotion or conviction; fervid; intense

vendetta   a grudge or feud characterized by acts of retaliation

verify   to establish as truth, confirm

vie   to strive for superiority; compete; rival

vignette   a short descriptive written piece

vivacious   lively in manner

wallow   to roll about pleasantly in water or mud; can also be used to mean to overindulge in something

ADITIONAL ONLINE PRACTICE ▶

Whether you need help building basic skills or preparing for an exam, visit the **LearningExpress Practice Center**! On this site, you can access FREE additional practice materials. This online practice will also provide you with:

- **Immediate scoring**
- **Detailed answer explanations**
- **Personalized recommendations for further practice and study**

Follow the directions below to access your free additional practice:

- Email **LXHub@learningexpresshub.com** for your access code. Please include your name, contact information, and complete book title in your email.
- Write "Free online practice code" in your email subject line.
- You will receive your access code by email.
- Go to **www.learningexpresshub.com/affiliate** and follow the easy registration steps. Be sure to have your access code handy!
  - ❏ If this is your first time registering, be sure to register as a new user.
  - ❏ If you've registered before with another product, be sure to follow the steps for **returning users**.

The email address you register with will become your username. You will also be prompted to create a password. For easy reference, record them here:

Username: _____

Password: _____

With your username and password, you can log in and access your additional practice. If you have any questions or problems, please contact LearningExpress customer service at 1-800-295-9556 ext. 2, or e-mail us at **customerservice@learningexpressllc.com.**